THE ALKALINE for HEALTHY WOMEN

Cookbook

More than **320 Healthy Recipes** to **Increase your Energy**, **Detox Your Body** and **Improve your Body Tone!**
Stay **FIT** with **The HEALTHIEST Diet** Overall!

3 BOOKS IN 1

By

Sarah Johnson

Table of Contents

Introduction

Would you like to have a healthy diet that allows you to <u>STAY FIT, FEEL ENERGY,</u> and ***prevent pathology in the future***?

Recently, scientists discovered that cancer cells were particularly active in acid environments: if there are too many acids in the body, it tends to accumulate them in our cells and unbalance the acid-base balance. Moreover, scientists discovered that cancer cells were particularly active in acid environments, and an unbalanced body can accelerate aging processing more easily and can't allow the body to work well.
Some foods form **alkaline waste** after digestion and others turn into **acidic toxins**.

What does it mean? <u>You must be careful what you eat. Each food you eat can create the right environmental condition or not; all it depends on if the food you eat forms acid or alkaline waste.</u>
Does a solution exist? <u>***YES:***</u> ***Follow the Alkaline diet!***

The alkaline diet is based on one simple law: *<u>do not eat foods considered acidic or acidic</u>*. By doing this, the body can produce the right amount of acidic metabolic wastes avoiding the accumulation of acids in the body. The results? Your muscles work well, and you can stay HEALTHY, TONE, and LIGHT!
Everyone can follow Alkaline diet: **beginners**, **young people**, **children**, and **adult people**. ***All of us should follow the Alkaline diet***: this is why I wrote ***over 10 books*** about the Alkaline Diet during my life! In my opinion, ***WOMEN*** should follow this diet ***<u>absolutely</u>***! Eating only foods considered alkaline, the body can produce the right amount of acidic metabolic wastes avoiding the accumulation of acids in the body: the body works better in all of its functions, such as weight loss and weight control!
This fantastic cookbook was born as a collection of the best recipes for the books "The Alkaline Diet *Cookbook*", "the Alkaline diet for Women *Cookbook*", and "The Alkaline Diet for Beginners *Cookbook*", to give my brilliant readers more than 320 Alkaline recipes to stay Tone and Healthy!

*Are you ready to discover **The Best** Alkaline Recipes for **Women**?*
<u>LET'S GO!</u>

Mains Acid-Forming Foods

- ✓ Coffee
- ✓ Red Meat
- ✓ Fish
- ✓ Light meat
- ✓ Cornmeal, Corn
- ✓ Rice
- ✓ Wheat Germ
- ✓ Cheese
- ✓ Mais
- ✓ Alcoholic drinks
- ✓ All sauces
- ✓ White flour
- ✓ Refined sugar
- ✓ Refined salt
- ✓ White vinegar
- ✓ Nutmeg

Main Alkalinizing Foods

- ✓ Peas
- ✓ Beans
- ✓ Grains: flax, millet, quinoa, and amaranth
- ✓ Potatoes
- ✓ Almonds, peanuts and nuts
- ✓ Coconut
- ✓ Fresh unsalted butter
- ✓ Raw yogurt
- ✓ Natural Fruit juices
- ✓ All vegetable juices
- ✓ Herbal teas
- ✓ Garlic
- ✓ Cayenne pepper
- ✓ Most herbs dressing
- ✓ All vegetables
- ✓ Unprocessed sea salt
- ✓ Raw honey
- ✓ Dried sugar cane

Chapter 1

BREAKFAST AND SNACKS

1) BOWL OF RASPBERRY AND BANANA SMOOTHIE

Preparation Time: 10 minutes	Cooking Time: 10 minutes	Servings: 2

Ingredients:

- ✓ 2 cups of fresh raspberries, split
- ✓ 2 large frozen bananas, peeled

Directions:

- ❖ In a blender, add the raspberries, bananas and almond milk and blend until smooth.

Ingredients:

- ✓ ½ cup of unsweetened almond milk
- ✓ 1/3 cup fresh mixed berries
- ❖ Transfer the smoothie to two serving bowls evenly.
- ❖ Top each bowl with berries and serve immediately.

2) APPLE AND WALNUT PORRIDGE

Preparation time: 10 minutes	Cooking time: 5 minutes	Servings: 4

Ingredients:

- ✓ 2 cups of unsweetened almond milk
- ✓ 3 tablespoons walnuts, chopped
- ✓ 3 tablespoons of sunflower seeds
- ✓ 2 large apples, peeled, pitted and grated

Directions:

- ❖ In a large skillet, stir together the milk, walnuts, sunflower seeds, applesauce, vanilla and cinnamon over medium-low heat and cook for about 3-5 minutes, stirring often.

Ingredients:

- ✓ ½ teaspoon of organic vanilla extract
- ✓ Pinch of cinnamon powder
- ✓ ½ small apple, core and slices
- ✓ 1 small banana, peeled and sliced
- ❖ Remove from heat and transfer oatmeal to serving bowls.
- ❖ Top with apple and banana slices and serve.

3) CHIA SEED PUDDING

Preparation Time: 10 minutes	Cooking Time: 10 minutes	Servings: 3

Ingredients:

- ✓ 2 cups of unsweetened almond milk
- ✓ ½ cup chia seeds
- ✓ 1 tablespoon maple syrup

Directions:

- ❖ In a large bowl, add the almond milk, chia seeds, maple syrup and vanilla extract and stir to combine well.

Ingredients:

- ✓ 1 teaspoon of organic vanilla extract
- ✓ 1/3 cup fresh strawberries, hulled and sliced
- ✓ 2 tablespoons of sliced almonds
- ❖ Cover the bowl and refrigerate for at least 3-4 hours, stirring occasionally.
- ❖ Serve with the strawberry and almond topping.

4) CAULIFLOWER AND RASPBERRY PORRIDGE

Preparation Time: 10 minutes	Cooking Time: 15 minutes	Servings: 2

Ingredients:

- ✓ 1 cup unsweetened coconut milk
- ✓ 1 cup cauliflower rice
- ✓ 1/3 cup fresh raspberries

Directions:

- ❖ In a skillet, add the coconut milk and cauliflower rice over medium heat and cook for about 2-3 minutes, stirring occasionally.

Ingredients:

- ✓ 3 tablespoons unsweetened coconut, shredded
- ✓ 3 drops of liquid stevia
- ❖ Add the raspberries and with the back of a spoon lightly crush them.
- ❖ Add the coconut and stevia and stir to combine.
- ❖ Cover the pan and cook for about 10 minutes, stirring occasionally.
- ❖ Serve hot.

5) SPICY QUINOA PORRIDGE

Preparation Time. 10 minutes	Cooking Time: 15 minutes	Servings: 4

Ingredients:

- ✓ 1 cup uncooked, rinsed and drained red quinoa
- ✓ 2 cups of alkaline water
- ✓ ½ teaspoon of organic vanilla extract
- ✓ ½ cup of coconut milk

Ingredients:

- ✓ ¼ teaspoon fresh lemon peel, finely grated
- ✓ 10-12 drops of liquid stevia
- ✓ 1 teaspoon of cinnamon powder
- ✓ ½ teaspoon of ground ginger
- ✓ Pinch of ground cloves
- ✓ 2 tablespoons of chopped almonds

Directions:

- ❖ In a large skillet, mix the quinoa, water and vanilla extract over medium heat and bring to a boil.
- ❖ Reduce heat to low and simmer, covered for about 15 minutes or until all liquid is absorbed, stirring occasionally.

- ❖ In the pan with the quinoa, add the coconut milk, lemon zest, stevia and spices and stir to combine.
- ❖ Immediately remove from heat and stir quinoa with a fork.
- ❖ Divide the quinoa mixture evenly among the serving bowls.
- ❖ Serve with a garnish of chopped almonds.

6) CHOCOLATE QUINOA PORRIDGE

Preparation Time: 15 minutes	Cooking Time: 30 minutes	Servings: 4

Ingredients:

- ✓ 1 cup uncooked quinoa, rinsed and drained
- ✓ 1 cup unsweetened almond milk
- ✓ 1 cup unsweetened coconut milk
- ✓ Pinch of sea salt

Ingredients:

- ✓ 2 spoons of cocoa powder
- ✓ 2 tablespoons of maple syrup
- ✓ ½ teaspoon of organic vanilla extract
- ✓ ½ cup fresh strawberries, hulled and sliced

Directions:

- ❖ Heat a small nonstick skillet over medium heat and cook quinoa for about 3 minutes or until lightly toasted, stirring often.
- ❖ Add the almond milk, coconut milk and a pinch of salt and stir to combine.
- ❖ Increase heat to high and bring to a boil.

- ❖ Reduce heat to low and cook, uncovered for about 20-25 minutes or until all liquid is absorbed, stirring occasionally.
- ❖ Remove from heat and immediately, stir in the cocoa powder, maple syrup and vanilla extract.
- ❖ Serve immediately with the garnish of strawberry slices.

7) BUCKWHEAT PORRIDGE WITH WALNUTS

Preparation Time: 15 minutes	Cooking Time: 7 minutes	Servings: 2

Ingredients:

- ✓ ½ cup buckwheat
- ✓ 1 cup of alkaline water
- ✓ 2 tablespoons of chia seeds
- ✓ 15-20 almonds
- ✓ 1 cup unsweetened almond milk

Ingredients:

- ✓ ½ teaspoon of cinnamon powder
- ✓ 1 teaspoon of organic vanilla extract
- ✓ 3-4 drops of liquid stevia
- ✓ ¼ cup of fresh mixed berries

Directions:

- ❖ In a large bowl, soak buckwheat groats in water overnight.
- ❖ In 2 other bowls, dip chia seeds and almonds, respectively.
- ❖ Drain the buckwheat and rinse well.
- ❖ In a nonstick skillet, add buckwheat and almond milk over medium heat and cook for about 7 minutes or until creamy.

- ❖ Drain chia seeds and almonds well.
- ❖ Remove the pan from the heat and stir in the almonds, chia seeds, cinnamon, vanilla extract and stevia.
- ❖ Serve warm with a berry garnish.

8) FRUITY OATMEAL

Preparation Time: 15 minutes	Cooking Time: 10 minutes	Servings: 4

Ingredients:

- ✓ 4 cups of alkaline water
- ✓ 1 cup steel cut dry oats
- ✓ 1 large banana, peeled and mashed

Ingredients:

- ✓ 1½ cups fresh mixed berries (your choice)
- ✓ ¼ cup walnuts, finely chopped

Directions:

- ❖ In a large skillet, add the water and oats over medium-high heat and bring to a boil.
- ❖ Reduce the heat to low and simmer for about 20 minutes, stirring occasionally.

- ❖ Remove from heat and cool slightly.
- ❖ Add the mashed banana and stir to combine.
- ❖ Top with strawberries and walnuts and serve.

9) BAKED WALNUT OATMEAL

Preparation Time: 15 minutes	Cooking time: 45 minutes	Servings: 5

Ingredients:

- ✓ 1 tablespoon of flaxseed meal
- ✓ 3 tablespoons of alkaline water
- ✓ 3 cups of unsweetened almond milk
- ✓ ¼ cup maple syrup
- ✓ 2 tablespoons of coconut oil, melted and cooled
- ✓ 2 teaspoons of organic vanilla extract

Ingredients:

- ✓ 1 teaspoon of cinnamon powder
- ✓ 1 teaspoon of organic baking powder
- ✓ ¼ teaspoon of sea salt
- ✓ 2 cups old rolled oats
- ✓ ½ cup almonds, chopped
- ✓ ½ cup walnuts, chopped

Directions:

- ❖ Lightly grease an 8x8-inch baking dish. Set aside.
- ❖ In a large bowl, add the flaxseed meal and water and beat until well combined. Set aside for about 5 minutes.
- ❖ In the bowl of the flax mixture, add the remaining ingredients except the oats and nuts and mix until well combined.
- ❖ Add the oats and nuts and stir gently to combine.
- ❖ Place the mixture in the prepared baking dish and spread it out in an even layer.

- ❖ Cover the pan with plastic wrap and refrigerate for about 8 hours.
- ❖ Preheat the oven to 350 degrees F. Arrange a rack in the center of the oven.
- ❖ Remove the pan from the refrigerator and let rest at room temperature for 15-20 minutes.
- ❖ Remove the plastic wrap and mix the oatmeal mixture well.
- ❖ Bake for about 45 minutes.
- ❖ Remove from oven and set aside to cool slightly.
- ❖ Serve hot.

10) BANANA WAFFLES

Preparation Time: 15 minutes	Cooking Time: 20 minutes	Servings: 5

Ingredients:

- ✓ 2 tablespoons of flax meal
- ✓ 6 tablespoons of warm alkaline water
- ✓ 2 bananas, peeled and mashed

Ingredients:

- ✓ 1 cup creamy almond butter
- ✓ ¼ cup whole coconut milk

Directions:

- ❖ In a small bowl, add the flax meal and warm water and whisk until well combined.
- ❖ Set aside for about 10 minutes or until mixture becomes thick.
- ❖ In a medium bowl, add bananas, almond butter and coconut milk, mix well.

- ❖ Add the flax meal mixture and stir until well combined.
- ❖ Preheat waffle iron and grease it lightly.
- ❖ Place desired amount of batter in preheated waffle iron.
- ❖ Bake for about 3-4 minutes or until waffles turn golden brown.
- ❖ Repeat with the remaining mixture.
- ❖ Serve hot.

11) BANANA AND ALMOND SMOOTHIE

Preparation Time: 10 minutes	Cooking Time: 0 minutes	Servings: 2

Ingredients:

- ✓ 2 large frozen bananas, peeled and sliced
- ✓ 1 tablespoon chopped almonds

Ingredients:

- ✓ 1 teaspoon of organic vanilla extract
- ✓ 2 cups of cooled unsweetened almond milk

❖ Pour the smoothie into two serving glasses and serve immediately

Directions:

❖ Place all ingredients in a high speed blender and pulse until smooth and creamy.

12) STRAWBERRY AND BEET SMOOTHIE

Preparation Time: 10 minutes	Cooking Time: 0 minutes	Servings: 2

Ingredients:

- ✓ 2 cups frozen strawberries, hulled
- ✓ 2/3 cup frozen beets, cut, peeled and chopped
- ✓ 1 teaspoon of fresh ginger root, peeled and grated

Ingredients:

- ✓ 1 teaspoon fresh turmeric root, peeled and grated
- ✓ ½ cup fresh orange juice
- ✓ 1 cup unsweetened almond milk

❖ Pour the smoothie into two serving glasses and serve immediately

Directions:

❖ Place all ingredients in a high speed blender and pulse until smooth and creamy.

13) RASPBERRY AND TOFU SMOOTHIE

Preparation Time: 10 minutes	Cooking Time:	Servings: 2

Ingredients:

- ✓ 1½ cups fresh raspberries
- ✓ 6 ounces of firm silken tofu, drained, pressed and chopped
- ✓ 1 teaspoon of stevia powder

Ingredients:

- ✓ 1/8 teaspoon of organic vanilla extract
- ✓ 1½ cups unsweetened almond milk
- ✓ ¼ cup ice cubes, crushed

❖ Pour the smoothie into two serving glasses and serve immediately

Directions:

❖ Place all ingredients in a high speed blender and pulse until smooth and creamy.

14) MANGO LEMON SMOOTHIE

Preparation Time: 10 minutes	Cooking Time:	Servings: 2

Ingredients:

- ✓ 2 cups frozen mango, peeled, pitted and chopped
- ✓ ¼ cup of almond butter
- ✓ pinch of ground turmeric

Ingredients:

- ✓ 2 tablespoons fresh lemon juice
- ✓ 1¼ cups unsweetened almond milk
- ✓ ¼ cup ice cubes, crushed

❖ Pour the smoothie into two serving glasses and serve immediately

Directions:

❖ Place all ingredients in a high speed blender and pulse until smooth and creamy.

15) PAPAYA AND BANANA SMOOTHIE

Preparation Time: 10 minutes	Cooking Time:	Servings: 2

- ✓ ½ of a medium papaya, peeled and coarsely chopped
- ✓ 1 large banana, peeled and sliced
- ✓ 2 tablespoons of agave nectar
- ✓ ¼ teaspoon ground turmeric

- ✓ 1 tablespoon fresh lime juice
- ✓ 1½ cups unsweetened almond milk
- ✓ ½ cup ice cubes, crushed

❖ Pour the smoothie into two serving glasses and serve immediately

Directions:

❖ Place all ingredients in a high speed blender and pulse until smooth and creamy.

16) ORANGE AND OAT SMOOTHIE

Preparation Time: 10 minutes	Cooking Time:	Servings: 2

Ingredients:

- ✓ 2/3 cups rolled oats
- ✓ 2 oranges, peeled, seeded and cut up
- ✓ 2 large bananas, peeled and sliced

Ingredients:

- ✓ 1½ cups unsweetened almond milk
- ✓ ½ cup ice cubes, crushed

❖ Pour the smoothie into two serving glasses and serve immediately

Directions:

❖ Place all ingredients in a high speed blender and pulse until smooth and creamy.

17) PINEAPPLE AND KALE SMOOTHIE

Preparation Time: 10 minutes	Cooking Time:	Servings: 2

Ingredients:

- ✓ 1½ cups fresh cabbage, hard ribs removed and chopped
- ✓ 1 large frozen banana, peeled and sliced
- ✓ ½ cup fresh pineapple, peeled and cut into pieces

Ingredients:

- ✓ ½ cup fresh orange juice
- ✓ 1 cup unsweetened coconut milk
- ✓ ½ cup ice cubes, crushed

❖ Pour the smoothie into two serving glasses and serve immediately

Directions:

❖ Place all ingredients in a high speed blender and pulse until smooth and creamy.

18) PUMPKIN AND BANANA SMOOTHIE

Preparation Time: 10 minutes	Cooking Time:	Servings: 2

- ✓ 1 cup homemade pumpkin puree
- ✓ 1 large banana, peeled and sliced
- ✓ 1 tablespoon maple syrup
- ✓ 1 teaspoon ground flaxseed

- ✓ ¼ teaspoon of cinnamon powder
- ✓ 1/8 teaspoon ground ginger
- ✓ 1½ cups unsweetened almond milk
- ✓ ¼ cup ice cubes, crushed

❖ Pour the smoothie into two serving glasses and serve immediately

Directions:

❖ Place all ingredients in a high speed blender and pulse until smooth and creamy.

19) CABBAGE AND AVOCADO SMOOTHIE

Preparation Time: 10 minutes	Cooking Time:	Servings: 2

Ingredients:

- ✓ 2 cups fresh cabbage, hard ribs removed and chopped
- ✓ ½ of a medium avocado, peeled, pitted and chopped
- ✓ ½ inch pieces of fresh ginger root, peeled and chopped

Ingredients:

- ✓ ½ inch pieces of fresh turmeric root, peeled and chopped
- ✓ 1½ cups unsweetened coconut milk
- ✓ ¼ cup ice cubes, crushed
- ❖ Pour the smoothie into two serving glasses and serve immediately

Directions:

- ❖ Place all ingredients in a high speed blender and pulse until smooth and creamy.

20) CUCUMBER AND HERB SMOOTHIE

Preparation Time: 10 minutes	Cooking Time:	Servings: 2

Ingredients:

- ✓ 2 cups fresh mixed greens (cabbage, beets), chopped and shredded
- ✓ 1 small cucumber, peeled and chopped
- ✓ ½ cup of lettuce, torn up
- ✓ ¼ cup of fresh parsley leaves
- ✓ ¼ cup of fresh mint leaves

Ingredients:

- ✓ 2-3 drops of liquid stevia
- ✓ 1 teaspoon fresh lemon juice
- ✓ 1½ cups of alkaline water
- ✓ ¼ cup ice cubes, crushed

Directions:

- ❖ Place all ingredients in a high speed blender and pulse until smooth and creamy.

21) HEMP SEED AND CARROT MUFFINS

Pour smoothie into two serving glasses and serve immediately

Preparation Time: 20-25 minutes	Cooking Time:	Servings: 12

Ingredients:

- ✓ Cashew butter, 6 tablespoons
- ✓ Shredded Carrot,
- ✓ Unrefined whole cane sugar, .5 c.
- ✓ Almond milk, 1 c.
- ✓ Oatmeal, 2 c.
- ✓ Ground flaxseed, 1 tablespoon

Ingredients:

- ✓ Water, 3 tablespoons
- ✓ Pinch of sea salt
- ✓ Powdered vanilla bean, one pinch
- ✓ Baking powder, 1 tablespoon
- ✓ Chopped cabbage, 1 tablespoon
- ✓ Hemp seeds, 2 tablespoons
- ❖ Mix everything together until well combined.
- ❖ Grease a 12-cup muffin pan and divide the batter between the cups. Bake for 20-25 minutes and enjoy.

Directions:

- ❖ Start by setting your oven to 350.
- ❖ Whisk the flax seeds and water together to make the flax egg.
- ❖ Pour everything into a larger bowl and then combine the salt, vanilla powder, baking powder, kale, hemp seeds, cashew butter, carrot, sugar, almond milk and oatmeal.

22) CHIA SEED AND STRAWBERRY PARFAIT

		Servings: 2

- ✓ Strawberry mixture -
- ✓ Brown rice syrup, 1-2 teaspoons
- ✓ Chia seeds, 1 teaspoon
- ✓ Diced strawberries, 1 c.
- ✓ Oat Blend -

- ✓ Quick rolled oats, 1 c.
- ✓ Powdered vanilla bean, one pinch
- ✓ Brown rice syrup, 1 tablespoon
- ✓ Coconut milk, 1 c.

Directions:

- ❖ To make the strawberry mixture, mix together the brown rice syrup, chia seeds and strawberries in a small bowl until well blended.
- ❖ In a separate bowl, mix together the vanilla bean powder, brown rice syrup, coconut milk and oats until well blended.

- ❖ Place one part of the oats in the base of two jars. Cover with some of the strawberry mixture. Repeat with the remaining ingredients.
- ❖ Put a lid on the jars and let them sit in the fridge overnight.
- ❖ The next morning, discover and enjoy.

23) PECAN PANCAKES

Preparation Time: 10 minutes	**Cooking Time:** 5 minutes	**Servings: 5**

Ingredients:

- ✓ Chopped pecans, .25 c.
- ✓ Nutmeg, .25 tsp
- ✓ Cinnamon, 0.5 teaspoons
- ✓ Vanilla, 1 teaspoon
- ✓ Melted butter, 2 tablespoons
- ✓ Unsweetened soy milk, .75 c.

Ingredients:

- ✓ Eggs, 2
- ✓ Salt, .25 tsp
- ✓ Baking powder, .25 tsp
- ✓ Granular sugar substitute, 1 tablespoon
- ✓ Almond flour, .75 c.
- ✓ Olive oil - cooking spray

Directions:

- ❖ Place the salt, sugar substitute, baking powder and almond flour in a bowl and mix well.
- ❖ In another bowl, place the vanilla, soy milk, butter and eggs. Mix well to incorporate everything.
- ❖ Place the egg mixture into the dried contents and mix well until well blended.
- ❖ Add the nutmeg, pecans and cinnamon. Stir for five minutes.

- ❖ Set a twelve-inch skillet over medium heat and sprinkle with cooking spray.
- ❖ Pour a tablespoon of batter into the preheated skillet and spread into a four-inch circle.
- ❖ Spoon three more spoonfuls into the pan and cook until bubbles have formed at the edges of the pancakes and the bottom is golden brown.
- ❖ Turn each one over and cook another two minutes.
- ❖ Repeat the process until all the batter has been used.
- ❖ Serve with a syrup of your choice.

24) QUINOA BREAKFAST

		Servings: 4

Ingredients:

- ✓ Maple syrup, 3 tablespoons
- ✓ 2 inch cinnamon stick
- ✓ Water, 2 c.
- ✓ Quinoa, 1 c.
- ✓ Optional Condiments:
- ✓ Yogurt
- ✓ Chopped cashews, 2 tablespoons

Ingredients:

- ✓ Whipped coconut cream, 3 tablespoons
- ✓ Lime juice, 1 teaspoon
- ✓ Nutmeg, .25 tsp
- ✓ Raisins, 2 tablespoons
- ✓ Strawberries, .5 c.
- ✓ Raspberries, .5 c.
- ✓ Blueberries, .5 c.

Directions:

- ❖ Place the quinoa in a colander and rinse under cold running water. Make sure there are no stones or anything else.
- ❖ Pour the water into a saucepan, add the quinoa and place the saucepan over medium heat. Bring to a boil.

- ❖ Add the cinnamon stick, put a lid on the saucepan, lower the hot temperature, also, simmer gently fifteen minutes until the water is swallowed.
- ❖ Remove from hot temperature and stir with a fork. Add the maple syrup and one of the toppings listed above.

25) OATMEAL

		Servings: 4

Ingredients:

- ✓ Halls
- ✓ Steel cut oats, 1.25 c.
- ✓ Water, 3.75 c.
- ✓ Optional Condiments:
- ✓ Nuts
- ✓ Dried fruits
- ✓ Sliced banana
- ✓ Diced Mango

Ingredients:

- ✓ Mixed berries
- ✓ Garam masala, 1 teaspoon
- ✓ Lemon pepper, .25 tsp
- ✓ Nutmeg, .25 tsp
- ✓ Cinnamon, 1 teaspoon

Directions:

- ❖ Place a saucepan on medium and add the water. Allow the water to boil.
- ❖ Pour in the oats with a pinch of salt and lower the heat to a simmer.

- ❖ Let simmer 25 minutes, stirring constantly.
- ❖ Once all the water has been absorbed, add one of the seasonings listed above if you want to add some flavor. If you want it creamier, add a tablespoon of coconut milk.

26) BAKED GRAPEFRUIT

		Servings: 1

Ingredients:

✓ Unsweetened grated coconut, 2 tablespoons

Ingredients:

- ✓ Halved grapefruit, 1

- ❖ Place in oven and bake 15 minutes or until coconut is tan.
- ❖ Carefully remove from oven and enjoy.

Directions:

- ❖ You need to heat your oven to 350.
- ❖ Take some foil and line a baking sheet with it.
- ❖ Place grapefruits cut in half with cut side up on aluminum foil. Top each with a tablespoon of coconut.

27) ALMOND FRITTERS

		Servings: 4

Ingredients:

- ✓ Coconut oil, 3 tablespoons
- ✓ Almond milk, 1 c.
- ✓ Baking powder, 1 teaspoon

Ingredients:

- ✓ Arrowroot powder, 2 tablespoons
- ✓ Almond flour, 1 c.

Directions:

- ❖ Place each of the dry fixings in a dish and whisk to mix.
- ❖ Add two tablespoons of coconut oil along with the almond milk to the dry elements and blend well until everything is blended.
- ❖ Place a skillet over medium heat and put a teaspoon of coconut in to melt. Swirl it around in the pan to coat it.

- ❖ Pour a ladleful of batter into the pan and use the bottom of the ladle to smooth the pancake.
- ❖ Bake for three minutes until the edges are bubbly and brown.
- ❖ Flip the pancake over and bake another three minutes until cooked through.
- ❖ Continue to cook the pancakes until all the batter has been used.

28) AMARANTH PORRIDGE

Preparation Time: 40 minutes	Cooking Time: 30 minutes	Servings: 2
✓ Cinnamon, 1 tablespoon ✓ Coconut oil, 2 tablespoons ✓ Amaranth, 1 c.		✓ Alkaline water, 2 c. ✓ Almond milk, 2 c.

Directions:	
❖ Run the water along with the milk into a pot. Set to medium-hot and allow to boil.	❖ Add the amaranth and turn the heat down to low. Stew for half an hour, stirring occasionally. ❖ Remove from hot, add copra oil and cinnamon, mix well, serve hot.

29) BANANA PORRIDGE

		Servings: 2
✓ Chopped almonds, .25 c. ✓ Liquid stevia, 3 drops ✓ Barley, .5 c.		✓ Sliced banana, 1 ✓ Unsweetened almond milk, 1 c.

Directions:	
❖ Mix stevia, 1/2 cup almond milk and barley in a bowl. ❖ Refrigerate, covered for six hours.	❖ Remove from refrigerator and stir in remaining milk. Pour into a saucepan and place on medium. Allow mixture to cook for five minutes.

30) ZUCCHINI MUFFINS

Preparation Time:	Cooking Time:	Servings: 16
✓ Halls ✓ Cinnamon, 1 teaspoon ✓ Baking powder, 1 tablespoon ✓ Almond flour, 2 c. ✓ Vanilla extract, 1 teaspoon ✓ Almond milk, .5 c. ✓ Grated zucchini, 2		✓ Overripe bananas, 3 ✓ Almond butter, .25 c. ✓ Alkaline water, 3 tablespoons ✓ Ground flaxseed, 1 tablespoon ✓ Optional Ingredients: ✓ Chopped walnuts, .25 c. ✓ Chocolate chips, .25 c.

Directions:	
❖ You need to heat your kitchen appliance to 375 degrees. Sprinkle a cupcake pan with cooking spray. ❖ Place the water and flaxseed in a bowl.	❖ Mash the bananas in a pot and put in all the leftover contents. Stir well. ❖ Separate the concoction evenly into a cupcake pan. ❖ Place in oven for 25 minutes.

31) SCRAMBLE OF TOFU WITH VEGETABLES

Preparation Time:	Cooking Time:	Servings: 4
✓ Halls ✓ Chopped basil, 2 tablespoons ✓ Chopped firm tofu, 3 c. ✓ Diced peppers (red, bell), 2 pieces. ✓ Olive oil, 1 tablespoon		Turmeric ✓ Chopped cherry tomatoes, 2 c. ✓ Chopped onions, 2 ✓ Cayenne

Directions:	
❖ Place a greased skillet over medium heat and heat the pan. ❖ Place peppers along with onions, prepare for five minutes.	❖ Toss in the tofu, cayenne, salt and turmeric. Cook an additional eight minutes. ❖ Garnish with the basil.

32) ZUCCHINI FRITTERS

Preparation Time: 10 minutes	Cooking Time: 5 minutes	Servings: 8

✓ Finely chopped shallots, .5 c. ✓ Jalapeno finely chopped, 2 ✓ Olive oil, 2 tablespoons ✓ Ground flaxseed, 4 tablespoons	✓ Halls ✓ Grated zucchini, 6 ✓ Alkaline water, 12 tablespoons

Directions:	❖ Add the flaxseed mixture and scallions and mix well.
❖ Place flaxseed and water in a bowl and mix well. Set aside. ❖ Place a large skillet over medium heat and heat the oil. Add the pepper, salt and zucchini. Cook three minutes and place zucchini in a bowl.	❖ Heat a griddle that has been sprayed with cooking spray. Pour some zucchini onto the preheated griddle and cook three minutes per side until golden brown. ❖ Repeat until the mixture is completely used up.

33) PUMPKIN QUINOA

Preparation Time:	Cooking Time:	Servings: 2

✓ Chia seeds, 2 teaspoons ✓ Pumpkin pie spice, 1 teaspoon ✓ Pumpkin puree, .25 c.	✓ Crushed banana, 1 ✓ Unsweetened almond milk, 1 c. ✓ Cooked quinoa, 1 c.

Directions:	❖ Refrigerate overnight.
❖ Place all ingredients in a container. ❖ Make sure the lid is sealed and shake well to combine.	❖ When it's ready to eat, take it out of the fridge and enjoy.

34) AVOCADO TOAST

Preparation Time: 10 minutes	Cooking Time: 10 minutes	Servings: 4

✓ Dulse flakes, sliced radish, sliced red onion, for garnish - optional ✓ Sea salt, 0.5 teaspoons ✓ Fresh coriander leaves, 1 tablespoon ✓ Chopped onion, 1 tablespoon	✓ Garlic, 2 cloves ✓ Jalapeno ✓ Avocado, 2 ✓ Sweet potato, unpeeled, cut into 4 thick slices lengthwise

Directions:	❖ While the sweet potato toast is cooking, add the salt, cilantro, onion, garlic, jalapeno and avocado to an extremely electric food processor and blend until creamy and smooth. Adjust the amount of salt as needed.
❖ Place each of the potato slices in a slot of the toaster and toast them for four cycles, or until they are cooked through. You can also toast them in the oven if you don't have a regular toaster oven. You want them to be tender enough that you can easily pierce them with a fork. Carefully arrange the cooked "toasts" on plates.	❖ Divide the avocado spread over each of the sweet potato toast slices. Top each slice with your desired toppings. Enjoy.

35) FROZEN BANANA BREAKFAST BOWL

		Servings: 1

✓ Chia seeds, hemp seeds, unsweetened coconut flakes, for garnish - optional ✓ Pumpkin seed protein powder, 4 tablespoons	✓ Bananas, 2

Directions:	❖ Process the pumpkin protein powder through the bananas until just combined.
❖ Peel and then slice the bananas. Place them thinly in a freezer safe container and freeze overnight. ❖ The next morning, add the bananas to a food processor and blend until you reach a creamy, smooth consistency, much like soft-serve ice cream.	❖ Pour into a serving dish and add desired toppings, if desired, and enjoy.

36) SAVORY SWEET POTATO WAFFLES

Preparation time: 10 minutes	Cooking Time: 20 minutes	Servings: 2

Ingredients:

- ✓ 1 medium sweet potato, peeled, grated and squeezed
- ✓ 1 teaspoon fresh thyme, chopped
- ✓ 1 teaspoon fresh rosemary, chopped

Ingredients:

- ✓ 1/8 teaspoon red pepper flakes, crushed
- ✓ Sea salt and freshly ground black pepper, to taste

Directions:

- ❖ Preheat the waffle iron and then grease it.
- ❖ In a large bowl, add all ingredients and mix until well combined.

- ❖ Place ½ of the sweet potato mixture into the preheated waffle iron and bake for about 8-10 minutes or until golden brown.
- ❖ Repeat with the remaining mixture.
- ❖ Serve hot.

37) FRUIT OATMEAL PANCAKES

Preparation Time: 10 minutes	Cooking Time: 15 minutes	Servings: 3

Ingredients:

- ✓ 1 cup rolled oats
- ✓ 1 medium banana, peeled and mashed
- ✓ ¼-½ cup unsweetened almond milk
- ✓ 1 tablespoon of organic baking powder

Ingredients:

- ✓ 1 tablespoon organic apple cider vinegar
- ✓ 1 tablespoon of agave nectar
- ✓ ½ teaspoon of organic vanilla extract
- ✓ ½ cup of fresh blackberries

Directions:

- ❖ Place all ingredients except blackberries in a large bowl and mix until well combined.
- ❖ Gently add the blackberries.
- ❖ Set the mixture aside for about 5-10 minutes.
- ❖ Preheat a large nonstick skillet over medium-low heat.
- ❖ Add about ¼ cup of the mixture and using a spatula, spread in an even layer.

- ❖ Immediately, cover the pan and cook for about 2-3 minutes or until golden brown.
- ❖ Flip the pancake and bake for another 1-2 minutes or until golden brown.
- ❖ Repeat with the remaining mixture.
- ❖ Serve hot.

38) TOFU AND MUSHROOM MUFFINS

Preparation Time: 15 minutes	Cooking Time: 30 minutes	Servings: 6

Ingredients:

- ✓ 1 teaspoon of olive oil
- ✓ 1½ cups fresh button mushrooms, chopped
- ✓ 1 shallot, chopped
- ✓ 1 teaspoon of minced garlic
- ✓ 1 teaspoon fresh rosemary, chopped
- ✓ Freshly ground black pepper, to taste

Ingredients:

- ✓ 1 (12.3ounce) package of firm silken tofu, drained, pressed and sliced
- ✓ ¼ cup of unsweetened almond milk
- ✓ 2 tablespoons of nutritional yeast
- ✓ 1 tablespoon arrowroot starch
- ✓ ¼ teaspoon ground turmeric
- ✓ 1 teaspoon coconut oil, softened

Directions:

- ❖ Preheat oven to 375 degrees F. Grease a 12-cup muffin pan.
- ❖ In a nonstick skillet, heat the oil over medium heat and sauté the shallots and garlic for about 1 minute.
- ❖ Add the mushrooms and cook for about 5-7 minutes, stirring often.
- ❖ Add the rosemary and black pepper and remove from heat.
- ❖ Set aside to cool slightly.
- ❖ In a food processor, add the tofu and remaining ingredients and pulse until smooth.

- ❖ Transfer the tofu mixture to a large bowl.
- ❖ Add the mushroom mixture.
- ❖ Divide the tofu mixture evenly among the prepared muffin cups.
- ❖ Bake for 20-22 minutes or until a toothpick inserted into the center comes out clean.
- ❖ Remove muffin pan from oven and place on a rack to cool for about 10 minutes.
- ❖ Carefully invert the muffins onto the wire rack and serve warm.

39) SIMPLE WHITE BREAD

Preparation Time: 10 minutes	Cooking Time: 1 hour and 10 minutes	Servings: 8

Ingredients:

- ✓ 4 cups of spelt flour
- ✓ 4 tablespoons of sesame seeds
- ✓ 1 teaspoon of baking soda

Ingredients:

- ✓ ¼ teaspoon of sea salt
- ✓ 10-12 drops of liquid stevia
- ✓ 2 cups plus 2 tablespoons of unsweetened almond milk

Directions:

- ❖ Preheat oven to 350 degrees F. Line a 9x5-inch baking dish with greased baking paper.
- ❖ In a large bowl, add all ingredients and with a fork, mix until well combined.
- ❖ Transfer the mixture to the prepared baking dish evenly.
- ❖ Bake for about 70 minutes or until a toothpick inserted into the center comes out clean.
- ❖ Remove from the oven and place the pan on a wire rack to cool for at least 10 minutes.
- ❖ Carefully flip the loaf of bread onto the rack to cool completely before slicing.
- ❖ Using a sharp knife, cut the loaf of bread into desired size slices and serve.

40) QUINOA BREAD

Preparation Time: 10 minutes	Cooking Time: 1 hour and a half	Servings: 12

Ingredients:

- ✓ ¼ cup chia seeds
- ✓ 1 cup of alkaline water, divided by
- ✓ 1¾ cups uncooked quinoa, soaked overnight and rinsed
- ✓ ½ teaspoon of baking soda

Ingredients:

- ✓ ¼ teaspoon of sea salt
- ✓ ¼ cup of olive oil
- ✓ 1 tablespoon fresh lemon juice

Directions:

- ❖ In a bowl, soak chia seeds in ½ cup of water overnight,
- ❖ Preheat oven to 320 degrees F. Line a baking sheet with baking paper.
- ❖ In a food processor, add the chia seed mixture and remaining ingredients and pulse for about 3 minutes.
- ❖ Place the bread mixture evenly in the prepared baking dish.
- ❖ Bake for about 1 1/2 hours or until a toothpick inserted into the center comes out clean.
- ❖ Remove the loaf pan from the oven and place on a rack to cool for about 10 minutes.
- ❖ Carefully flip the loaf of bread onto the rack to cool completely before slicing.
- ❖ Using a sharp knife, cut the loaf of bread into desired size slices and serve.

41) ZUCCHINI AND BANANA BREAD

Preparation Time: 15 minutes	Cooking Time: 45 minutes	Servings: 6

- ✓ ½ cup almond flour, sifted
- ✓ 1½ teaspoons of baking soda
- ✓ ½ teaspoon of cinnamon powder
- ✓ ¼ teaspoon ground cardamom

- ✓ 1/8 teaspoon clove powder
- ✓ 1½ cups banana, peeled and sliced
- ✓ ¼ cup almond butter, softened
- ✓ 2 teaspoons of organic vanilla extract
- ✓ 1 cup zucchini, shredded and squeezed

- ❖ Preheat oven to 350 degrees F. Grease a 6x3-inch baking dish.
- ❖ In a large bowl, add the flour, baking soda and spices and with a fork, mix well.
- ❖ In another bowl, add the banana and use a fork to mash it completely.
- ❖ In the bowl of the banana, add the almond butter and vanilla extract and beat until well combined.
- ❖ Add the flour mixture and stir until just combined.
- ❖ Gently add the grated zucchini.
- ❖ Spoon the flour mixture evenly into the prepared baking dish.
- ❖ Bake for about 40-45 minutes or until a toothpick inserted into the center comes out clean.
- ❖ Remove from the oven and place the pan on a wire rack to cool for at least 10 minutes.
- ❖ Carefully invert the bread onto the rack to cool completely before slicing.

42) GRANOLA WITH COCONUT, NUTS AND SEEDS

Preparation Time: 15 minutes	Cooking Time: 23 minutes	Servings: 8

Ingredients:

- ✓ ½ cup unsweetened coconut flakes
- ✓ 1 cup raw almonds
- ✓ 1 cup raw walnuts
- ✓ ½ cup raw sunflower seeds, shelled
- ✓ ¼ cup of coconut oil

Ingredients:

- ✓ ½ cup maple syrup
- ✓ 1 teaspoon of organic vanilla extract
- ✓ ½ cup golden raisins
- ✓ ½ cup of black raisins
- ✓ Sea salt, to taste

Directions:

- ❖ Preheat oven to 275 F. Line a large baking sheet with baking paper.
- ❖ In a food processor, add the coconut flakes, almonds, nuts and seeds and pulse until finely chopped.
- ❖ Meanwhile, in a medium nonstick skillet, add the oil, maple syrup and vanilla extract and cook for 3 minutes over medium-high heat, stirring constantly.
- ❖ Remove from heat and immediately stir in nut mixture.
- ❖ Transfer the mixture to the prepared baking sheet and spread evenly.
- ❖ Cook for about 25 minutes, stirring twice.

- ❖ Remove the pan from the oven and immediately stir in the raisins.
- ❖ Sprinkle with a little salt.
- ❖ With the back of a spatula, flatten the surface of the mixture.
- ❖ Set aside to cool completely.
- ❖ Next, break the granola into uniformly sized pieces.
- ❖ Serve this granola with your choice of non-dairy milk and fruit toppings.
- ❖ To store, transfer this granola to an airtight container and store in the refrigerator.

43) CHIA SEED PUDDING

Preparation Time: 10minutes	Cooking Time: 10minutes	Servings: 3

Ingredients:

- ✓ 2 cups of unsweetened almond milk
- ✓ ½ cup chia seeds
- ✓ 1 tablespoon maple syrup

Ingredients:

- ✓ 1 teaspoon of organic vanilla extract
- ✓ 1/3 cup fresh strawberries, hulled and sliced
- ✓ 2 tablespoons of sliced almonds

Directions:

- ❖ In a large bowl, add the almond milk, chia seeds, maple syrup and vanilla extract and stir to combine well.

- ❖ Cover the bowl and refrigerate for at least 3-4 hours, stirring occasionally.
- ❖ Serve with the strawberry and almond topping.

❖

44) CAULIFLOWER AND RASPBERRY PORRIDGE

Preparation Time: 10 minutes	Cooking Time: 15 minutes	Servings: 2

- ✓ 1 cup unsweetened coconut milk
- ✓ 1 cup cauliflower rice
- ✓ 1/3 cup fresh raspberries

- ✓ 3 tablespoons unsweetened coconut, shredded
- ✓ 3 drops of liquid stevia

- ❖ In a skillet, add the coconut milk and cauliflower rice over medium heat and cook for about 2-3 minutes, stirring occasionally.

- ❖ Add the raspberries and with the back of a spoon lightly crush them.
- ❖ Add the coconut and stevia and stir to combine.
- ❖ Cover the pan and cook for about 10 minutes, stirring occasionally.
- ❖ Serve hot.

45) SPICY QUINOA PORRIDGE

Preparation Time: 10 minutes	Cooking Time: 15 minutes	Servings: 4

✓ 1 cup uncooked, rinsed and drained red quinoa ✓ 2 cups of alkaline water ✓ ½ teaspoon of organic vanilla extract ✓ ½ cup of coconut milk	✓ ¼ teaspoon fresh lemon peel, finely grated ✓ 10-12 drops of liquid stevia ✓ 1 teaspoon of cinnamon powder ✓ ½ teaspoon of ground ginger ✓ Pinch of ground cloves ✓ 2 tablespoons of chopped almonds

Directions:

- ❖ In the pan with the quinoa, add the coconut milk, lemon zest, stevia and spices and stir to combine.
- ❖ Immediately remove from heat and stir quinoa with a fork.
- ❖ Divide the quinoa mixture evenly among the serving bowls.
- ❖ Serve with a garnish of chopped almonds.

- ❖ In a large skillet, mix the quinoa, water and vanilla extract over medium heat and bring to a boil.
- ❖ Reduce heat to low and simmer, covered for about 15 minutes or until all liquid is absorbed, stirring occasionally.

46) CHOCOLATE QUINOA PORRIDGE

Preparation Time: 15 minutes	Cooking Time: 30 minutes	Servings: 4

✓ 1 cup uncooked quinoa, rinsed and drained ✓ 1 cup unsweetened almond milk ✓ 1 cup unsweetened coconut milk ✓ Pinch of sea salt	✓ 2 spoons of cocoa powder ✓ 2 tablespoons of maple syrup ✓ ½ teaspoon of organic vanilla extract ✓ ½ cup fresh strawberries, hulled and sliced

Directions:

- ❖ Heat a small nonstick skillet over medium heat and cook quinoa for about 3 minutes or until lightly toasted, stirring often.
- ❖ Add the almond milk, coconut milk and a pinch of salt and stir to combine.
- ❖ Increase heat to high and bring to a boil.

- ❖ Reduce heat to low and cook, uncovered for about 20-25 minutes or until all liquid is absorbed, stirring occasionally.
- ❖ Remove from heat and immediately, stir in the cocoa powder, maple syrup and vanilla extract.
- ❖ Serve immediately with the garnish of strawberry slices.

47) BUCKWHEAT PORRIDGE WITH WALNUTS

Preparation Time: 15minutes	Cooking Time: 7 minutes	Servings: 2

Ingredients:

- ✓ ½ cup buckwheat
- ✓ 1 cup of alkaline water
- ✓ 2 tablespoons of chia seeds
- ✓ 15-20 almonds
- ✓ 1 cup unsweetened almond milk

Ingredients:

- ✓ ½ teaspoon of cinnamon powder
- ✓ 1 teaspoon of organic vanilla extract
- ✓ 3-4 drops of liquid stevia
- ✓ ¼ cup of fresh mixed berries

Directions:

- ❖ In a large bowl, soak buckwheat groats in water overnight.
- ❖ In 2 other bowls, dip chia seeds and almonds, respectively.
- ❖ Drain the buckwheat and rinse well.
- ❖ In a nonstick skillet, add buckwheat and almond milk over medium heat and cook for about 7 minutes or until creamy.

- ❖ Drain chia seeds and almonds well.
- ❖ Remove the pan from the heat and stir in the almonds, chia seeds, cinnamon, vanilla extract and stevia.
- ❖ Serve warm with a berry garnish.

48) FRUITY OATMEAL

Preparation Time: 15 minutes	Cooking Time: 10 minutes	Servings: 4

- ✓ 4 cups of alkaline water
- ✓ 1 cup steel cut dry oats
- ✓ 1 large banana, peeled and mashed

- ✓ 1½ cups fresh mixed berries (your choice)
- ✓ ¼ cup walnuts, finely chopped

Directions:

- ❖ In a large skillet, add the water and oats over medium-high heat and bring to a boil.
- ❖ Reduce the heat to low and simmer for about 20 minutes, stirring occasionally.

- ❖ Remove from heat and cool slightly.
- ❖ Add the mashed banana and stir to combine.
- ❖ Top with strawberries and walnuts and serve.

49) BAKED WALNUT OATMEAL

Preparation Time: 15minutes	Cooking Time: 45 minutes	Servings: 5

- ✓ 1 tablespoon of flaxseed meal
- ✓ 3 tablespoons of alkaline water
- ✓ 3 cups of unsweetened almond milk
- ✓ ¼ cup maple syrup
- ✓ 2 tablespoons of coconut oil, melted and cooled
- ✓ 2 teaspoons of organic vanilla extract

- ✓ 1 teaspoon of cinnamon powder
- ✓ 1 teaspoon of organic baking powder
- ✓ ¼ teaspoon of sea salt
- ✓ 2 cups old rolled oats
- ✓ ½ cup almonds, chopped
- ✓ ½ cup walnuts, chopped

Directions:

- ❖ Lightly grease an 8x8-inch baking dish. Set aside.
- ❖ In a large bowl, add the flaxseed meal and water and beat until well combined. Set aside for about 5 minutes.
- ❖ In the bowl of the flax mixture, add the remaining ingredients except the oats and nuts and mix until well combined.
- ❖ Add the oats and nuts and stir gently to combine.
- ❖ Place the mixture in the prepared baking dish and spread it out in an even layer.

- ❖ Cover the pan with plastic wrap and refrigerate for about 8 hours.
- ❖ Preheat the oven to 350 degrees F. Arrange a rack in the center of the oven.
- ❖ Remove the pan from the refrigerator and let rest at room temperature for 15-20 minutes.
- ❖ Remove the plastic wrap and mix the oatmeal mixture well.
- ❖ Bake for about 45 minutes.
- ❖ Remove from oven and set aside to cool slightly.
- ❖ Serve hot.

50) BANANA WAFFLES

Preparation Time: 15 minutes	Cooking Time: 20 minutes	Servings: 5

Ingredients:

- ✓ 2 tablespoons of flax meal
- ✓ 6 tablespoons of warm alkaline water
- ✓ 2 bananas, peeled and mashed

Ingredients:

- ✓ 1 cup creamy almond butter
- ✓ ¼ cup whole coconut milk

Directions:

- ❖ In a small bowl, add the flax meal and warm water and whisk until well combined.
- ❖ Set aside for about 10 minutes or until mixture becomes thick.
- ❖ In a medium bowl, add bananas, almond butter and coconut milk, mix well.

- ❖ Add the flax meal mixture and stir until well combined.
- ❖ Preheat waffle iron and grease it lightly.
- ❖ Place desired amount of batter in preheated waffle iron.
- ❖ Bake for about 3-4 minutes or until waffles turn golden brown.
- ❖ Repeat with the remaining mixture.
- ❖ Serve hot.

51) SAVORY SWEET POTATO WAFFLES

Preparation Time: 10 minutes	Cooking Time: 20 minutes	Servings: 2

Ingredients:

- ✓ 1 medium sweet potato, peeled, grated and squeezed
- ✓ 1 teaspoon fresh thyme, chopped
- ✓ 1 teaspoon fresh rosemary, chopped

Ingredients:

- ✓ 1/8 teaspoon red pepper flakes, crushed
- ✓ Sea salt and freshly ground black pepper, to taste

Directions:

- ❖ Preheat the waffle iron and then grease it.
- ❖ In a large bowl, add all ingredients and mix until well combined.

- ❖ Place ½ of the sweet potato mixture into the preheated waffle iron and bake for about 8-10 minutes or until golden brown.
- ❖ Repeat with the remaining mixture.
- ❖ Serve hot.

❖

52) FRUIT OATMEAL PANCAKES

Preparation Time: 10 minutes	Cooking Time: 15 minutes	Servings: 3

Ingredients:

- ✓ 1 cup rolled oats
- ✓ 1 medium banana, peeled and mashed
- ✓ ¼-½ cup unsweetened almond milk
- ✓ 1 tablespoon of organic baking powder

Ingredients:

- ✓ 1 tablespoon organic apple cider vinegar
- ✓ 1 tablespoon of agave nectar
- ✓ ½ teaspoon of organic vanilla extract
- ✓ ½ cup of fresh blackberries

Directions:

- ❖ Place all ingredients except blackberries in a large bowl and mix until well combined.
- ❖ Gently add the blackberries.
- ❖ Set the mixture aside for about 5-10 minutes.
- ❖ Preheat a large nonstick skillet over medium-low heat.
- ❖ Add about ¼ cup of the mixture and using a spatula, spread in an even layer.

- ❖ Immediately, cover the pan and cook for about 2-3 minutes or until golden brown.
- ❖ Flip the pancake and bake for another 1-2 minutes or until golden brown.
- ❖ Repeat with the remaining mixture.
- ❖ Serve hot.

❖

53) TOFU AND MUSHROOM MUFFINS

Preparation Time: 15 minutes	Cooking Time: 30 minutes	Servings: 6

Ingredients:

- ✓ 1 teaspoon of olive oil
- ✓ 1½ cups fresh button mushrooms, chopped
- ✓ 1 shallot, chopped
- ✓ 1 teaspoon of minced garlic
- ✓ 1 teaspoon fresh rosemary, chopped
- ✓ Freshly ground black pepper, to taste

Ingredients:

- ✓ 1 (12.3ounce) package of firm silken tofu, drained, pressed and sliced
- ✓ ¼ cup of unsweetened almond milk
- ✓ 2 tablespoons of nutritional yeast
- ✓ 1 tablespoon arrowroot starch
- ✓ ¼ teaspoon ground turmeric
- ✓ 1 teaspoon coconut oil, softened

Directions:

- ❖ Preheat oven to 375 degrees F. Grease a 12-cup muffin pan.
- ❖ In a nonstick skillet, heat the oil over medium heat and sauté the shallots and garlic for about 1 minute.
- ❖ Add the mushrooms and cook for about 5-7 minutes, stirring often.
- ❖ Add the rosemary and black pepper and remove from heat.
- ❖ Set aside to cool slightly.
- ❖ In a food processor, add the tofu and remaining ingredients and pulse until smooth.
- ❖

- ❖ Transfer the tofu mixture to a large bowl.
- ❖ Add the mushroom mixture.
- ❖ Divide the tofu mixture evenly among the prepared muffin cups.
- ❖ Bake for 20-22 minutes or until a toothpick inserted into the center comes out clean.
- ❖ Remove muffin pan from oven and place on a rack to cool for about 10 minutes.
- ❖ Carefully invert the muffins onto the wire rack and serve warm.

54) SIMPLE WHITE BREAD

Preparation Time: 10 minutes	Cooking Time: 1 hour and 10 minutes	Servings: 8

Ingredients:

- ✓ 4 cups of spelt flour
- ✓ 4 tablespoons of sesame seeds
- ✓ 1 teaspoon of baking soda

Ingredients:

- ✓ ¼ teaspoon of sea salt
- ✓ 10-12 drops of liquid stevia
- ✓ 2 cups plus 2 tablespoons of unsweetened almond milk

Directions:

- ❖ Preheat oven to 350 degrees F. Line a 9x5-inch baking dish with greased baking paper.
- ❖ In a large bowl, add all ingredients and with a fork, mix until well combined.
- ❖ Transfer the mixture to the prepared baking dish evenly.
- ❖ Bake for about 70 minutes or until a toothpick inserted into the center comes out clean.
- ❖

- ❖ Remove from the oven and place the pan on a wire rack to cool for at least 10 minutes.
- ❖ Carefully flip the loaf of bread onto the rack to cool completely before slicing.
- ❖ Using a sharp knife, cut the loaf of bread into desired size slices and serve.

55) QUINOA BREAD

Preparation Time: 10 minutes	Cooking Time: 1 hour and a half	Servings: 12

Ingredients:

- ✓ ¼ cup chia seeds
- ✓ 1 cup of alkaline water, divided by

Ingredients:

- ✓ ¼ teaspoon of sea salt
- ✓ ¼ cup of olive oil
- ✓ 1 tablespoon fresh lemon juice

✓ 1¾ cups uncooked quinoa, soaked overnight and rinsed ✓ ½ teaspoon of baking soda	

Directions: ❖ In a bowl, soak chia seeds in ½ cup of water overnight, ❖ Preheat oven to 320 degrees F. Line a baking sheet with baking paper. ❖ In a food processor, add the chia seed mixture and remaining ingredients and pulse for about 3 minutes. ❖ Place the bread mixture evenly in the prepared baking dish. ❖ Bake for about 1 1/2 hours or until a toothpick inserted into the center comes out clean.	❖ Remove the loaf pan from the oven and place on a rack to cool for about 10 minutes. ❖ Carefully flip the loaf of bread onto the rack to cool completely before slicing. ❖ Using a sharp knife, cut the loaf of bread into desired size slices and serve.

Chapter 2

LUNCH

56) TOMATO AND VEGETABLE SALAD

Preparation Time: 15 minutes.		Servings: 4

Ingredients:

- ✓ 6 cups of fresh vegetables
- ✓ 2 cups of cherry tomatoes
- ✓ 2 shallots, chopped

Directions:

- ❖ Place all ingredients in a large bowl and mix to coat well.

Ingredients:

- ✓ 2 tablespoons of extra virgin olive oil
- ✓ 2 tablespoons fresh orange juice
- ✓ 1 tablespoon fresh lemon juice
- ❖ Cover the bowl and refrigerate for about 6-8 hours.
- ❖ Remove from refrigerator and mix well before serving.

57) STRAWBERRY AND APPLE SALAD

Preparation time: 15 minutes.		Servings: 4

Ingredients:

For the salad:
- ✓ 4 cups of mixed lettuce, ripped up
- ✓ 2 apples, core and slices
- ✓ 1 cup fresh strawberries, hulled and sliced
- ✓ ¼ cup pecans, chopped

For the dressing:

Directions:

- ❖ For the salad, place all ingredients in a large bowl and mix well.
- ❖ For the dressing, place all ingredients in a bowl and whisk until well combined.

Ingredients:

- ✓ 3 tablespoons of apple cider vinegar
- ✓ 3 tablespoons of olive oil
- ✓ 1 tablespoon of agave nectar
- ✓ 1 teaspoon poppy seeds
- ❖ Pour the dressing over the salad and toss to coat well.
- ❖ Serve immediately.

58) CAULIFLOWER SOUP

Preparation Time: 15 minutes	Cooking Time: 30 minutes.	Servings: 4

Ingredients:

- ✓ 2 tablespoons of olive oil
- ✓ 1 yellow onion, chopped
- ✓ 2 carrots, peeled and cut into pieces
- ✓ 2 garlic cloves, minced
- ✓ 1 Serrano bell pepper, finely chopped
- ✓ 2 stalks of celery, chopped
- ✓ 1 teaspoon ground turmeric
- ✓ 1 teaspoon of ground coriander

Directions:

- ❖ Heat the oil over medium heat in a large soup pot and sauté the onion, carrot and celery for about 4-6 minutes.
- ❖ Add the garlic, serrano pepper and spices and sauté for about 1 minute.
- ❖ Add the cauliflower and cook for about 5 minutes, stirring occasionally.

Ingredients:

- ✓ 1 teaspoon of ground cumin
- ✓ ¼ teaspoon of red pepper flakes, crushed
- ✓ 1 head of cauliflower, chopped
- ✓ 4 cups of homemade vegetable broth
- ✓ 1 cup unsweetened coconut milk
- ✓ Sea salt and freshly ground black pepper, to taste
- ✓ 2 tablespoons fresh chives, finely chopped

- ❖ Add the broth and coconut milk and bring to a boil over medium-high heat.
- ❖ Reduce the heat to low and simmer for about 15 minutes.
- ❖ Season the soup with salt and black pepper and remove from heat.
- ❖ Using an immersion blender, blend the soup until smooth.
- ❖ Serve warm and garnish with chives.

59) ASIAN PUMPKIN SALAD

		Servings:

- ✓ Diced avocado (.5)
- ✓ Pomegranate seeds (.25 c.)
- ✓ Lemon juice (1 tablespoon)
- ✓ Sliced cabbage (4 c.)
- ✓ Olive oil (1.5 tablespoons)
- ✓ Diced pumpkin (2 c.)
- ✓ Salt (.5 tsp.)

- ✓ Red pepper flakes (.25 tsp.)
- ✓ Ground mustard (.25 tsp.)
- ✓ Ground Garlic (.25 tsp.)
- ✓ Ground cloves (.25 tsp.)
- ✓ Black sesame seeds (1 tablespoon)
- ✓ White sesame seeds (1 tablespoon)

Directions:

- ❖ Turn on the oven and give it time to heat to 400 degrees. Prepare a baking sheet with baking paper.
- ❖ In a large dish, combine the black and white sesame seeds with the salt, chili flakes, mustard, garlic and cloves.
- ❖ Drizzle the squash with a little olive oil and then roll each cube in the sesame seed mixture, pressing down a little to coat it.

- ❖ Add the squash to the baking dish and place it in the oven. It will take about half an hour to bake.
- ❖ While the squash is cooking, add the kale to a large bowl and pour in the salt, lemon juice and the rest of the olive oil. Massage the mixture into the kale and then set aside.
- ❖ When the squash is ready, add it on top of the kale and garnish with the avocado and pomegranate seeds before serving.

60) SWEET POTATO ROLLS

		Servings:

- ✓ Avocado (1)
- ✓ Alfalfa sprouts (1 c.)
- ✓ Sliced red onion (.5)
- ✓ Spinach (1 c.)
- ✓ Cooked quinoa (.5 c.)
- ✓ Swiss chard greens (4)
- ✓ Sweet potato hummus
- ✓ Crushed black pepper (.25 tsp.)

- ✓ Salt (.25 tsp.)
- ✓ Cinnamon powder (.25 tsp.)
- ✓ Chilli powder (.25 tsp.)
- ✓ Garlic clove (1)
- ✓ Lemon juice (.5)
- ✓ Olive oil (.25 c.)
- ✓ Tahini (.33 c.)
- ✓ Diced sweet potato (1)

Directions:

- ❖ Take the sweet potatoes and add them to a pan. Cover with water and bring to a boil. When it reaches a boil, reduce the flame and let it cook for a while to make the potatoes tender.
- ❖ When these are ready, drain the water and add them to the food processor along with pepper, salt, cinnamon, chili powder, garlic, lemon juice, olive oil and tahini.

- ❖ Process until the mixture is smooth.
- ❖ Lay out each of the green collards and then spread sweet potato hummus on each.
- ❖ Add the avocado, sprouts, onion, spinach and quinoa. Roll everything up and secure with toothpicks. Repeat until the vegetables and filling are done.

61) SPICY CABBAGE BOWL

Preparation Time:	Cooking Time:	Servings:

Ingredients:

- ✓ Sesame seeds (1 tablespoon)
- ✓ Green onion (.25 c.)
- ✓ Cabbage (2 c.)
- ✓ Coconut amino acids (1 teaspoon)
- ✓ Tamari (2 tablespoons)
- ✓ Chopped kimchi cabbage (1 c.)

Ingredients:

- ✓ Cooked brown rice (1 c.)
- ✓ Chopped garlic (1 teaspoon)
- ✓ Grated ginger (.5 tsp.)
- ✓ Sesame oil (2 tablespoons)

Directions:

- ❖ Take out a frying pan and heat the sesame oil in it. When the oil is hot, add together the coconut amino acid, tamari, kimchi, brown rice, garlic and ginger.

- ❖ After five minutes of cooking these ingredients, add the green onions and cabbage and toss to combine.
- ❖ Cook for a little longer. Then you can garnish the dish with some sesame seeds before serving.

62) CITRUS AND FENNEL SALAD

		Servings:

Ingredients:

- ✓ Diced avocado (.5)
- ✓ Pomegranate seeds (2 tablespoons)
- ✓ Pepper (.5 tsp.)
- ✓ Salt (.25 tsp.)
- ✓ Olive oil (.25 c.)
- ✓ Orange juice (2 tablespoons)
- ✓ Lemon juice (2 tablespoons)

Directions:

- ❖ To start this recipe, bring out a large bowl and combine together the parsley, mint, fennel slices, grapefruit wedges, and orange wedges. Stir to combine.
- ❖ In another bowl, whisk together the pepper, salt, olive oil, orange juice and lemon juice.

Ingredients:

- ✓ Chopped mint (1 tablespoon)
- ✓ Chopped parsley (.5 c.)
- ✓ Sliced fennel bulbs (2)
- ✓ Red grapefruit segmented (.5)
- ✓ Segmented orange (1)

- ❖ When combined, pour over the fennel and citrus mixture in the large bowl, stirring to coat.
- ❖ Move to a plate and garnish with the avocado and pomegranate seeds. Serve immediately.

63) VEGAN BURGER

Preparation Time:	Cooking Time:	Servings: 4 hamburger patties

- ✓ 1/4 to 1/2 cup of spring water
- ✓ 1/2 teaspoon of cayenne powder
- ✓ 1/2 teaspoon of ginger powder
- ✓ Grape oil
- ✓ 1 teaspoon of dill
- ✓ 2 teaspoons of sea salt
- ✓ 2 teaspoons of onion powder

Directions:

- ❖ Mix the vegetables and seasonings in a large bowl, then add the flour. Gently add the spring water and stir the mixture until combined. In case the dough is too soft, add more flour.

- ✓ 2 teaspoons of oregano
- ✓ 2 teaspoons of basil
- ✓ ¼ cup cherry tomatoes, diced
- ✓ 1/2 cup of cabbage, diced
- ✓ 1/2 cup green peppers, diced
- ✓ 1/2 cup onions, diced
- ✓ 1 cup of chickpea flour

- ❖ Divide the dough into 4 meatballs. Cook patties in grapeseed oil, in a skillet over medium heat for about 2 to 3 minutes per side. Continue flipping until the burger is brown on all sides.
- ❖ Serve the burger on a bun and enjoy.

64) ALKALINE SPICY CABBAGE

		Servings: 1 portion

Ingredients:

- ✓ Grape oil
- ✓ 1/4 teaspoon of sea salt
- ✓ 1 teaspoon crushed red pepper

Directions:

- ❖ First wash the cabbage well and then fold each cabbage leaf in half. Cut off and discard the stems. Cut the prepared cabbage into bite-size portions and use the salad spinner to remove the water.
- ❖ In a wok, add 2 tablespoons of grapeseed oil and heat the oil over high heat.

Ingredients:

- ✓ 1/4 cup red bell bell pepper, diced
- ✓ 1/4 cup onion, diced
- ✓ 1 bunch of cabbage

- ❖ Fry the peppers and onions in the oil for about 2-3 minutes and then season with a little sea salt.
- ❖ Lower the heat and add the cabbage, cover the wok with a lid and simmer for about 5 minutes.
- ❖ Open the lid and add the crushed pepper, mix well and cover again. Cook until tender, or for about 3 more minutes.

65) ELECTRIC SALAD

		Servings: 4

✓ 3 jalapenos ✓ 2 red onions ✓ 1 orange bell pepper ✓ 1 yellow bell pepper ✓ 1 cup cherry tomatoes, chopped	✓ 1 bunch of cabbage ✓ 1 handful of romaine lettuce ✓ Extra virgin olive oil ✓ Juice of 1 lime

❖ Place ingredients in a bowl and drizzle with olive oil and lime juice to your preferred taste.

Directions:

❖ First wash and rinse the ingredients well. Dry the ingredients and then cut them into bite-size pieces, or as required.

66) KALE SALAD

Preparation Time:	Cooking Time:	Servings: 2

✓ 1/4 teaspoon of cayenne ✓ 1/2 teaspoon of sea salt ✓ 1/2 cup of cooked chickpeas ✓ 1/2 cup of red onions ✓ 1/2 cup sliced red, orange, yellow, and green peppers ✓ 4 cups chopped cabbage	✓ 1/2 cup alkaline garlic sauce (recipe included). ✓ Alkaline Garlic Sauce ✓ 1/4 teaspoon of dill ✓ 1/4 teaspoon of sea salt ✓ 1/2 teaspoon of ginger ✓ 1 tablespoon of onion powder ✓ 1/4 cup shallots, chopped ✓ 1 cup of grape oil

❖ Prepare the dressing by mixing the ingredients for the "Alkaline Electric Garlic Sauce".
❖ Drizzle with half a cup of sauce and then serve.

Directions:

❖ In a bowl, mix all the ingredients for the coleslaw and toss.

67) WALNUT, DATE, ORANGE AND KALE SALAD

Preparation Time:	Cooking Time:	Servings: 2

Ingredients:

✓ /2 red onion, very thinly sliced
✓ 2 bunches of cabbage, or 6 full cups of sprouts
✓ 6 medjool dates, pitted
✓ 1/3 cup whole walnuts
✓ For the dressing

Ingredients:

✓ 5 tablespoons of olive oil
✓ Pinch of coarse salt
✓ 1 medjool date
✓ 4 tablespoons orange juice, freshly squeezed
✓ 2 tablespoons of lime juice

❖ Then wash, dry and chop the cabbage and place in a large bowl. Thinly slice the onion and add it to the bowl.
❖ Now prepare the dressing by combining the ingredients for the "dressing" in the blender apart from the olive oil.
❖ Blend the mixture to break up the dates and then pour in the oil in a steady stream to emulsify the dressing.
❖ Finally, saute the cabbage and onion mixture along with the orange and walnut dressing.
❖ Move to a serving bowl and sprinkle with the walnut and date mixture. Enjoy!

Directions:

❖ Preheat the oven to 375 degrees F and then place the walnuts on a baking sheet. Roast the walnuts for about 7-8 minutes, or until the skin begins to darken and crack.
❖ Once done, transfer the walnuts while still warm and let them steam for 15 minutes wrapped in a kitchen towel.
❖ Once cooled, squeeze and turn firmly to remove the skin, all this time still wrapped in the towel.
❖ In a food processor, place the pitted dates along with the walnuts and puree until completely mixed and finely chopped. Set aside to cover the salad.

68) TOMATOES WITH BASIL-SNACK

		Servings: 1 portion

Ingredients:

- ✓ ¼ teaspoon of sea salt
- ✓ 2 tablespoons of lemon juice
- ✓ 2 tablespoons of olive oil

Ingredients:

- ✓ ¼ cup basil, fresh
- ✓ 1 cup chopped tomatoes, cherry or Roma

Directions:

- ❖ Start by slicing the cherry tomatoes and placing them in a medium sized bowl.
- ❖ Then finely chop your basil and add it to the bowl of tomatoes.

- ❖ Drizzle the tomatoes and basil with a little olive oil and lemon juice.
- ❖ Add a little sea salt to taste.
- ❖ Serve.

69) SPELT, ZUCCHINI AND EGGPLANT PASTA

		Servings: 4

Ingredients:

- ✓ 2 teaspoons of dried basil leaves
- ✓ 1 teaspoon of oregano
- ✓ 2/3 cup vegetable broth
- ✓ 2/3 cup of dried, diced cherry tomatoes
- ✓ 1 large zucchini, diced
- ✓ 3 medium-sized ripe cherry tomatoes, diced

Ingredients:

- ✓ 2-3 ginger, crushed
- ✓ 1-2 white onions, finely chopped
- ✓ 3 tablespoons of cold-pressed extra virgin olive oil
- ✓ 1 large eggplant cut into cubes
- ✓ 300g of spelt pasta
- ✓ Sea salt to taste

Directions:

- ❖ Over medium heat, heat a little oil in a skillet and then sauté the eggplant, ginger and onion for about 8-10 minutes, stirring constantly.
- ❖ Then add the oregano, tomatoes and zucchini and let cook for 6-8 minutes, stirring occasionally.

- ❖ Now heat the water and cook the pasta until it is firm to the bite, and then add the vegetable broth to the pan.
- ❖ Season with fresh pepper, salt and dried basil. Allow the mixture to simmer for a few minutes, covered.
- ❖ Once cooked, you can serve the sauce over pasta and garnish with fresh basil leaves.

70) ALKALIZING MILLET DISH

		Servings: 2

Ingredients:

- ✓ 1/2 teaspoon of sea salt
- ✓ 2 1/2 cups of water

Ingredients:

- ✓ 1 cup millet

Directions:

- ❖ In a pot with a tight-fitting lid, add the millet and then dry-fry over medium heat, stirring constantly.
- ❖ As soon as the millet turns golden brown, add the sea salt and water and cover the ingredients with a lid.
- ❖ Then bring the mixture to a boil and let it simmer until all the water has been absorbed, or for about 25-35 minutes.

- ❖ Alternatively, you can cook on an electric stove. Just cover the lid and bring to a boil, simmer for a couple of minutes and then turn off the stove.
- ❖ Allow the contents to cool for about 30 minutes with the lid on to allow the millet to dry out.
- ❖ Then serve and enjoy the millet.

71) GREEN NOODLE SALAD

		Servings: 2

Ingredients:

- ✓ 1 pinch of sea salt
- ✓ 1 cup chopped fresh basil
- ✓ 2 tablespoons lemon juice, fresh
- ✓ ¼ cup unleavened vegetable broth

Ingredients:

- ✓ 1" ginger knob
- ✓ 1 cup of kale
- ✓ 1 cup zucchini, chopped
- ✓ 1 handful of lettuce
- ✓ 1 cup millet noodles

Directions:

- ❖ First, cook the noodles according to package directions. Once ready, drain and rinse under cold running water. Once done, set aside and allow to cool.
- ❖ Thinly slice the zucchini and shred the kale. Steam the two vegetables very lightly for a few minutes until the color pops. Make sure they still remain crisp.

- ❖ Wash and cut the lettuce and discard the stalks.
- ❖ Start by making the dressing: combine the vegetable broth and lemon juice in a food processor, and then add the chopped ginger. Blend the ingredients for about 15-30 seconds.
- ❖ Now mix the basil, shredded lettuce, zucchini, cabbage and noodles in a bowl and pour the dressing over it. Mix well and then season with salt.
- ❖ Serve and enjoy.

72) PUMPKIN RATATOUILLE

		Servings: 4

Ingredients:

- ✓ 1 cup of spring water
- ✓ Pinch of cayenne pepper
- ✓ Sea salt or organic salt
- ✓ 4 tablespoons of cold-pressed extra virgin olive oil
- ✓ 2 teaspoons of thyme
- ✓ 1 fennel bulb

Ingredients:

- ✓ 2 large onions
- ✓ 1 cup cherry tomatoes, chopped
- ✓ 1 red bell pepper
- ✓ 1 yellow bell pepper
- ✓ 16 ounces of fresh pumpkin

Directions:

- ❖ Cut the bell bell pepper, tomatoes and fresh squash into small portions. Then dice the fennel and onions.
- ❖ In a pot, heat some olive oil and then sauté the fennel and onions for a few minutes.

- ❖ Now add the bell bell pepper and the squash. Then sauté the mixture for about 8 minutes.
- ❖ Once done, add the alkaline water, thyme and tomatoes and cook until the vegetables are quite tender but not too soft.

73) ROASTED VEGETABLES

		Servings: 2

Ingredients:

- ✓ A sprinkle of cayenne pepper
- ✓ A drizzle of olive oil
- ✓ 2 fennel bulbs, chopped
- ✓ 1/2 onion, sliced

Ingredients:

- ✓ 1 yellow pumpkin, sliced
- ✓ 1 zucchini, sliced
- ✓ 1 bunch of green beans, ends cut off

Directions:

- ❖ Preheat the oven to 450 degrees F.
- ❖ Then, on a pitted baking sheet, place the fennel bulbs and vegetables and then drizzle everything with a little olive oil.

- ❖ Add a little cayenne pepper and stir.
- ❖ Cook vegetables for about 16 minutes, stirring at 8-minute intervals.
- ❖ As soon as the vegetables are lightly browned, remove from heat and serve.

74) CROCKPOT SUMMER VEGETABLES

		Servings: 6

Ingredients:

- ✓ 1 tablespoon chopped thyme, fresh
- ✓ 2 tablespoons chopped basil, fresh
- ✓ ½ cup olive oil
- ✓ Juice of 1 lemon
- ✓ 1 cup sliced mushrooms

Ingredients:

- ✓ 2 ½ cups sliced zucchini
- ✓ 2 cups sliced bell bell pepper, yellow
- ✓ 1 ½ cup chopped onions
- ✓ 1 cup chopped cherry tomatoes
- ✓ 2 cups of sliced okra

Directions:

- ❖ Mix the vegetables in a bowl, then stir in the olive oil and lemon juice in a separate bowl.
- ❖ Stir in the thyme and basil and place the vegetables in a slow stove.

- ❖ Top with the marinade and stir to coat.
- ❖ Cook vegetables over high heat for 3 hours, stirring every hour.
- ❖ Once cooked, serve and enjoy.

75) BRAZILIAN CABBAGE

		Servings: 2

Ingredients:

- ✓ Juice of 1/2 lime
- ✓ 1/4 teaspoon cayenne pepper
- ✓ 1/4 teaspoon salt

Ingredients:

- ✓ 2 bunches of cabbage, thin strips
- ✓ 2 fennel bulbs, peeled, cut and crushed
- ✓ 2 tablespoons of olive oil

Directions:

- ❖ Remove the rinds from the cabbage, stack the leaf halves together and slice the cabbage.
- ❖ Crush the fennel bulbs using the flat end of a chef's knife or a pestle and mortar.
- ❖ In a large skillet, heat the olive oil on medium for a minute and then add the fennel.

- ❖ Sauté for 1 minute or until aromatic, and then add the cayenne pepper, salt and cabbage.
- ❖ Lower the heat to medium low and sauté to soften the greens and get a vibrant color or about 3-4 minutes.
- ❖ Then squeeze in the lime juice and add more salt and cayenne pepper if needed. Serve and enjoy.

76) SEAWEED WRAPS WITH QUINOA AND VEGETABLES

		Servings: 2 rolls

Ingredients:

- ✓ 1 tablespoon sesame seed oil
- ✓ 1 tablespoon raw sesame seeds
- ✓ 1 teaspoon fresh ginger root, finely grated
- ✓ 1 teaspoon fresh red chili pepper with seeds and finely chopped
- ✓ 1 finely chopped fennel bulb

Ingredients:

- ✓ ¼ cup finely chopped fresh culantro leaves
- ✓ ¼ cup of raw cucumber sticks
- ✓ ¼ cup raw parsnips
- ✓ ½ cup of cooked quinoa

Directions:

- ❖ Spread 2 sheets of nori individually on a work surface.
- ❖ Mix quinoa with chili, ginger, fennel, seeds and culantro leaves.
- ❖ In this mixture, add the sesame seed oil and mix well.
- ❖ Spread the seed and quinoa mixture between two sheets of nori, placing it along the edge of each sheet.

- ❖ Top the quinoa mixture with the parsnip sticks and cucumber. Now roll up the sheets and gently wrap the contents.
- ❖ If you want, you can slide the nori rolls around until they look like sushi rolls.

77) LETTUCE WRAPS

	Servings: 4 wrappers

Ingredients:

- ✓ ½ cup coarsely chopped raw walnuts
- ✓ ½ cup fresh strawberries, sliced
- ✓ ½ of a ripe avocado, pitted and cut into slices

Ingredients:

- ✓ 1 cup raw green beans
- ✓ 4 large lettuce leaves

Directions:

- ❖ Spread the lettuce leaves on a kitchen work surface or plate.
- ❖ Divide the green beans among the individual lettuce leaves, placing them at a 90-degree angle to the edge.
- ❖ Now divide the avocado slices between the individual lettuce leaves placing them on top of the spears.

- ❖ Also divide berries between individual lettuce leaves and place on top of avocado.
- ❖ Then divide the nuts between the lettuce leaves and place them on top of the berries.
- ❖ Finally, roll up the leaves and wrap all the contents around them.

78) RAINBOW SALAD WITH MEYER LEMON DRESSING

	Servings: 4

Ingredients:

- ✓ 1/2 avocado, sliced
- ✓ Micro green or sprouts
- ✓ 1 cup of pea shoots
- ✓ ½ yellow bell pepper, sliced
- ✓ 1/8 red onion, thinly sliced
- ✓ ½ cup diced cherry tomatoes
- ✓ 1 parsnip, ribbon with peeler
- ✓ Arugula and other vegetables
- ✓ Chopped or chipped raw nuts

Ingredients:

For the dressing
- ✓ 1 tablespoon of agave sugar
- ✓ 1/16 teaspoon of sea salt
- ✓ 1/6 cup of cold-pressed extra virgin olive oil
- ✓ 3 stalks of fresh dill
- ✓ 3 basil leaves
- ✓ 3/4 teaspoon of chopped red onion
- ✓ ½ avocado
- ✓ 1 Meyer lemon, squeezed

Directions:

- ❖ Place a handful of arugula in each serving bowl.
- ❖ Add the rest of the vegetables followed by the micro greens and pea shoots.
- ❖ Then, top with the walnuts and set aside.

- ❖ Now move the ingredients for the dressing to a blender and blend until smooth and creamy.
- ❖ Pour the dressing into a serving bowl and then pour it over the salad and enjoy!

79) ALKALINE QUINOA & HUMMUS WRAPS

	Servings: 4 wrappers

Ingredients:

- ✓ 1 cup avocado
- ✓ 1 cup hummus
- ✓ 1 cup of quinoa
- ✓ 1/2 cup parsnips

Ingredients:

- ✓ 1/2 cup of lettuce
- ✓ 1/2 cup of sprouts
- ✓ 4 large baby cabbage

Directions:

- ❖ Place 1 cup of quinoa in a skillet with 2 cups of water. Bring the water to a boil and lower the heat to a simmer until the quinoa is soft and the water has evaporated.
- ❖ Cut the cabbage leaves from the plant, wash them and lay them out like a regular wrap. Spread hummus over each cabbage to help hold the other ingredients in place.

- ❖ Now slice and place the avocado in a line from top to bottom and down the center of the cabbage leaf.
- ❖ Once done, place the quinoa evenly between the cabbage leaves and fill with the rest of the ingredients.
- ❖ Finally wrap the leaf. Fold it down and then roll it up. Consider using a toothpick to help keep things in place.

80) GRILLED ZUCCHINI SALAD

		Servings: 2

Ingredients:

- ✓ 3 ounces of watercress
- ✓ 6 zucchinis
- ✓ Sea Salt
- ✓ Chili pepper and mint dressing:
- ✓ 6 tablespoons of extra virgin olive oil

Ingredients:

- ✓ ½ cup of fresh basil leaves
- ✓ 1 red hot pepper
- ✓ Zest and juice of 1/2 lemon
- ✓ Cayenne Pepper
- ✓ Halls

Directions:

- ❖ Clean the watercress and zucchini. Then slice the zucchini into thin strips. Salt the strips and let them soften slightly in the salt.
- ❖ Meanwhile, start preparing the dressing. Wash the basil leaves, chili pepper and lemon and set aside.
- ❖ Discard the seeds of the chili and chop well. Then shred the leaves and set aside.
- ❖ In a bowl, whisk together the olive oil, basil, red pepper and lemon zest and then season with cayenne pepper and salt.

- ❖ Now place the watercress in a serving dish.
- ❖ Fire up your barbecue for direct heat at 220 degrees F. Place the salt-softened strips on a rack and close the lid.
- ❖ Now grill the zucchini until spots develop, or for about 3 to 4 minutes per side.
- ❖ Then remove them from the grill and let them cool. To serve, place the zucchini on the watercress and then pour the dressing over it.

81) CREAMY CABBAGE SALAD WITH AVOCADO AND TOMATO

		Servings: 2

Ingredients:

- ✓ 1/2 teaspoon of cayenne pepper
- ✓ 1 tablespoon of agave syrup
- ✓ 1 funnel-shaped bulb, chopped
- ✓ Juice of 1 lime

Ingredients:

- ✓ ½ cup chopped cherry tomatoes
- ✓ 1 medium ripe avocado
- ✓ 2 large handfuls of cabbage

Directions:

- ❖ Clean and chop the tomatoes and cabbage and then place them in a bowl or large glass bowl.
- ❖ Then peel the avocado and place it in the bowl.

- ❖ Squeeze the lime and now add it along with the rest of the ingredients in the mixing bowl.
- ❖ Rub the ingredients together and serve the salad.

82) RICE WITH SESAME AND GINGER

		Servings: 4

Ingredients:

- ✓ 1/2 teaspoon celtic sea salt
- ✓ 2 teaspoons of fresh lime juice
- ✓ ½ cup culantro, finely chopped
- ✓ 4 cups mushrooms (any kind except shiitake), finely chopped
- ✓ 6 green onions, finely chopped
- ✓ 1 fennel bulb, chopped

Ingredients:

- ✓ 2 tablespoons fresh chopped ginger
- ✓ 1 small green chili pepper, ribbed, seeded and chopped
- ✓ 2 tablespoons of toasted sesame oil
- ✓ 2 tablespoons of grape oil
- ✓ 1 cup of cooked wild rice

Directions:

- ❖ Heat oil in a deep skillet or wok over medium-high heat.
- ❖ Once hot, sauté the mushrooms, green onions, fennel, ginger and chili along with a little salt until soft and combined, or for about 5 minutes.

- ❖ Add the tamari and rice and keep on the heat for another 2-3 minutes.
- ❖ Add the lime juice, culantro and ¼ teaspoon salt and taste.

83) MACARONI AND 'CHEESE

Preparation Time: 20 minutes.	Cooking Time: 50 minutes.	Servings: 8-10

Ingredients:

- ✓ 12 ounces of any alkaline pasta
- ✓ 1/4 cup of chickpea flour
- ✓ 1 cup of raw Brazil Nuts
- ✓ 1/2 teaspoon of Achiote Ground
- ✓ 2 teaspoons of onion powder

Ingredients:

- ✓ 1 teaspoon of Pure Sea Salt
- ✓ 2 teaspoons of Oil Sed Grape
- ✓ 1 cup of milk Homemade Hempseed
- ✓ 1 cup of spring water + an addition for juice of 1/2 Key Lime

Directions:

- ❖ Place the Brazil Nuts in a lunch bowl and add the soy water. Stand right side up.
- ❖ Coook your favorite alkaline pasta.
- ❖ Preheat our oven to 350 degrees Fahrenheit.
- ❖ Place the processed dough in a cooking dish and pour a little semi-fat oil to prevent it from sticking to the bread.

- ❖ Add all ingredients to a blender and blend for 2 to 4 minutes until done.
- ❖ Pour the Brazil nut sauce over the macaroni and mix well.
- ❖ Place the pan in the oven and bake for about 30 minutes.
- ❖ Serve and enjoy your Macaroni and 'Cheese'!
- ❖ Useful Tips:
- ❖ If you don't have Homemad Hempsed Milk milk, add Coconut Milk insted. If you want to make the dish crispy, bake it for about 5 minutes.

84) CREAMY KAMUT PASTA

Preparation Time: 25 minutes.	Cooking Time: 50 Minutes.	Servings: 6

Ingredients:

Pasta:
- ✓ 12 ounces of Kamut Spaghetti
- ✓ 1 tablespoon of tarragon
- ✓ 1 teaspoon of Onion Powder.
- ✓ 1 teaspoon of pure sea Salt
- ✓ 2 tablespoons of Grape Seed Oil 6 to 8 cups of Spring Water (for boiling the pasta)

Sauce:
- ✓ 2 cups of chopped Kale
- ✓ 12 Cherry chopped tomatoes
- ✓ 1/2 diced Onion
- ✓ 2 sliced mushrooms

Ingredients:

- ✓ 1/4 cup of Garbanzo Bean Flour
- ✓ 2 teaspoons of Onion Powder
- ✓ 1 tablespoon of Oregano
- ✓ 1 teaspoon of Tarragon
- ✓ 1 teaspoon of Basil
- ✓ 1/4 teaspoon of Pure Sea Salt + extra 1/2 teaspoon
- ✓ 1/8 teaspoon of Cayenne Powder + extra 1/8 teaspoon
- ✓ 2 tablespoons of Grape Seed Oil
- ✓ 2 cups of coconut Milk
- ✓ 2 cups of Spring Water

Directions:

- ❖ Pasta:
- ❖ In a large pot, bring the Spring Water to a boil. Add the Pure Sea Salt to taste.
- ❖ Add Kamut spaghetti to the boiling water. Cook for about 8-10 minutes until the noodles are dry.
- ❖ Drink the pasta and put it in a glass. Add the pure sea salt, peanut butter, onion powder, and ground olive oil to maximize the fluctuation.
- ❖ Mix the dough thoroughly.
- ❖ Sauce:
- ❖ Add 1 tablespoon of Grape Seed Oil to a medium saucepan. Heat over medium heat.
- ❖ Add sliced Mushrooms and diced Onions to the top. Coook for 3 to 5 minutes, stirring occasionally.
- ❖ Sprinkle 1/4 teaspoon of pure sea salt and 1/8 teaspoon of Cayenne over the vegetables and stir.

- ❖ Place the chickpea flour and another tablespoon of grain oil in the bowl. Stir until everything is well combined and there is no trace of dry flour.
- ❖ Add the nut milk, soybean oil, 1/2 teaspoon of Pure Sea Salt, Onion Powder, Oregano, Tarragon, and Basil and stir.
- ❖ Simmer for 20 minutes until slightly thickened.
- ❖ Add the cooked pasta, chopped tomatoes and cabbage to the pot. Submerge 3 to 5 minutes until the cabbage has dried out and withdrawn from the heat.
- ❖ Serve and enjoy your Creamy Kamut Pasta!
- ❖ Helpful Hints:
- ❖ Don't go swimming in your own time!
- ❖ Creamy Kamut Pasta can be stored in the refrigerator for 3-4 days.

85) BASIL AVOCADO PASTA

Preparation Time: 10 minutes.	**Cooking Time:** 20 Minutes.	**Servings:** 4

Ingredients:

- ✓ 4 cups of cooked Spelt pasta
- ✓ 1 medium diced Avocado
- ✓ 2 cups of halved Cherry Tomatoes
- ✓ 1 fresh basil chopped

Ingredients:

- ✓ 1 teaspoon of Agave Syrup
- ✓ 1 tablespoon of Key Lime Juice.
- ✓ 1/4 cup o of olive oil

Directions:

- ❖ Place the cooked meat in a large container.
- ❖ Add the Avocado dicedo, Cherry Tomatoes, and chopped Basil to the bowl.
- ❖ Hold all of the ingredients still until they are removed.

- ❖ Blend the agave syrup, olive oil and Pure Sea Salt a Key Lime in a separate bowl.
- ❖ Pour into the container and stir until well bottled.
- ❖ Enjoy your avocado pasta Basil!

86) JAMAICAN JERK PATTIES

Preparation Time: 35 minutes.	**Cooking Time:** 1 Hour.	**Servings:** 3-4

Ingredients:

- ✓ Filling:
- ✓ 1 cup of cooked Garbanzo Beans
- ✓ 1/2 cup pepper, diced
- ✓ 1 dried plum
- ✓ 2 cups of chopped Mushroms
- ✓ 1 cup of chopped Butternut Squash
- ✓ 1/2 cup of diced Onions
- ✓ 1 tablespoon of onion Powder
- ✓ 1 teaspoon of Ginger
- ✓ 2 teaspoons of thyme
- ✓ 1 tablespoon of Agave Syrup
- ✓ 1/2 teaspoon of Cayenne Powder
- ✓ 1 teaspoon of Allspice.

Ingredients:

- ✓ 1/4 teaspoon of cloves
- ✓ 1 teaspoon of Pure Sea Salt
- ✓ Crust:
- ✓ 1 1/2 cups of Spelt Flour
- ✓ 1/4 cup of Aquafaba
- ✓ 1 teaspoon of Pure Sea Salt
- ✓ 1/8 teaspoon of Ginger powder
- ✓ 1 teaspoon of Onion Powder.
- ✓ 1 tablespoon of Grape Seed Oil
- ✓ 1 cup of spring water

Directions:

- ❖ Preheat the oven to 350 degrees Fahrenheit.
- ❖ Add all vegetables, excluding Cherry Tomatoes, to a refrigerator. Wipe a couple of times to make them stiffer.
- ❖ Mix vegetables with seasonings and tomatoes in a cup. This constitutes the filling for the patties.
- ❖ In a separate glass jar, place the Spelt Flour, Grape Seed Oil and seasonings.
- ❖ Pour in 1/2 quart of water and knead the dough into a loaf, adding more water or flour if necessary.
- ❖ Allow to rest for 5 to 10 minutes. Knead for a few minutes and then divide into 8 parts.

- ❖ Make a piece of wood into a pile and then roll the pile into a 6 to 7 cm box.
- ❖ Take a circle dough and put 1/2 cup of filling in the center. Brush all the edges of the dough with the Aquafaba, top it and slide the edge with a knife.
- ❖ Repeat step 8 until all dough circles are filled.
- ❖ Lightly coat a baking sheet with a little Grape Seed Oil.
- ❖ Bake the filled patties for about 25-30 minutes until golden brown.
- ❖ Serve and enjoy your Jamaican Jerk Patties!
- ❖ Tips useful:
- ❖ You can serve Jamaican Jerk Patties with our Fragrant Tomato Sauce.

87) TOMATO SOUP

Preparation Time: 15 minutes	Cooking Time: 45 minutes	Servings: 4

Ingredients:

- ✓ 2 tablespoons of coconut oil
- ✓ 2 carrots, coarsely chopped
- ✓ 1 large white onion, coarsely chopped
- ✓ 3 garlic cloves, minced
- ✓ 5 large tomatoes, coarsely chopped

Ingredients:

- ✓ 1 tablespoon of homemade tomato paste
- ✓ 3 cups of homemade vegetable broth
- ✓ ¼ cup fresh basil, chopped
- ✓ ¼ cup unsweetened coconut milk
- ✓ Sea salt and freshly ground black pepper, to taste

Directions:

- ❖ Melt the coconut oil in a large soup pot over medium heat and cook the carrot and onion for about 10 minutes, stirring often.
- ❖ Add the garlic and sauté for about 1-2 minutes.
- ❖ Add the tomatoes, tomato paste, basil, broth, salt and black pepper and bring to a boil.
- ❖ Reduce the heat to low and simmer uncovered for about 30 minutes.
- ❖ Add the coconut milk and remove from heat.
- ❖ Using an immersion blender, blend the soup until smooth.
- ❖ Serve hot.

88) GARLIC BROCCOLI

Preparation Time: 10 minutes	Cooking Time: 8 minutes	Servings: 2

Ingredients:

- ✓ 1 tablespoon of extra virgin olive oil
- ✓ 3-4 garlic cloves, minced

Ingredients:

- ✓ 2 cups of broccoli florets
- ✓ 2 tablespoons of tamari

Directions:

- ❖ Heat the oil over medium heat in a large skillet and sauté the garlic for about 1 minute.
- ❖ Add the broccoli and sauté for about 2 minutes.
- ❖ Add the tamari and sauté for about 4-5 minutes or until desired doneness.
- ❖ Remove from heat and serve hot.

89) OKRA CURRY

Preparation Time: 10 minutes	Cooking Time: 15 minutes	Servings: 3

Ingredients:

- ✓ 1 tablespoon of olive oil
- ✓ ½ teaspoon of cumin seeds
- ✓ ¾ lb okra pods, trimmed and cut into 2-inch pieces
- ✓ ½ teaspoon of curry powder

Ingredients:

- ✓ ½ teaspoon of red chili powder
- ✓ 1 teaspoon of ground coriander
- ✓ Sea salt and freshly ground black pepper, to taste

Directions:

- ❖ Heat oil in a large skillet over medium heat
- ❖ For about 30 seconds, sauté the cumin seeds
- ❖ Add the okra and sauté for about 1-1½ minutes.
- ❖ Reduce heat to low and cook covered for about 6-8 minutes, stirring occasionally.
- ❖ Add the curry powder, red pepper and cilantro and stir to combine.
- ❖ Increase the heat to medium and cook uncovered for another 2-3 minutes or so.
- ❖ Season with the salt and pepper and remove from heat.
- ❖ Serve hot.

90) MUSHROOMS CURRY

Preparation Time: 20 minutes	Cooking Time: 20 minutes	Servings: 4

Ingredients:

- ✓ 2 cups of tomatoes, chopped
- ✓ 1 green chili pepper, chopped
- ✓ 1 teaspoon fresh ginger, chopped
- ✓ 2 tablespoons of olive oil
- ✓ ½ teaspoon of cumin seeds
- ✓ ¼ teaspoon ground coriander
- ✓ ¼ teaspoon ground turmeric

Ingredients:

- ✓ ¼ teaspoon of red chili powder
- ✓ 2 cups fresh shiitake mushrooms, sliced
- ✓ 2 cups fresh button mushrooms, sliced
- ✓ 1¼ cup of water
- ✓ ¼ cup unsweetened coconut milk
- ✓ Sea salt and freshly ground black pepper, to taste

Directions:

- ❖ In a food processor, add the tomatoes, green chiles and ginger and pulse until it forms a smooth paste.
- ❖ Heat the oil in a skillet over medium heat.
- ❖ For about 1 minute, sauté the cumin seeds.
- ❖ Add the spices and sauté for about 1 minute.

- ❖ Add the tomato mixture and cook for about 5 minutes.
- ❖ Add the mushrooms, water and coconut milk and bring to a boil.
- ❖ Cook for about 10-12 minutes, stirring occasionally.
- ❖ Season with the salt and black pepper and remove from heat.
- ❖ Serve hot.

91) FROSTED BRUSSELS SPROUTS

Preparation Time: 15 minutes	Servings: 15 minutes	Servings: 3

Ingredients:

- ✓ 3 cups Brussels sprouts, cut and halved
- ✓ Sea salt, to taste
- ✓ 2 tablespoons of coconut oil, melted
- ✓ For the orange frosting:
- ✓ 1 tablespoon of coconut oil
- ✓ 2 small shallots, thinly sliced

Ingredients:

- ✓ 2 tablespoons of fresh orange zest, finely grated
- ✓ ¼ teaspoon ground ginger
- ✓ 2/3 cup fresh orange juice
- ✓ 1 tablespoon of sambal oelek (raw chili paste)
- ✓ 2 tablespoons of coconut amino acids
- ✓ 1 teaspoon of tapioca starch
- ✓ Sea salt, to taste

Directions:

- ❖ Preheat oven to 400 degrees F. Line a baking sheet with baking paper.
- ❖ In a bowl, add the Brussels sprouts, a little salt and oil and toss to coat well.
- ❖ Transfer the mixture to the prepared baking dish.
- ❖ Roast for about 10-15 minutes, turning once halfway through.
- ❖ Meanwhile, prepare the frosting.
- ❖ In a skillet, melt the coconut oil over medium heat and sauté the scallions for about 5 minutes.
- ❖ Add the orange zest and sauté for about 1 minute.

- ❖ Stir in the ginger, orange juice, sambal oelek and coconut amino acid and cook for about 5 minutes.
- ❖ Slowly add the tapioca starch, whisking constantly.
- ❖ Cook for about 2-3 minutes longer, stirring often.
- ❖ Add salt and remove from heat.
- ❖ Transfer roasted Brussels sprouts to a serving platter. Top evenly with the orange glaze.
- ❖ Serve immediately garnished with scallions.

92) SAUTEED MUSHROOMS

Preparation Time: 15 minutes	Cooking Time: 16 minutes	Servings: 2

- ✓ 2 tablespoons of olive oil
- ✓ ½ teaspoon cumin seeds, lightly crushed
- ✓ 2 medium onions, thinly sliced

- ✓ ¾ lb fresh mushrooms, chopped
- ✓ Sea salt and freshly ground black pepper, to taste

- ❖ Heat oil in a frying pan over medium heat
- ❖ For about 1 minute, sauté the cumin seeds.
- ❖ Add the onion and sauté for about 4-5 minutes.

- ❖ Add the mushrooms and sauté for about 5-7 minutes.
- ❖ Add the salt and black pepper and sauté for about 2-3 minutes.
- ❖ Remove from heat and serve hot.

93) SWEET AND SOUR CABBAGE

Preparation Time: 10 minutes	Cooking Time: 20 minutes	Servings: 4

✓ 1 tablespoon of extra virgin olive oil ✓ 1 lemon, with seeds and thinly sliced ✓ 1 onion, chopped ✓ 3 garlic cloves, minced	✓ 2 pounds fresh cabbage, hard ribs removed and chopped ✓ ½ cup shallots, chopped ✓ 1 tablespoon of agave nectar ✓ Sea salt and freshly ground black pepper, to taste
Directions: ❖ In a large skillet, heat the oil over medium heat and cook the lemon slices for about 5 minutes. ❖ Using a slotted spoon, remove the lemon slices.	❖ In the same skillet, add the onion and garlic and sauté for about 5 minutes. ❖ Add the cabbage, scallions, agave nectar, salt and black pepper and cook for about 8-10 minutes, stirring occasionally. ❖ Remove from heat and serve hot.

94) BRUSSELS SPROUTS WITH WALNUTS

Preparation Time: 15 minutes	Cooking Time: 15 minutes	Servings: 2

✓ ½ pound Brussels sprouts, halved ✓ 1 tablespoon of olive oil ✓ 2 garlic cloves, minced ✓ ½ teaspoon of red pepper flakes, crushed	✓ Sea salt and freshly ground black pepper, to taste ✓ 1 tablespoon fresh lemon juice ✓ 1 tablespoon pine nuts
❖ Place a steamer basket in a large pot of boiling water. ❖ Place Brussels sprouts in the basket of the steamer and steam, covered for about 6-8 minutes. ❖ Drain Brussels sprouts well. ❖ In a large skillet, heat the oil over medium heat and sauté the garlic and red pepper flakes for about 40 seconds.	❖ Add the Brussels sprouts, salt and black pepper and sauté for about 4-5 minutes. ❖ Add the lemon juice and sauté for about 1 minute more. ❖ Add pine nuts and remove from heat. ❖ Serve hot.

95) ROASTED BUTTERNUT SQUASH

Preparation Time: 15 minutes	Cooking Time: 45 minutes	Servings: 6

✓ 8 cups butternut squash, peeled, seeded and diced ✓ 2 tablespoons of melted almond butter ✓ ½ teaspoon ground cinnamon	✓ ½ teaspoon of ground cumin ✓ ¼ teaspoon of red pepper flakes ✓ Sea salt, to taste
❖ Preheat oven to 425 degrees F. Place foil pieces on 2 baking sheets. ❖ In a large bowl, add all ingredients and mix to coat well.	❖ Arrange the pumpkin pieces on the prepared baking sheets in a single layer. ❖ Roast for about 40-45 minutes. ❖ Remove from oven and serve.

96) BROCCOLI WITH PEPPERS

Preparation Time: 15 minutes	Cooking Time: 10 minutes	Servings: 4

✓ 2 tablespoons of olive oil ✓ 4 garlic cloves, minced ✓ 1 large white onion, sliced ✓ 2 cups of small broccoli florets	✓ 3 red peppers, seeded and sliced ✓ ¼ cup homemade vegetable broth ✓ Sea salt and freshly ground black pepper, to taste
❖ In a large skillet, heat the oil over medium heat and sauté the garlic for about 1 minute.	❖ Add the onion, broccoli and peppers and sauté for about 5 minutes. ❖ Add the broth and sauté for about 4 more minutes. ❖ Serve hot.

97) SHRIMP WITH TAMARI

Preparation time: 15 minutes	Cooking Time: 6 minutes	Servings: 2

Ingredients:

- ✓ 1 tablespoon of olive oil
- ✓ 2 garlic cloves, minced
- ✓ ½ pound of raw, peeled and deveined jumbo shrimps

Directions:

- ❖ In a large skillet, heat the oil over medium heat and sauté the garlic for about 1 minute.

Ingredients:

- ✓ 2 tablespoons of tamari
- ✓ Freshly ground black pepper, to taste

- ❖ Stir in the shrimp, tamari and black pepper and cook for about 4-5 minutes or until completely done.
- ❖ Serve hot.

98) VEGETARIAN KEBABS

Preparation Time: 20 minutes	Cooking time: 10 minutes	Servings: 4

Ingredients:

For the marinade:
- ✓ 2 garlic cloves, minced
- ✓ 2 teaspoons fresh basil, chopped
- ✓ 2 teaspoons fresh oregano, chopped
- ✓ ½ teaspoon of cayenne pepper
- ✓ Sea salt and freshly ground black pepper, to taste
- ✓ 2 tablespoons fresh lemon juice

Directions:

- ❖ For the marinade: in a large bowl, add all ingredients and mix until well combined.
- ❖ Add the vegetables to the marinade and toss to coat well.
- ❖ Cover and refrigerate to marinate the vegetables for at least 6-8 hours.
- ❖ In a large bowl of water, soak the wooden skewers for at least 30 minutes.

Ingredients:

- ✓ 2 tablespoons of olive oil

For vegetables:
- ✓ 2 large zucchini, cut into thick slices
- ✓ 8 large button mushrooms, quartered
- ✓ 1 yellow bell pepper, seeded and diced
- ✓ 1 red bell pepper, seeded and diced

- ❖ Preheat grill to medium-high heat. Generously grease the grill grate.
- ❖ Remove the vegetables from the bowl and discard the marinade.
- ❖ Thread the vegetables onto the pre-soaked wooden skewers, starting with the zucchini, mushrooms and peppers.
- ❖ Grill for about 8-10 minutes or until fully done, turning occasionally.

99) FRIED ONION SPROUT

Preparation Time: 5 minutes	Cooking Time: 10 minutes	Servings: 4

Ingredients:

- ✓ 2½ pounds Brussels sprouts, cut4 slices bacon, cut into 1-inch pieces
- ✓ 1 tablespoon of extra virgin coconut oil
- ✓ 1 tomato, chopped
- ✓ 1 onion, chopped

Directions:

- ❖ Add sprouts to boiling water in a pot.
- ❖ Let them cook for about 3-5 minutes.
- ❖ Drain them and set them aside.
- ❖ Saute onions in a greased skillet for 4 minutes.

Ingredients:

- ✓ 4 sprigs of thyme or savory, divided
- ✓ 1 teaspoon celtic sea salt, iodine-free
- ✓ Freshly ground pepper to taste
- ✓ 2 teaspoons of lemon juice (optional)

- ❖ Mix with salt, pepper and thyme
- ❖ Add the drained sprouts to the skillet and stir for 3 minutes.
- ❖ Remove and discard sprigs of grasses.
- ❖ Serve warm with lemon juice and chopped spring onion on top.

100)   SOUTHWESTERN STUFFED SWEET POTATOES

- ✓ Sliced avocado (1)
- ✓ Pinch of cumin
- ✓ Pinch of dried red chili flakes
- ✓ Spinach (3 c.)
- ✓ Sliced shallot (1)
- ✓ Black beans (.5 c.)
- ✓ Coconut oil (2 tablespoons)
- ✓ Sweet potatoes

- ✓ Medication
- ✓ Pepper and salt
- ✓ Chopped coriander (1 handful)
- ✓ Cumin (1 teaspoon)
- ✓ Lime Juice (1)
- ✓ Olive oil (3 tablespoons)

Directions:

- ❖ Turn on the oven and give it time to heat up to 400 degrees. Clean the sweet potatoes and pierce them a few times with a fork.
- ❖ Add baking paper to a baking sheet and place sweet potatoes on top. Add to the oven to bake.
- ❖ After 50 minutes, the potatoes should be soft. Remove them from the oven and give them time to cool.
- ❖ Meanwhile, take a skillet and add the coconut oil along with the black beans and shallots.

- ❖ Cook these for a few minutes before adding the cumin, chili flakes and spinach, stirring to mix well.
- ❖ Finally, take a small bowl and whisk the ingredients for the dressing well.
- ❖ Slice the sweet potatoes down the middle before stuffing them with the black bean mixture you made.
- ❖ Add a few avocado slices and some of the dressing poured over them before serving.

101)   ZOODLES WITH CREAM SAUCE

- ✓ Toasted pepitas (2 tablespoons)
- ✓ Pepper (.5 tsp.)
- ✓ Salt (1 teaspoon)
- ✓ Chopped coriander (2 tablespoons)
- ✓ Water (1 tablespoon)

- ✓ Lemon juice (.5)
- ✓ Olive oil (2 tablespoons)
- ✓ Pitted avocado (1)
- ✓ Spiral zucchini (1)
- ✓ Coconut oil (1 tablespoon)

Directions:

- ❖ Add a little coconut oil to melt in a skillet before adding the zucchini noodles. Cook for 5 minutes before turning off the heat.
- ❖ Take out a blender and combine together the pepper, salt, 1 tablespoon cilantro, water, lemon juice, oil and avocado. Mix well and cook to make the cream.

- ❖ Add the sauce to the pan with the noodles and stir to combine. Move to a serving bowl and top with the rest of the cilantro and toasted pepitas before serving.

102)   RAINBOW PAD THAI

Ingredients:

- ✓ Avocado cubes (1)
- ✓ Chopped coriander (1 c.)
- ✓ Shredded daikon radish (1 c.)
- ✓ Chopped broccoli (1 c.)
- ✓ Shredded red cabbage (1 c.)
- ✓ Sliced shallots (3)
- ✓ Shredded carrots (2)
- ✓ Spiral Zucchini (3)

Ingredients:

For the dressing
- ✓ Chopped ginger (1 teaspoon)
- ✓ Chopped garlic clove (1)
- ✓ Sesame oil (1 tablespoon)
- ✓ Tahini (.25 c.)
- ✓ Lime Juice (1)

Directions:

- ❖ Add ingredients for Pad Thai, except avocado, to a large bowl and mix.
- ❖ Blend together all the ingredients you have for the dressing until creamy and combined.

- ❖ Top the vegetables with the diced avocado and pour the dressing over them before serving.

103) LENTILS AND VEGETABLES

Ingredients:

- ✓ Avocado (1)
- ✓ Crushed almonds (1 tablespoon)
- ✓ Crushed black pepper (1 teaspoon)
- ✓ Salt (1 teaspoon)
- ✓ Arugula (1 c.)
- ✓ Brown or green lentils (.5 c.)

Ingredients:

- ✓ Cooked wild rice (1 c.)
- ✓ Lemon juice (.5)
- ✓ Diced Carrot (1)
- ✓ Broccoli florets (.5 c.)
- ✓ Sliced Pak choi (.5 c.)
- ✓ Vegetable stock (.25 c.)

❖ Add the vegetable broth to a skillet over medium heat. Let it begin to simmer before adding the lemon juice, carrot, broccoli and pak choi.

❖ After 5 minutes, turn off the heat and stir in the almonds, pepper, salt, arugula, lentils and wild rice.

❖ Move this mixture to plates and top with a few slices of avocado before serving.

104) VEGETABLE DISH WITH SESAME

Ingredients:

- ✓ Sesame seeds (1 teaspoon)
- ✓ Lemon juice (.5)
- ✓ Tamari Sauce (2 tablespoons)
- ✓ Chopped garlic clove (1)
- ✓ Diced red bell pepper (.5 c.)

Ingredients:

- ✓ Finely chopped broccoli florets (2 c.)
- ✓ Cubed tofu (8 ounces)
- ✓ Olive oil (2 tablespoons)
- ✓ Sesame oil, toasted (1.5 tablespoons)

❖ Heat half a tablespoon of sesame oil and one tablespoon of olive oil in a skillet. Add the tofu and let it cook for a bit.

❖ After ten minutes, remove the tofu and add a little more of the two oils.

❖ Stir in the garlic, red bell bell pepper and broccoli until they soften a bit. Add the tofu and also stir in the lemon juice and soy sauce.

❖ Top this dish with a few sesame seeds before serving.

105) SWEET SPINACH SALAD

Ingredients:

- ✓ Crushed black pepper (1 teaspoon)
- ✓ Salt (1 teaspoon)
- ✓ Nutmeg (1 teaspoon)
- ✓ Cinnamon (1 teaspoon)
- ✓ Chopped spinach (4 c.)
- ✓ Chopped parsley (2 tablespoons)

Ingredients:

- ✓ Chopped walnuts (.25 c.)
- ✓ Raisins (.25 c.)
- ✓ Sliced apple (.5 c.)
- ✓ Yogurt (.5 c.)
- ✓ Lime juice (1 tablespoon)
- ✓ Shredded carrots (.75 c.)

❖ To start this recipe, bring out a large bowl and combine all the ingredients together.

❖ Place the bowl in the refrigerator to chill for about ten minutes before serving.

106) STEAMED GREEN BOWL

- ✓ Chopped coriander (2 tablespoons)
- ✓ Salt (1 teaspoon)
- ✓ Sliced green onions (2)
- ✓ Ground cashews (1 c.)
- ✓ Coconut milk (2 c.)
- ✓ Green peas (.5 c.)
- ✓ Sliced zucchini (1)

- ✓ Head of broccoli (1)
- ✓ Grated ginger (1 inch piece)
- ✓ Turmeric (1 teaspoon)
- ✓ Chopped garlic clove (1)
- ✓ Sliced onion (1)
- ✓ Coconut oil (1 tablespoon)

❖ Heat some coconut oil in a pan and when hot, add the ginger, turmeric, garlic and onion.

❖ After five minutes of cooking, add the coconut milk, peas, zucchini and broccoli to this mixture.

❖ Let the ingredients come to a boil before reducing the heat and simmering for a bit.

❖ After another 15 minutes, stir in the cilantro, salt, green onions and cashews before serving.

107) VEGETABLE AND BERRY SALAD

✓ Raspberries (.5 c.) ✓ Sliced tangerine (.5) ✓ Alfalfa sprouts (1 c.) ✓ Shredded red cabbage (.5 head) ✓ Lemon juice 1 ✓ Olive oil (3 tablespoons) ✓ Diced cucumber (1) ✓ Avocado (1) ✓ Sliced shallot (1)	✓ Sliced cabbage (4 leaves) ✓ Chopped parsley (1 tablespoon) ✓ Sliced red bell pepper (.5) ✓ Shredded Carrot (1) ✓ Crushed almonds (1 tablespoon) ✓ Pumpkin seeds (2 tablespoons)
❖ Take a large bowl and add all the ingredients to it.	❖ Stir well to combine before seasoning the fruits and vegetables with a little lemon juice and a little oil. ❖ Serve this immediately.

108) BOWL OF QUINOA AND CARROTS

✓ Sliced green onions (2 tablespoons) ✓ Black sesame seeds (2 tablespoons) ✓ Salt (.25 tsp.) ✓ Chopped parsley (3 tablespoons) ✓ Lemon juice (.5) ✓ Cooked quinoa (2 c.)	✓ Sliced fennel bulb (1) ✓ Carrots, chopped (1 bunch) ✓ Olive oil (1 tablespoon) ✓ Miso (1 tablespoon) ✓ Water (1 c.)
❖ Whisk together the miso and water in a bowl. Then get a frying pan and heat some oil inside. ❖ When the oil is hot, add the fennel bulb and carrots and cook for a few minutes, turning when three minutes have passed.	❖ Add the water and miso mixture to the pan and reduce the heat to low. Cook with the lid on for a bit. This will take about 20 minutes. ❖ While this mixture is cooking, combine together the quinoa with the parsley, lemon juice and salt in a bowl. ❖ When the carrots are ready, add the mixture over the quinoa. Sprinkle the green onions and sesame seeds on top before serving.

109) GRAB AND GO WRAPS

✓ Carrot cut into julienne (1) ✓ Red bell pepper (.5) ✓ Swiss chard greens (4) ✓ Salt (.25 tsp.) ✓ Diced jalapeno bell pepper (.5)	✓ Diced shallots (1) ✓ Chopped coriander leaves (.25 c.) ✓ Lime Juice (1) ✓ Avocado (1) ✓ Steamed green peas (1 c.)
❖ Get out your blender or food processor and combine the salt, jalapeno, shallots, cilantro, lime, avocado and peas together. Process to combine, but leave some texture to still be there.	❖ Lay the collards out on the counter and then spread your pea and avocado mixture on top. ❖ Add the carrot and bell pepper strips before rolling the collards and secure with a toothpick. ❖ Repeat with all ingredients before serving.

110) WALNUT TACOS

✓ Chopped coriander (1 tablespoon) ✓ Nutritional yeast (2 tablespoons) ✓ Romaine lettuce leaves (6) ✓ Cooked red quinoa (.25 c.) ✓ Salt (.25 tsp.) ✓ Tamari (1 tablespoon) ✓ Coconut amino acids (1 teaspoon) ✓ Smoked paprika (.25 tsp.)	✓ Onion powder (.25 tsp.) ✓ Garlic Powder (.25 tsp.) ✓ Chilli powder (.25 tsp.) ✓ Ground Coriander (1 teaspoon) ✓ Ground Cumin (1 teaspoon) ✓ Olive oil (2 tablespoons) ✓ Chopped dried tomatoes (.25 c.) ✓ Raw chipped almonds (.25 c.) ✓ Walnuts (.5 c.)
❖ To get started with this recipe, add the almonds and walnuts to the food processor and puree. ❖ Add the tomatoes and give it a couple of pulses until you have a nice crumbly mixture. ❖ From here, add the salt, tamari, coconut aminos, paprika, onion, garlic, chili, cilantro, cumin, and olive oil.	❖ Pulse a few more times to get fully combined. ❖ Add the tomato and walnut mixture to a bowl and combine with the quinoa. ❖ Divide this mixture among the romaine lettuce leaves and top with the cilantro and nutritional yeast before serving.

111) BRUSSELS SPROUTS WITH WALNUTS

Preparation Time: 15 minutes	Cooking Time: 15 minutes	Servings: 2

Ingredients:

- ✓ ½ pound of Brussels sprouts, cut and halved
- ✓ 1 tablespoon of olive oil
- ✓ 2 cloves of garlic, minced
- ✓ ½ teaspoon of red pepper flakes, crushed

Ingredients:

- ✓ Sea salt and freshly ground black pepper, to taste
- ✓ 1 tablespoon fresh lemon juice
- ✓ 1 tablespoon pine nuts

Directions:

- ❖ In a large pot of boiling water, arrange a steamer basket.
- ❖ Place the asparagus in the steamer basket and steam, covered, for about 6-8 minutes.
- ❖ Drain the asparagus well.

- ❖ In a large skillet, heat the oil over medium heat and sauté the garlic and red pepper flakes for about 30-40 seconds.
- ❖ Add the Brussels sprouts, salt and black pepper and sauté for about 4-5 minutes.
- ❖ Add the lemon juice and sauté for about 1 minute more.
- ❖ Add pine nuts and remove from heat.
- ❖ Serve hot.

❖

112) BROCCOLI WITH CABBAGE

Preparation Time: 20 minutes	Cooking Time: 1 hour and 20 minutes	Servings: 8

Ingredients:

- ✓ 3 tablespoons of coconut oil, divided by
- ✓ ¼ small yellow onion, chopped
- ✓ 1 teaspoon of minced garlic
- ✓ 1 teaspoon fresh ginger root, peeled and chopped
- ✓ 1 cup of broccoli florets

Ingredients:

- ✓ 2 cups fresh cabbage, hard ribs removed and chopped
- ✓ ½ cup of coconut cream
- ✓ ¼ teaspoon of red pepper flakes, crushed
- ✓ 1 teaspoon fresh parsley, finely chopped

Directions:

- ❖ In a large skillet, melt 2 tablespoons of coconut oil over medium-high heat and sauté the onion for about 3-4 minutes.
- ❖ Add the garlic and ginger and sauté for about 1 minute.
- ❖ Add the broccoli and stir to combine well.
- ❖ Immediately, reduce heat to medium-low and cook for about 2-3 minutes, stirring constantly.

- ❖ Add the kale and cook for about 3 minutes, stirring often.
- ❖ Add the coconut cream and remaining coconut oil and mix until smooth.
- ❖ Add the red pepper flakes and simmer for about 5-10 minutes, stirring occasionally or until the curry is the desired thickness.
- ❖ Remove from heat and serve hot with the parsley garnish.

❖

113) MUSHROOMS WITH PARSLEY

Preparation Time: 15 minutes	Cooking Time: 15 minutes	Servings: 2

Ingredients:

- ✓ 2 tablespoons of olive oil
- ✓ 2-3 tablespoons of chopped onion
- ✓ ½ teaspoon of minced garlic

Ingredients:

- ✓ 12 ounces of fresh, sliced mushrooms
- ✓ 1 tablespoon fresh parsley, chopped
- ✓ Sea salt and freshly ground black pepper, to taste

Directions:

- ❖ In a skillet, heat the oil over medium heat and sauté the onion and garlic for 2-3 minutes.

- ❖ Add mushrooms and cook for 8-10 minutes or until desired doneness, stirring often.
- ❖ Add the parsley, salt and black pepper and remove from heat.
- ❖ Serve hot.

❖

114) GARLIC BROCCOLI

Preparation Time: 15 minutes	**Cooking Time**: 8 minutes	**Servings: 3**

Ingredients:

- ✓ 1 tablespoon of olive oil
- ✓ 2 cloves of garlic, minced
- ✓ 2 cups of broccoli florets

Ingredients:

- ✓ 2 tablespoons of alkaline water
- ✓ Sea salt and freshly ground black pepper, to taste

Directions:

- ❖ In a large skillet, heat the oil over medium heat and sauté the garlic for about 1 minute.
- ❖ Add the broccoli and sauté for about 2 minutes.

- ❖ In a large skillet, heat the oil over medium heat and sauté the garlic for about 1 minute.
- ❖ Add the broccoli and sauté for about 2 minutes.

❖

115) BROCCOLI WITH PEPPERS

Preparation Time: 15 minutes	**Cooking Time**: 10 minutes	**Servings: 5**

Ingredients:

- ✓ 2 tablespoons of olive oil
- ✓ 4 cloves of garlic, minced
- ✓ 1 large white onion, sliced
- ✓ 2 cups of small broccoli florets

Ingredients:

- ✓ 3 red peppers, seeded and sliced
- ✓ ¼ cup of homemade vegetable broth
- ✓ Sea salt and freshly ground black pepper, to taste

Directions:

- ❖ In a large skillet, heat the oil over medium heat and sauté the garlic for about 1 minute.

- ❖ Add the onion, broccoli and peppers and sauté for about 5 minutes.
- ❖ Add the broth and sauté for about 4 more minutes.
- ❖ Serve hot.

❖

116) SPICY OKRA

Preparation Time: 15 minutes	**Cooking Time**: 13 minutes	**Servings: 2**

Ingredients:

- ✓ 1 tablespoon of olive oil
- ✓ ½ teaspoon of caraway seeds
- ✓ ¾ pound okra pods, trimmed and cut into 2 inch pieces

Ingredients:

- ✓ ½ teaspoon of red chili powder
- ✓ 1 teaspoon of ground coriander
- ✓ Sea salt and freshly ground black pepper, to taste

Directions:

- ❖ In a large skillet, heat the oil over medium heat and sauté the cumin seeds for 30 seconds.
- ❖ Add the okra and sauté for 1-1½ minutes.
- ❖ Reduce heat to low and cook, covered for 6-8 minutes, stirring occasionally.

- ❖ Uncover and increase heat to medium.
- ❖ Add the chili powder and cilantro and cook for another 2-3 minutes.
- ❖ Season with salt and remove from heat.
- ❖ Serve hot.

❖

117) SPICY CAULIFLOWER

Preparation Time: 15 minutes	Cooking Time: 20 minutes	Servings: 4

Ingredients:

- ✓ ¼ cup of alkaline water
- ✓ 2 medium fresh tomatoes, chopped
- ✓ 2 tablespoons of extra virgin olive oil
- ✓ 1 small white onion, chopped
- ✓ ½ tablespoon fresh ginger root, peeled and chopped
- ✓ 3 medium garlic cloves, minced
- ✓ 1 jalapeño bell pepper, seeded and chopped
- ✓ 1 teaspoon of ground cumin

Ingredients:

- ✓ 1 teaspoon of ground coriander
- ✓ 1 teaspoon of cayenne pepper
- ✓ ¼ teaspoon ground turmeric
- ✓ 3 cups cauliflower, chopped
- ✓ Sea salt and freshly ground black pepper, to taste
- ✓ ½ cup of hot alkaline water
- ✓ ¼ cup fresh parsley leaves, chopped

Directions:

- ❖ In a blender, add ¼ cup water and the tomatoes and pulse until pureed. Set aside.
- ❖ In a large skillet, heat the oil over medium heat and sauté the onion for about 4-5 minutes.
- ❖ Add the ginger, garlic, jalapeño pepper and spices and sauté for about 1 minute.

- ❖ Add the tomato puree and cauliflower and cook for about 3-4 minutes, stirring constantly.
- ❖ Add the hot water and bring to a boil.
- ❖ Reduce heat to medium-low and simmer, covered for about 8-10 minutes or until desired doneness of cauliflower.
- ❖ Remove from heat and serve hot with the parsley garnish.

118) EGGPLANT CURRY

Preparation Time: 15 minutes	Cooking Time: 35 minutes	Servings: 3

Ingredients:

- ✓ 1 tablespoon of coconut oil
- ✓ 1 medium onion, finely chopped
- ✓ 2 cloves of garlic, minced
- ✓ ½ tablespoon fresh ginger root, peeled and chopped
- ✓ 1 Serrano bell pepper, seeded and chopped

Ingredients:

- ✓ Sea salt and freshly ground black pepper, to taste
- ✓ 1 medium tomato, finely chopped
- ✓ 1 large eggplant, diced
- ✓ 1 cup unsweetened coconut milk
- ✓ 2 tablespoons fresh parsley, chopped

Directions:

- ❖ In a large skillet, melt the coconut oil over medium heat and sauté the onion for 8-9 minutes.
- ❖ Add the garlic, serrano pepper and salt and sauté for 1 minute.
- ❖ Add the tomato and cook for 3-4 minutes, mashing with the back of a spoon.

- ❖ Add eggplant and salt and cook for 1 minute, stirring occasionally.
- ❖ Stir in the coconut milk and bring to a gentle boil.
- ❖ Reduce heat to medium-low and simmer, covered for 15-20 minutes or until completely done.
- ❖ Remove from heat and serve with parsley garnish.

119) LEMON CABBAGE WITH SHALLOTS

Preparation Time: 15 minutes	Cooking Time: 20 minutes	Servings: 4

Ingredients:

- ✓ 1 tablespoon of extra virgin olive oil
- ✓ 1 lemon, seeded and thinly sliced
- ✓ 1 white onion, thinly sliced
- ✓ 3 cloves of garlic, minced

Ingredients:

- ✓ 2 pounds fresh cabbage, hard ribs removed and chopped
- ✓ ½ cup shallots, chopped
- ✓ Sea salt and freshly ground black pepper, to taste

Directions:

- ❖ In a large skillet, heat the oil over medium heat and cook the lemon slices for 5 minutes.
- ❖ Using a slotted spoon, remove the lemon slices from the pan and set aside.

- ❖ In the same skillet, add the onion and garlic and sauté for about 5 minutes.
- ❖ Add the cabbage, scallions, salt and pepper and cook for 8-10 minutes.
- ❖ Add the lemon slices and stir until well combined.
- ❖ Remove from heat and serve hot.

120) VEGETABLES WITH APPLE

Preparation Time: 15 minutes	Cooking Time: 16 minutes	Servings: 4

Ingredients:

For the sauce:
- ✓ 3 small cloves of garlic, minced
- ✓ 1 teaspoon fresh ginger root, peeled and chopped
- ✓ 1 tablespoon fresh orange zest, finely grated
- ✓ ½ cup fresh orange juice
- ✓ 1 tablespoon maple syrup
- ✓ 2 tablespoons of tamari
- ✓ 2 tablespoons organic apple cider vinegar

Ingredients:

For the vegetables and apple:
- ✓ 1 tablespoon of olive oil
- ✓ 2 cups of carrots, peeled and julienned
- ✓ 1 head of broccoli, cut into florets
- ✓ 1 cup red onion, chopped
- ✓ 2 apples, core and slices

- ❖ For the sauce: in a large bowl, add all ingredients and with a wire whisk, beat until well combined. Set aside.
- ❖ In a large skillet, heat the oil over medium-high heat and sauté the carrot and broccoli for about 4-5 minutes.

- ❖ Add the onion and sauté for about 4-5 minutes.
- ❖ Add the sauce and cook for about 2-3 minutes, stirring often.
- ❖ Stir in the apple slices and cook for about 2-3 minutes.
- ❖ Remove from heat and serve hot.

121) CABBAGE WITH APPLE

Preparation Time: 15 minutes	Cooking Time: 12 minutes	Servings: 4

Ingredients:

- ✓ 2 teaspoons of coconut oil
- ✓ 1 large apple, cored and thinly sliced
- ✓ 1 onion, thinly sliced
- ✓ 1½ pounds of cabbage, finely chopped

Ingredients:

- ✓ 1 tablespoon fresh thyme, chopped
- ✓ 1 fresh red chili pepper, chopped
- ✓ 1 tablespoon organic apple cider vinegar

Directions:

- ❖ In a nonstick skillet, melt 1 teaspoon of coconut oil over medium heat and sauté the apple for about 2-3 minutes.
- ❖ Transfer the apple to a bowl.
- ❖ In the same skillet, melt 1 teaspoon of coconut oil over medium heat and sauté the onion for about 2-3 minutes.

- ❖ Add the kale and sauté for about 4-5 minutes.
- ❖ Add the cooked apple slices, thyme and vinegar and cook, covered, for about 1 minute.
- ❖ Remove from heat and serve hot.

❖

122) ASPARAGUS WITH HERBS

Preparation Time: 15 minutes	Cooking Time: 10 minutes	Servings: 4

Ingredients:

- ✓ 2 tablespoons of olive oil
- ✓ 2 tablespoons fresh lemon juice
- ✓ 1 tablespoon organic apple cider vinegar
- ✓ 1 teaspoon of minced garlic

Ingredients:

- ✓ 1 tablespoon fresh parsley, chopped
- ✓ 1 teaspoon of dried oregano
- ✓ Sea salt and freshly ground black pepper, to taste
- ✓ 1 pound fresh asparagus, without ends

Directions:

- ❖ Preheat oven to 400 degrees F. Lightly grease a rimmed baking sheet.
- ❖ In a bowl, add the oil, lemon juice, vinegar, garlic, herbs, salt and black pepper and whisk until well combined.

- ❖ Arrange the asparagus on the prepared baking sheet in a single layer.
- ❖ Cover with half of the herb mixture and stir to coat.
- ❖ Roast for about 8-10 minutes.
- ❖ Remove from oven and transfer asparagus to a serving platter.
- ❖ Sprinkle with the remaining herb mixture and serve immediately.

123) VEGETARIAN KABOBS

Preparation Time: 20 minutes	Cooking Time: 10 minutes	Servings: 4

For the marinade:
- ✓ 2 cloves of garlic, minced
- ✓ 2 teaspoons fresh basil, chopped
- ✓ 2 teaspoons fresh oregano, chopped
- ✓ ½ teaspoon of cayenne pepper
- ✓ Sea salt and freshly ground black pepper, to taste
- ✓ 2 tablespoons fresh lemon juice
- ✓ 2 tablespoons of olive oil

For vegetables:
- ✓ 16 large button mushrooms, in quarters
- ✓ 1 yellow bell pepper, seeded and diced
- ✓ 1 red bell pepper, seeded and diced
- ✓ 1 orange bell pepper, seeded and diced
- ✓ 1 green bell pepper, seeded and diced

Directions:

- ❖ For the marinade: in a large bowl, add all ingredients and mix until well combined.
- ❖ Add the vegetables and toss to coat them well.
- ❖ Cover the bowl and refrigerate to marinate for at least 6-8 hours.
- ❖ Preheat grill to medium-high heat. Generously grease the grill grate.

- ❖ Remove vegetables from bowl and thread onto pre-soaked wooden skewers.
- ❖ Place the skewers on the grill and cook for about 8-10 minutes or until fully done, turning occasionally.
- ❖ Remove from grill and serve hot.

124) TOFU WITH BRUSSELS SPROUTS

Preparation Time: 15 minutes	Cooking Time: 15 minutes	Servings: 4

- ✓ 1 tablespoon olive oil, divided
- ✓ 8 ounces of extra-fine tofu, drained, pressed and sliced
- ✓ 2 garlic cloves, minced
- ✓ 1/3 cup pecans, toasted and chopped

- ✓ 1 tablespoon unsweetened applesauce
- ✓ ¼ cup fresh parsley, chopped
- ✓ ½ pound Brussels sprouts, trimmed and cut into wide ribbons

Directions:

- ❖ In a skillet, heat ½ tablespoon oil over medium heat and sauté the tofu and for about 6-7 minutes or until golden brown.
- ❖ Add the garlic and pecans and sauté for about 1 minute.
- ❖ Add the applesauce and cook for about 2 minutes.
- ❖ Add the parsley and remove from heat.

- ❖ With a slotted spoon, transfer tofu to a plate and set aside
- ❖ In the same skillet, heat the remaining oil over medium-high heat and cook the Brussels sprouts for about 5 minutes.
- ❖ Stir in the cooked tofu and remove from heat.
- ❖ Serve immediately.

125) TOFU WITH BROCCOLI

Preparation Time: 15 minutes	Cooking Time: 13 minutes	Servings: 3

Ingredients:

- ✓ 1 (12-ounce) package of solid tofu, drained, pressed and cut into 5 slices
- ✓ 2 tablespoons of coconut oil, divided
- ✓ 2 cups of small broccoli florets

Ingredients:

- ✓ ¼ cup of alkaline water
- ✓ ½ tablespoon chopped garlic
- ✓ ½ tablespoon fresh ginger root, chopped
- ✓ Sea salt and freshly ground black pepper, to taste

Directions:

- ❖ In a large nonstick skillet, melt 1 tablespoon coconut oil over medium-high heat and cook tofu for 4-5 minutes per side or until crispy.
- ❖ Using a slotted spoon, place the tofu slices on a paper towel-lined plate to absorb the extra oil.
- ❖ Next, cut each slice of tofu into equal sized pieces.
- ❖ Meanwhile, in a large microwave-safe bowl, add the broccoli florets and water.

- ❖ Cover the bowl and microwave on High for about 5 minutes.
- ❖ Remove from microwave and drain broccoli.
- ❖ In the same skillet, melt the remaining coconut oil over medium heat and sauté the garlic and ginger for about 1 minute.
- ❖ Add the tofu, broccoli and black pepper and cook for 2 minutes, tossing occasionally.
- ❖ Remove from heat and serve hot.

126) TEMPEH IN TOMATO SAUCE

Preparation Time: 20 minutes	Cooking Time: 1 hour and 20 minutes	Servings: 4

- ✓ ½ cup of extra virgin olive oil, divided
- ✓ 2 packages of tempeh (8 ounces), cut into half-inch horizontal slices
- ✓ 1 large yellow onion, chopped
- ✓ 3 cloves of garlic, minced
- ✓ 1 teaspoon dried oregano, crushed
- ✓ 1 teaspoon dried thyme, crushed
- ✓ ½ teaspoon of red chili powder

- ✓ ½ teaspoon of red pepper flakes, crushed
- ✓ 1 large green bell pepper, seeded and thinly sliced
- ✓ 1 large yellow bell pepper, seeded and thinly sliced
- ✓ 2 cups fresh tomatoes, finely chopped
- ✓ ¼ cup of homemade tomato paste
- ✓ 1 teaspoon organic apple cider vinegar
- ✓ 1 tablespoon maple syrup

Directions:

- ❖ Preheat the oven to 350 degrees F.
- ❖ In a large bowl, add 2 tablespoons oil and the tempeh slices and toss to coat well.
- ❖ In a large skillet, heat ¼ cup oil over medium-high heat and cook tempeh slices for about 5-7 minutes.
- ❖ Carefully switch sides and cook for about 5-7 minutes.
- ❖ Transfer the cooked tempeh slices to a plate lined with paper towels.
- ❖ Set aside to drain.
- ❖ Meanwhile, in another nonstick skillet, heat the remaining oil over medium-low heat and sauté the onion, garlic, herbs and spices for about 8-10 minutes.

- ❖ Add the peppers and sauté for about 4-5 minutes, stirring occasionally.
- ❖ Add the remaining ingredients and mix until well combined.
- ❖ Remove from heat.
- ❖ In the bottom of a large casserole dish, arrange the tempeh slices.
- ❖ Spoon the tomato mixture over the tempeh slices evenly.
- ❖ With a piece of foil, cover the casserole dish tightly.
- ❖ Bake for about 1 hour.
- ❖ Remove from oven and set aside to cool slightly.
- ❖ Serve hot.

127) SOUTHWESTERN STUFFED SWEET POTATOES

Preparation Time: 30 minutes	Cooking Time: 30 minutes	Servings: 2

- ✓ 2 sweet potatoes
- ✓ 2 tablespoons of coconut oil
- ✓ ½ cup black beans, rinsed and drained
- ✓ 1 shallot, sliced
- ✓ 3 cups of spinach
- ✓ A pinch of dried red chili pepper
- ✓ Pinch of cumin
- ✓ 1 avocado, peeled and sliced

Seasoning
- ✓ 3 tablespoons of olive oil
- ✓ 1 lime, squeezed
- ✓ 1 teaspoon of cumin
- ✓ Handful of coriander, chopped
- ✓ Salt and pepper

Directions:

- ❖ Preheat oven to 400°F/205°C. Clean the sweet potatoes and pierce them several times with a fork. Place sweet potatoes on a baking sheet lined with baking paper and bake about 50 minutes or until soft.
- ❖ Allow sweet potatoes to cool for 5 minutes.
- ❖ While the sweet potatoes are cooling, heat the skillet over medium heat and add the coconut oil, shallots and black beans.

- ❖ Cook for 5 minutes then add the spinach, dried chili flakes and cumin. Cook another 1 minute.
- ❖ In a small bowl, whisk together the dressing ingredients.
- ❖ Slice sweet potatoes in center and stuff with black bean mixture. Top with avocado slices.
- ❖ Pour the dressing over the sweet potatoes and serve.

128) COCONUT CAULIFLOWER WITH HERBS AND SPICES

Preparation Time: 30 minutes		Servings: 2

- ✓ ¼ cup coconut oil, melted
- ✓ ½ tablespoon ground cumin
- ✓ ¼ teaspoon ground coriander
- ✓ 1 teaspoon ground turmeric
- ✓ ¼ teaspoon black pepper, ground
- ✓ 1 large cauliflower, cut into small florets

- ✓ 2 tablespoons of toasted pine nuts
- ✓ 1 tablespoon coriander, chopped
- ✓ ½ tablespoon of mint, coarsely chopped
- ✓ 1 tablespoon of raisins
- ✓ Himalayan Salt

Directions:

- ❖ Preheat oven to 425°F/220°C. In a large bowl, mix together coconut oil, cumin, coriander, turmeric and black pepper. Add cauliflower and stir until well coated.

- ❖ Spread the cauliflower on the baking sheet and place in the oven for 20 minutes. Remove from oven and transfer to serving bowl.
- ❖ Mix the pine nuts, cilantro, mint, raisins and salt with the cauliflower and serve hot.

129) QUINOA AND BRUSSELS SPROUTS SALAD

Preparation Time: 5 minutes	Cooking Time: 0 minutes	Servings: 2

- ✓ ¼ cup quinoa, cooked
- ✓ ½ pound (227 g) Brussels sprouts, halved, diced, roasted
- ✓ 2 tablespoons of dried blueberries
- ✓ 1 medium white onion, peeled, sliced and caramelized

- ✓ ⅓ teaspoon of salt
- ✓ ⅛ teaspoon of cayenne pepper
- ✓ ½ orange, squeezed
- ✓ ½ teaspoon of orange zest
- ✓ 1 tablespoon of lime juice

Directions:

- ❖ Take a small bowl, pour in the orange juice and lime juice, add the orange zest and then stir until blended.
- ❖ Take a salad bowl, put in the remaining ingredients, drizzle with the orange juice mixture and then toss until mixed.
- ❖ Serve immediately.

130) MANGO AND JICAMA SALAD

Preparation Time: 5 minutes	Cooking Time: 15 minutes	Servings: 1

- ✓ 1 mango, peeled and cut into pieces
- ✓ 1 cup of sliced jicama
- ✓ 1 cup sliced bell bell pepper

- ✓ Juice of 1 lime
- ✓ 1 tablespoon of chili powder

Directions:

- ❖ In a small bowl, combine the mango, bell bell pepper and jicama.
- ❖ Squeeze lime juice over vegetables. Sprinkle with the chili powder.
- ❖ Refrigerate for 15 minutes to allow the flavors to meld and taste.

131) ASPARAGUS AND ROASTED MUSHROOM SALAD

Preparation Time: 10 minutes	Cooking Time: 15 minutes	Servings: 2

- ✓ ½ bunch of asparagus, blunted
- ✓ 1 pint of cherry tomatoes
- ✓ ½ cup mushrooms, halved
- ✓ 1 carrot, peeled and cut into small pieces

- ✓ 1 red or yellow bell pepper, with seeds and cut into small pieces
- ✓ 1 tablespoon of coconut oil
- ✓ 1 tablespoon garlic powder
- ✓ 1 teaspoon of sea salt

Directions:

- ❖ Preheat the oven to 425ºF (220ºC).
- ❖ In a bowl, add the asparagus, tomatoes, mushrooms, carrot and bell bell pepper. Add the coconut oil, garlic powder and salt. Stir to coat the vegetables evenly.
- ❖ Transfer vegetables to a baking sheet, place in preheated oven and roast for 15 minutes, or until vegetables are tender.
- ❖ Transfer vegetables to a large bowl. Refrigerate, if desired.
- ❖ Divide the vegetables between two bowls and serve hot or cold.

132) THAI GREEN SALAD

Preparation Time: 10 minutes	Cooking Time: 0 minutes	Servings: 2

- ✓ 4 cups chopped iceberg lettuce
- ✓ 1 cup of bean sprouts
- ✓ 2 carrots, cut into thin slices or spirals
- ✓ 1 zucchini, cut into thin strips or spirals
- ✓ 1 shallot, finely chopped
- ✓ 2 tablespoons of chopped almonds

- ✓ Juice of 1 lime
- ✓ 1 garlic clove
- ✓ 1 teaspoon of tamarind paste
- ✓ 1 packet of stevia
- ✓ ½ teaspoon of sea salt

Directions:

- ❖ In a large bowl, combine the lettuce, bean sprouts, carrots, zucchini, scallion and almonds.
- ❖ In a small food processor bowl, add the lime juice, garlic, tamarind, stevia and salt. Blend to combine.
- ❖ Pour the dressing over the vegetables and mix well.
- ❖ Divide evenly between two bowls and serve.

133) AVOCADO AND QUINOA SALAD

Preparation Time: 10 minutes	Cooking Time: 0 minutes	Servings: 2

✓ 1 cup of cooked, cooled quinoa ✓ 1 avocado, diced ✓ 1 cup cherry tomatoes, halved ✓ 1 cup cucumber, peeled and diced ✓ ¼ cup chopped cilantro	✓ 1 tablespoon garlic powder ✓ 1 tablespoon of onion powder ✓ 1 teaspoon of sea salt ✓ 1 tablespoon freshly squeezed lemon juice

Directions:	❖ Chill for 15 minutes to allow the flavors to meld. ❖ Serve immediately or store in the refrigerator for 2 to 3 days.
❖ In a large bowl, mix together the quinoa, avocado, tomatoes, cucumber, cilantro, garlic powder, onion powder, salt and lemon juice.	

134) CAPRESE SALAD

Preparation Time: 5 minutes	Cooking Time: 0 minutes	Servings: 2

✓ 2 large heirloom tomatoes, sliced ✓ 1 avocado, sliced	✓ 1 bunch of basil leaves ✓ 1 teaspoon of sea salt

Directions:	❖ Repeat the pattern with all remaining tomato slices, avocado slices and basil leaves. ❖ Season with salt and serve.
❖ n a serving plate, layer 1 tomato slice, 1 avocado slice and 1 basil leaf.	

135) TAGLIATELLE WITH PUMPKIN AND BROCCOLI SALAD

Preparation Time: 10 minutes	Cooking Time: 50 minutes	Servings: 4

✓ 1 spaghetti squash ✓ 2 tablespoons of coconut oil ✓ 2 cups of cooked broccoli florets ✓ 1 red bell pepper, seedless and cut into strips ✓ 1 shallot, chopped	✓ 1 tablespoon of sesame oil ✓ 1 teaspoon of red pepper flakes ✓ 2 teaspoons of sea salt, divided ✓ 2 tablespoons of toasted sesame seeds

Directions:	❖ Prepare spaghetti squash "noodles" by removing the inside of the roasted squash with a fork to a large bowl. ❖ Add the broccoli, red bell bell pepper and shallots. ❖ In a small bowl, combine sesame oil, red pepper flakes and remaining salt. Pour over the vegetables. Stir gently to combine. ❖ Garnish with the sesame seeds and serve.
❖ Preheat the oven to 350ºF (180ºC). ❖ To roast a squash, cut it in half lengthwise and scrape out the seeds. Brush each half with coconut oil and season with 1 teaspoon of sea salt. Place the squash halves with the cut side up on a baking sheet and roast in the preheated oven for about 50 minutes, or until tender to the fork.	

136) BROCCOLI AND MANDARIN SALAD

Preparation Time: 5 minutes	Cooking Time: 0 minutes	Servings: 4

✓ 4 cups of cooked, cooled broccoli florets ✓ 2 tangerines without seeds, peeled and separated ✓ ⅓ cup of freshly squeezed orange juice ✓ 2 tablespoons of sesame oil	✓ 2 garlic cloves, minced ✓ ½ teaspoon of sea salt ✓ ¼ teaspoon of red pepper flakes

Directions:	❖ Pour the dressing over the broccoli salad. Refrigerate for 1 hour to blend flavors. ❖ Serve cold.
❖ In a large bowl, combine the broccoli and tangerine sections. ❖ In a blender, combine the orange juice, sesame oil, garlic, salt, and red pepper flakes. Blend until smooth.	

❖

137) SPINACH AND MUSHROOM SALAD

Preparation Time: 2 minutes	Cooking Time: 5 minutes	Servings: 2

✓ 1 (6-ounce / 170-g) packet of baby spinach leaves ✓ ½ cup of toasted and chopped almonds ✓ 1 tablespoon of sesame oil ✓ 1 tablespoon apple cider vinegar	✓ 1 teaspoon of sea salt ✓ 1 cup chopped shiitake mushrooms ✓ Water, as needed
Directions: ❖ In a large bowl, combine the spinach and almonds. ❖ In a small saucepan over low heat, combine the sesame oil, cider vinegar, salt, and mushrooms.	❖ Cook for about 5 minutes, or until mushrooms are softened, adding water if necessary. ❖ Pour the mushroom dressing over the spinach. Stir well to coat the spinach leaves. ❖ Serve immediately.

138) BROCCOLI, ASPARAGUS AND QUINOA SALAD

Preparation Time: 5 minutes	Cooking Time: 0 minutes	Servings: 4

✓ 1 cup cooked broccoli florets, coarsely chopped ✓ 1 cup cut and cooked asparagus, coarsely chopped ✓ 2 cups of cooked, cooled quinoa ✓ ½ cup of water	✓ 2 tablespoons of freshly squeezed lemon juice ✓ 2 tablespoons of coconut oil ✓ ½ teaspoon of sea salt
Directions: ❖ In a large bowl, combine the broccoli and asparagus. ❖ Stir in the quinoa. ❖ In a blender, combine the water, lemon juice, coconut oil, and salt. ❖ Blend until the ingredients emulsify.	❖ Pour the dressing over the salad. Stir to combine. ❖ Refrigerate the salad for 15 minutes to chill. ❖ Serve cold.

139) ROOT VEGETABLE SALAD

Preparation Time: 15 minutes	Cooking Time: 0 minutes	Servings: 2

✓ 1 red beet, peeled and chopped ✓ 1 golden beet, peeled and chopped ✓ 2 carrots, peeled and chopped	✓ 2 tablespoons of hazelnuts ✓ 2 tablespoons of golden raisins ✓ ½ teaspoon of sea salt
Directions: ❖ In a medium bowl, mix together the red beet, golden beet, carrots, hazelnuts, golden raisins and salt.	❖ Refrigerate for 15 minutes to blend flavors. Serve.

140) LUSH SUMMER SALAD

Preparation Time: 5 minutes	Cooking Time: 0 minutes	Servings: 4

✓ 4 cups chopped iceberg or romaine lettuce ✓ 2 cups of cherry tomatoes, halved ✓ 1 (14.5-ounce / 411-g) can of whole green beans, drained ✓ ½ cup shredded carrot	✓ 1 shallot, sliced ✓ 1 cucumber, peeled and sliced ✓ 2 radishes, thinly sliced
Directions: ❖ In a large bowl, combine the lettuce, tomatoes, green beans, carrot, scallion, cucumber and radishes.	❖ Mix well with 2 tablespoons of the dressing of your choice and serve immediately.

❖

141) SALAD OF SEA VEGETABLES AND ALGAE

Preparation Time: 5 minutes	**Cooking Time**: 0 minutes	**Servings**: 2

✓ 1 cup of dried sea vegetables ✓ 1 ounce (28 g) of dried seaweed ✓ 1 teaspoon of spirulina	✓ 1 teaspoon apple cider vinegar ✓ 1 packet of stevia ✓ 1 teaspoon of sesame seeds

Directions:	❖ Drain the sea vegetables and seaweed. Squeeze out excess moisture and place in a medium bowl. Add the spirulina mixture and toss to combine. ❖ Refrigerate for 1 hour to blend flavors. ❖ Add the sesame seeds and serve.
❖ Reconstitute sea vegetables and dried seaweed according to package directions. ❖ Meanwhile, in a small bowl, mix together the spirulina, cider vinegar and stevia.	

142) RAINBOW SALAD

Preparation Time: 10 minutes	**Cooking Time**: 0 minutes	**Servings**: 2

✓ 1 mango, peeled, boned and cut into cubes ✓ ¼ onion, chopped ✓ ½ cup cherry tomatoes, halved ✓ ½ cucumber, seedless, sliced	✓ ½ of a green bell pepper, seedless, sliced ✓ ⅓ teaspoon of salt ✓ ¼ teaspoon cayenne pepper ✓ ¼ key lime, squeezed

Directions:	❖ Season with salt and cayenne pepper, toss until combined, and let the salad sit in the refrigerator for a minimum of 20 minutes. ❖ Serve immediately.
❖ Take a medium bowl, place the mango pieces in it, add the onion, tomatoes, cucumber and bell bell pepper and then drizzle with the lime juice.	

143) ARUGULA SALAD WITH BASIL

Preparation Time: 5 minutes	**Cooking Time**: 10 minutes	**Servings**: 2

✓ 4 ounces (113 g) arugula ✓ ½ cup cherry tomatoes, halved ✓ ¼ cup of basil leaves ✓ ½ key lime, squeezed	✓ 2 tablespoons of walnuts ✓ ¼ teaspoon salt ✓ ⅛ teaspoon of cayenne pepper ✓ ½ tablespoon of tahini butter

Directions:	❖ Take a medium bowl, place the arugula, tomatoes and basil leaves, pour in the dressing and then massage with your hands. ❖ Let the salad sit for 20 minutes, then taste to adjust the dressing and serve.
❖ Prepare the dressing and for that, take a small bowl, put the lime juice in it, add the butter tahini, salt and cayenne pepper and then whisk until combined.	

144) GREEN SALAD OF CUCUMBERS AND ARUGULA

Preparation Time: 5 minutes	**Cooking Time**: 0 minutes	**Servings**: 2

✓ ½ cucumber, seedless ✓ 4 ounces (113 g) arugula ✓ ⅛ teaspoon of salt	✓ 1 tablespoon of lime juice ✓ 1 tablespoon of olive oil ✓ ⅛ teaspoon of cayenne pepper

Directions:	❖ Mix together the lime juice and oil until combined, pour over the salad and then season with salt and cayenne pepper. ❖ Stir until blended and then serve.
❖ Slice the cucumber, add it to a salad bowl and then add the arugula.	

❖

145) STRAWBERRY AND DANDELION SALAD

Preparation Time: 10 minutes	**Cooking Time:** 7 minutes	**Servings: 2**

Ingredients:

- ✓ ½ of onion, peeled, sliced
- ✓ 5 strawberries, sliced
- ✓ 2 cups of dandelion greens, rinsed

Ingredients:

- ✓ 1 tablespoon of lime juice
- ✓ 1 tablespoon of grape oil
- ✓ ¼ teaspoon salt

Directions:

- ❖ Take a medium skillet, place it over medium heat, add the oil and let it heat until hot.
- ❖ Add onion, season with ⅛ teaspoon salt, stir until combined, and then cook 3 to 5 minutes until tender and golden brown.
- ❖ Meanwhile, take a small bowl, place the strawberry slices in it, drizzle with ½ tablespoon of lime juice and then toss until coated.

- ❖ When the onions have turned golden brown, add the remaining lime juice, stir until combined, and then cook for 1 minute.
- ❖ Remove the skillet from the heat, transfer the onions to a large salad bowl, add the strawberries with their juice and dandelion, and then sprinkle with the remaining salt. Stir until combined and then serve.

❖

146) WAKAME AND BELL PEPPER SALAD

Preparation Time: 15 minutes	**Cooking Time:** 0 minutes	**Servings: 2**

Ingredients:

- ✓ 1 cup of wakame stems
- ✓ ½ tablespoon chopped red bell pepper
- ✓ ½ teaspoon of onion powder
- ✓ ½ tablespoon of lime juice

Ingredients:

- ✓ ½ tablespoon of agave syrup
- ✓ ½ tablespoon of sesame seeds
- ✓ ½ tablespoon of sesame oil

Directions:

- ❖ Place the wakame stems in a bowl, cover with water, let them soak for 10 minutes and then drain.
- ❖ Meanwhile, prepare the dressing and for that, take a small bowl, add the lime juice, onion, agave syrup and sesame oil and then whisk until combined.

- ❖ Place the drained wakame stems in a large dish, add the bell bell pepper, pour in the dressing and toss until coated.
- ❖ Sprinkle the salad with sesame seeds and serve.

❖

147) GREEN SALAD OF ORANGE AND AVOCADO

Preparation Time: 5 minutes	**Cooking Time:** 0 minutes	**Servings: 2**

Ingredients:

- ✓ 1 orange, peeled, sliced
- ✓ 4 cups of vegetables
- ✓ ½ avocado, peeled, pitted and diced
- ✓ 2 tablespoons of chipped red onion
- ✓ ½ cup of coriander

Ingredients:

- ✓ ¼ teaspoon salt
- ✓ ¼ cup olive oil
- ✓ 2 tablespoons of lime juice
- ✓ 2 tablespoons of orange juice

Directions:

- ❖ Prepare the dressing and for that, put the cilantro in a food processor, pour in the orange juice, lime juice and oil, add the salt and then pulse until blended.

- ❖ Pour the dressing into a jar. Add remaining ingredients, toss until coated and add to a salad bowl or serve in the jar.

❖

148) GREEN SALAD WITH CUCUMBERS AND MUSHROOMS

Preparation Time: 5 minutes	Cooking Time: 0 minutes	Servings: 2

Ingredients:

- ✓ ½ medium cucumber, seedless, chopped
- ✓ 6 lettuce leaves, broken into pieces
- ✓ 4 mushrooms, chopped
- ✓ 6 cherry tomatoes, chopped

Ingredients:

- ✓ 10 olives
- ✓ ½ of a lime, squeezed
- ✓ 1 teaspoon of olive oil
- ✓ ¼ teaspoon salt

❖ Serve immediately.

Directions:

- ❖ Take a medium salad bowl, put in all the ingredients and then toss until mixed.

❖

149) CHICKPEA, VEGETABLE AND FONIO SALAD

Preparation Time: 10 minutes	Cooking Time: 5 minutes	Servings: 2

Ingredients:

- ✓ ½ cup of cooked chickpeas
- ✓ ¼ cup chopped cucumber
- ✓ ½ cup crushed red pepper
- ✓ ½ cup cherry tomatoes, halved
- ✓ ½ cup of fonio

Ingredients:

- ✓ ⅓ teaspoon of salt
- ✓ 1 tablespoon of grape oil
- ✓ ⅛ teaspoon of cayenne pepper
- ✓ 1 Key lime, squeezed
- ✓ 1 cup of spring water

❖ Cover the pan with its lid, let the fonio stand for 5 minutes, mash it with a fork and then let it cool for 15 minutes.

❖ Take a salad bowl, put in the lime juice and oil and then stir in the salt and cayenne pepper until combined.

❖ Add the remaining ingredients, including the fonio, stir until combined, and then serve.

Directions:

- ❖ Take a medium saucepan, set it over high heat, pour in the water and bring it to a boil.
- ❖ Add the fonio, turn the heat to low, cook for 1 minute and then remove the pan from the heat.

❖

150) AVOCADO AND CHICKPEA SALAD

Preparation Time: 10 minutes	Cooking Time: 20 minutes	Servings: 2

Ingredients:

- ✓ ½ cucumber, seedless, sliced
- ✓ 2 avocados, peeled, pitted and diced
- ✓ 1 medium white onion, peeled, diced
- ✓ 2 cups of cooked chickpeas
- ✓ ¼ cup chopped cilantro
- ✓ 1 teaspoon of onion powder

Ingredients:

- ✓ ½ teaspoon of cayenne pepper
- ✓ 1 teaspoon of sea salt
- ✓ 2 tablespoons hemp seeds, shelled
- ✓ 1 Key lime, squeezed
- ✓ 1 tablespoon of olive oil

❖ Bake the chickpeas for 20 minutes or until golden brown and crispy, then let them cool for 10 minutes.

❖ Transfer chickpeas to a bowl, add remaining ingredients and stir until combined. Serve immediately.

Directions:

- ❖ Turn on the oven, then set it to 425ºF (220ºC) and let it preheat.
- ❖ Meanwhile, take a baking sheet, place the chickpeas on it, season with salt, onion powder and pepper, drizzle with oil and then toss until combined.

151) AMARANTH, CUCUMBER AND CHICKPEA SALAD

Preparation Time: 5 minutes	Cooking Time: 10 minutes	Servings: 2

Ingredients:

- ✓ 1 small white onion, peeled, chopped
- ✓ 1 cup of cooked amaranth
- ✓ ½ cucumber, seedless, chopped
- ✓ 1 cup of cooked chickpeas

Ingredients:

- ✓ ½ of a medium red bell pepper, chopped
- ✓ ⅓ teaspoon of sea salt
- ✓ ⅛ teaspoon of cayenne pepper
- ✓ 2 tablespoons of lime juice

- ❖ Take a small bowl, put in the lime juice, add salt and stir until combined.
- ❖ Place remaining ingredients in a salad bowl, drizzle with lime juice mixture, toss and serve.

152) AVOCADO AND ARUGULA SALAD WITH CITRUS FRUITS

Preparation Time: 5 minutes	Cooking Time: 0 minutes	Servings: 2

Ingredients:

- ✓ 4 slices of onion
- ✓ ½ avocado, peeled, pitted and sliced
- ✓ 4 ounces (113 g) arugula
- ✓ 1 orange, peeled and cut into slices
- ✓ 1 teaspoon of agave syrup

Ingredients:

- ✓ ⅛ teaspoon of salt
- ✓ ⅛ teaspoon of cayenne pepper
- ✓ 2 tablespoons of lime juice
- ✓ 2 tablespoons of olive oil

- ❖ Distribute avocado, oranges, onion and arugula between two plates.
- ❖ Mix together the oil, salt, cayenne pepper, agave syrup and lime juice in a small bowl and then stir until combined.
- ❖ Pour the dressing over the salad and then serve.

153) AVOCADO SALAD AND SPELT NOODLES

Preparation Time: 10 minutes	Cooking Time: 0 minutes	Servings: 2

Ingredients:

- ✓ ½ cup avocado, peeled, pitted and chopped
- ✓ ½ cup of basil leaves
- ✓ ½ cup of cherry tomatoes
- ✓ 2 cups of cooked spelt noodles

Ingredients:

- ✓ 1 teaspoon of agave syrup
- ✓ 1 tablespoon of lime juice
- ✓ 2 tablespoons of olive oil

- ❖ Pour the lime juice mixture over the pasta, stir until combined and then serve.

Directions:

- ❖ Take a large bowl, put the pasta in it, add the tomato, avocado and basil and then mix until everything is combined.
- ❖ Take a small bowl, add the agave syrup and salt, pour in the lime juice and olive oil, and then whisk until combined.

❖ Calories: 388 | fat: 16.5g | protein: 9.3g | carbohydrates: 54.2g | fibre: 8.5g

154) LETTUCE SALAD WITH BASIL

Preparation Time: 10 minutes	**Cooking Time**: 10 minutes	**Servings**: 2

✓ 2 small heads of romaine lettuce, cut in half ✓ 1 tablespoon chopped basil ✓ 1 tablespoon chopped red onion ✓ ¼ teaspoon of onion powder ✓ ½ tablespoon of agave syrup	✓ ½ teaspoon salt ✓ ¼ teaspoon cayenne pepper ✓ 2 tablespoons of olive oil ✓ 1 tablespoon of lime juice
❖ Take a large skillet, place it over medium heat and when it is heated, place the heads of lettuce in it, cut side down, and then cook them for 4 to 5 minutes per side until they are golden brown on both sides. ❖ When done, transfer the heads of lettuce to a plate and let them cool for 5 minutes.	❖ Meanwhile, prepare the dressing and for that, place the remaining ingredients in a small bowl and then mix until combined. ❖ Pour the dressing over the lettuce heads and then serve.

155) CABBAGE AND SPROUTS SALAD

Preparation Time: 5 minutes	**Cooking Time**: 0 minutes	**Servings**: 2

✓ 2 cups of kale leaves ✓ 1 cup of sprouts ✓ 1 cup of cherry tomatoes ✓ ½ avocado, peeled, pitted and diced	✓ 1 Key lime, squeezed ✓ 1 teaspoon of agave syrup ✓ ½ tablespoon of olive oil ✓ ⅛ teaspoon of cayenne pepper
❖ Take a small bowl, put the lime juice in it, add the oil and agave syrup and then stir until mixed.	❖ Take a salad bowl, put in the remaining ingredients, drizzle with the lime juice mixture and then toss until mixed. ❖ Serve immediately.

156) WATERCRESS AND CUCUMBER SALAD

Preparation Time: 5 minutes	**Cooking Time**: 0 minutes	**Servings**: 2

✓ 2 cups of torn watercress ✓ ½ sliced cucumber ✓ 1 tablespoon of lime juice	✓ 2 tablespoons of olive oil ✓ Pure sea salt, to taste ✓ Cayenne powder, to taste
❖ Pour the lime juice and olive oil into a salad bowl and mix well to combine. ❖ Slice the cucumber and add it to the bowl.	❖ Tear up the watercress and add it to the bowl. ❖ Sprinkle cayenne powder and pure sea salt according to your taste. ❖ Mix thoroughly. ❖ Serve immediately.

157) WATERCRESS AND ORANGE SALAD

Preparation Time: 10 minutes	**Cooking Time**: 0 minutes	**Servings**: 2

✓ 4 cups of torn watercress ✓ 1 avocado sliced ✓ 2 thinly sliced red onions ✓ 1 Seville orange chopped ✓ 2 tablespoons of lime juice	✓ 2 teaspoons of agave syrup ✓ ⅛ teaspoon of pure sea salt ✓ Cayenne powder, to taste ✓ 2 tablespoons of olive oil
❖ Prepare the avocado. cut it in half, peel it, remove the seeds and slice it. ❖ Peel the Seville orange and cut it into medium cubes. ❖ Remove the skin from the red onions and thinly slice them.	❖ Place onions, avocado, oranges and watercress in a salad bowl. ❖ Combine the olive oil, cayenne powder, pure sea salt, lime juice and agave syrup in a separate bowl, mix well. ❖ Pour the dressing over the top of the salad. ❖ Serve immediately.

158) MUSHROOM AND OLIVE SALAD

Preparation Time: 10 minutes	Cooking Time: 0 minutes	Servings: 2

✓ 5 mushrooms cut in half ✓ 6 halved cherry (plum) tomatoes ✓ 6 lettuce leaves, rinsed ✓ 10 olives	✓ ½ chopped cucumber ✓ Juice of ½ lime ✓ 1 teaspoon of olive oil ✓ Pure sea salt, to taste
❖ Cut the rinsed lettuce leaves into medium pieces and place in a medium salad bowl. ❖ Add the mushroom halves, chopped cucumber, olives, and cherry tomato halves to the bowl.	❖ Mix well. ❖ Pour the olive oil and lime juice over the salad. ❖ Add pure sea salt to taste. mix until well combined. ❖ Serve immediately.

159) TEX-MEX BOWL

✓ Nutritional yeast (2 tablespoons) ✓ Cilantro (2 tablespoons) ✓ Sliced avocado (1) ✓ Salt (.25 tsp.) ✓ Olive oil (.25 c.) ✓ Apple Cider Vinegar (.25 c.) ✓ Lime juice and zest (1) ✓ Lemon juice and zest (1) ✓ Squeezed Oranges (2) ✓ Chopped garlic cloves (2) ✓ Sliced red onion (1) ✓ Sliced peppers ✓ For the brown rice ✓ Hind beans (.5 c.)	✓ Garlic powder (.5 tsp.) ✓ Cayenne pepper (.5 tsp.) ✓ Paprika (1 teaspoon) ✓ Salt (1 teaspoon) ✓ Garlic powder (1.5 teaspoons) ✓ Chili powder (2 teaspoons) ✓ Cooked brown rice (1 c.) ✓ Sauce ✓ Juice of a lime ✓ Salt (.25 tsp.) ✓ Diced Cilantro (.25 c.) ✓ Diced red onion (.5) ✓ Diced Tomatoes (2)
❖ Pull out a large bowl and combine together the salt, olive oil, vinegar, lime zest and juice, lemon zest and juice, garlic, red onion, and bell bell pepper. ❖ Cover and let sit for about five hours to marinate a bit. While the peppers marinate a bit in the refrigerator, it's time to work on the sauce. ❖ To make the sauce, add all ingredients to a small bowl and mix well to combine. Cover the bowl and place in the refrigerator.	❖ In a medium bowl, add all the ingredients for the brown rice. Mix well and set aside. ❖ Heat your skillet and add the peppers with some of the marinade. Cook for a bit until the onion and peppers are soft. ❖ Add the rice to a few serving bowls and top with the bell pepper and onion mixture, salsa and avocado. Add the nutritional yeast and cilantro before serving.

160) AVOCADO AND SALMON SOUP

✓ Cilantro (2 tablespoons) ✓ Crushed pepper (1 teaspoon) ✓ Olive oil (1 tablespoon) ✓ Flaked salmon (1 can) ✓ Salt (.25 tsp.) ✓ Cumin (.25 tsp.) ✓ Vegetable stock (1.5 c.)	✓ Whole coconut cream (2 tablespoons) ✓ Lemon juice (4 tablespoons) ✓ Sliced green onion (1 tablespoon) ✓ Chopped Shallot (1) ✓ Pitted Avocado (3)

Directions:

❖ Take out a blender and combine together the salt, cumin, vegetable broth, coconut cream, two tablespoons of lemon juice, green onion, scallion, and avocado.
❖ Blend until smooth and then chill in the refrigerator for an hour.

❖ Meanwhile, take out a bowl and combine together a tablespoon of cilantro, two tablespoons of lemon juice, the pepper, olive oil and salmon.
❖ Add the cooled avocado soup to the bowls and top each with the salmon and the rest of the cilantro. Serve immediately.

Chapter 3.
DINNER

161) STEW WITHOUT BEEF

Ingredients:

- ✓ Dried oregano, 1 teaspoon
- ✓ Celery, diced, 2 stalks
- ✓ Large diced potato
- ✓ Sliced carrot, 3 c.
- ✓ Water, 2 c.
- ✓ Vegetable broth, 3 c.

Directions:

- ❖ Heat the avocado oil in a top pan. Put in the pepper, salt, garlic cloves and onion bulbs. Cook everything for two to three minutes, or until the onion is soft.
- ❖ Add the bay leaf, oregano, celery, potato, carrot, water and broth. Allow to simmer, then lower the heat and prepare for 30-45 minutes, or until the carrots and potatoes become soft.

Ingredients:

- ✓ Pepper, one teaspoon
- ✓ Sea salt, one teaspoon
- ✓ Garlic puree, 2 bulbs
- ✓ Diced onion, 1 c.
- ✓ Avocado oil, 1 tablespoon
- ✓ Laurel

- ❖ Taste and adjust the seasonings as needed. If it's too thick, you can add more water or broth.
- ❖ Divide among four bowls and enjoy.

162) EMMENTHAL SOUP

Ingredients:

- ✓ Cayenne
- ✓ Nutmeg
- ✓ Pumpkin seeds, 1 tablespoon
- ✓ Chopped chives, 2 tablespoons

Directions:

- ❖ Place the potato and cauliflower in a saucepan with the vegetable broth until tender.
- ❖ Place in a blender and blend.

Ingredients:

- ✓ Diced Emmenthal cheese, 3 tablespoons
- ✓ Vegetable broth, 2 c.
- ✓ Diced potato, 1
- ✓ Cauliflower chunks, 2 c.

- ❖ Add the spices and adjust to taste.
- ❖ Pour into bowls, add chives and cheese and mix well.
- ❖ Garnish with pumpkin seeds. Enjoy.

163) SPAGHETTI WITH BROCCOLI

Ingredients:

- ✓ Pepper
- ✓ Halls
- ✓ Vegetable broth, 1 teaspoon
- ✓ Oregano plant, 1 teaspoon
- ✓ Lemon juice, 1 tablespoon
- ✓ Sliced carrots, 3
- ✓ Diced tomatoes, 3

Directions:

- ❖ Place a pot of water halfway up and add the salt. Allow to boil and add the pasta. Prepare according to box instructions. Empty.
- ❖ Place broccoli in another bowl and cover with h2O. Prepare for five minutes.
- ❖ Place a skillet over normal heat and put two tablespoons of olive oil in the pan and heat. Place the bulbs, garlic and onion in and prepare until soft and fragrant. Remove from the skillet and set aside.

Ingredients:

- ✓ Broccoli cut into florets, 1 head
- ✓ Sliced bell pepper - red - bell, one
- ✓ Sliced onion bulb, one
- ✓ Diced garlic bulbs, two cloves
- ✓ EVOO, 4 tablespoons
- ✓ Buckwheat pasta, 1 lb.

- ❖ carrots. Cook for five minutes, then put in the sweet bell pepper and prepare for another five minutes, now put in the tomatoes and prepare for two minutes.
- ❖ Drain the broccoli completely and add it to the skillet with the rest of the vegetables. Return the onions and garlic to the skillet.
- ❖ Add the vegetable broth, oregano and lemon juice. Add a little pepper and salt, taste and adjust seasonings if needed. Stir well to combine.
- ❖ Place the cooked pasta on a serving plate. Pour over the vegetable mixture and toss to combine.

164)   INDIAN LENTIL CURRY

		Servings: 4 - 6

✓ Lime Juice	✓ Chopped garlic, 1 clove
✓ Chopped coriander	✓ Grated ginger, 1 inch
✓ Halls	✓ Turmeric, .5 tsp
✓ EVOO, 1 tablespoon	✓ Cumin seeds, .5 tsp
✓ Diced tomatoes, 2	✓ Chopped green peppers, 2
✓ Sliced onion, 1	✓ Fine red lentils, 1 c.

Directions:

❖ Place lentils in a bowl, cover with water and let stand for six hours.
❖ After six hours, drain the lentils completely.
❖ Place a bowl over normal heat. Place the lentils and cover with cool water. Allow to boil. Add the turmeric. Lower the heat and simmer until the lentils are cooked through.
❖ Take out of the pot and into a bowl. Place these on the side.

❖ In another skillet over medium heat, heat the olive oil. Add the turmeric, cumin, ginger and onions. Cook until the onions are soft and the ginger is fragrant.
❖ Add the chiles and tomatoes and cook. Add the salt and cook for five minutes.
❖ Pour the lentil into this mixture and bring back to a simmer. As soon as it starts to cook, remove it from the hot temperature. Squeeze a little lemon
❖ Sprinkle with cilantro and serve with rice.

165)   VEGETABLES WITH WILD RICE

		Servings: 4

Ingredients:

✓ Halls
✓ Basil
✓ Cilantro
✓ Juice of a lime
✓ Chopped red pepper, 1
✓ Vegetable broth, .5 c.

Ingredients:

✓ Bean sprouts, 1 c.
✓ Chopped carrots, 2 c.
✓ Beans - green - diced, 1 c.
✓ Broccoli, cut, 1 c.
✓ Pak Choi, 1 c.
✓ Wild rice, 1 c.

Directions:

❖ Place all the chopped vegetables in a pan and add the vegetable broth.
❖ Steam fry the vegetables until cooked but still crispy.

❖ Using a mortar and pestle, grind the chili, basil and cilantro until a paste is formed. Add the lime juice and mix well.
❖ Place the rice on a serving plate. Add the vegetables on top and drizzle with the dressing.

166)   SPICY LENTIL SOUP

		Servings: 4

Ingredients:

✓ Halls
✓ Turmeric, .25 tsp
✓ Chopped garlic, 3 cloves
✓ Grated ginger, 1.5 inch piece
✓ Chopped tomato, 1

Ingredients:

✓ Chopped Serrano chili pepper, 1
✓ Rinsed red lentils, 2 c.
✓ Topping:
✓ Coconut yogurt, .25 c.

Directions:

❖ Place lentils in a colander and place under running water. Rinse until the soil and stones are released.
❖ Pour rinsed lentils into a pot. Add enough water to cover the lentils. Place the pot over medium heat and allow to boil.

❖ Lower the heat and simmer for ten minutes.
❖ Put in the leftover contents and then mix well to combine.
❖ Cook again until lentils are soft.
❖ Garnish with a spoonful of coconut yogurt.

167) LEEK SOUP WITH MUSHROOMS

Servings: 4

- ✓ Sherry vinegar, 1.5 tablespoons
- ✓ Almond milk, .5 c.
- ✓ Cream of coconut, .66 c.
- ✓ Vegetable broth, 3 c.
- ✓ Chopped dill, 1 tablespoon
- ✓ Pepper
- ✓ Halls

- ✓ Almond flour, 5 tablespoons
- ✓ Cleaned and sliced mushrooms, 7 c.
- ✓ Chopped garlic, 3 cloves
- ✓ Chopped leeks, 2.75 c.
- ✓ Vegetable oil, 3 tablespoons

Directions:

- ❖ Set a Dutch oven on medium and heat the oil. Add the leeks and bulb garlic and prepare until soft.
- ❖ Toss in the mushrooms, stir, and cook an additional 10 minutes.

- ❖ Add the salt, dill, pepper and flour. Mix well, until combined.
- ❖ Put the soup in and let it simmer. Reduce the heat and put in the rest of the ingredients. Stir well. Cook another ten minutes.
- ❖ Serve hot with almond flour bread.

168) FRESH VEGETARIAN PIZZA

Servings: 4

- ✓ Crust -
- ✓ Garlic bulb flavored powder, 0.5 teaspoon
- ✓ Sea salt, 0.5 teaspoon
- ✓ Coconut oil, 3 tablespoons
- ✓ Almond flour, 1.25 c.
- ✓ Tahini-Bee Spread -
- ✓ Pepper, pinch

- ✓ Sea salt, a pinch
- ✓ Garlic, 2 cloves
- ✓ Lemon juice, one tablespoon
- ✓ Avocado oil, one tablespoon
- ✓ Middle Eastern Pasta, one tablespoon
- ✓ Beets peeled and diced, 2

Directions:

- ❖ Start by setting your oven to 375. Place some parchment on a tray.
- ❖ Mix together the salt, garlic powder, coconut oil and almond flour.
- ❖ Place it on the tray and squish it into a ball shape. Place another piece of parchment on top and roll out the dough into a 7x7 square. Bake for 14 minutes, or until it starts to brown.

- ❖ While the crust is cooking, add the pepper, salt, garlic, lemon juice, avocado oil, tahini and beets to a food processor. Blend until creamy.
- ❖ To make your pizza, spread the crust with beet sauces and then top with your favorite alkaline friendly vegetables. Cut it into four and enjoy.

169) SPICY LENTIL BURGER

Servings: 4

Ingredients:

- ✓ Avocado oil, 1 tablespoon
- ✓ Coconut flour, 1 tablespoon
- ✓ Crushed garlic, 2 cloves
- ✓ Diced Jalapeno
- ✓ Chopped cilantro, .5 c.

Ingredients:

- ✓ Diced onion, .5 c.
- ✓ Pepper, .5 tsp
- ✓ Sea salt, 0.5 teaspoons
- ✓ Almond flour, .5 c.
- ✓ Dried lentils, .5 c.

- ❖ Cook lentils according to package directions and set aside to cool.
- ❖ Mix together the garlic, jalapeno, cilantro, onion, pepper, salt, almond meal and lentils until everything is well combined.
- ❖ Add half of the lentil mixture to a food processor and process until it reaches a paste-like consistency.
- ❖ Pour this into the bowl with the rest of the lentil mixture and mix everything together.

- ❖ The mixture will be very moist. Stir in the coconut flour to help get rid of the moisture and to help hold them together.
- ❖ Divide the mixture into quarters. Squeeze a quarter of the mixture between your hands to flatten it into a hamburger shape. Do this for the remaining three sections.
- ❖ Heat the oil in an oversized pan and place the burgers in it. Prepare the burgers 4 to 6 minutes on both sides, or until golden brown. When you flip them, do so carefully so they don't fall apart. Enjoy.

170) ROASTED CAULIFLOWER ROLLS

		Servings: 2

✓ Cauliflower -	✓ Apple cider vinegar, 2 tablespoons
✓ Pepper, .25 tsp	✓ Garlic, 2 cloves
✓ Sea salt, .25 tsp	✓ Habanero Pepper
✓ Garlic powder, .5 tsp	✓ Mango cubes, 1 c.
✓ Nutritional yeast, .25 c.	✓ Assembly -
✓ Almond flour, .25 c.	✓ Canola greens, 2 leaves
✓ Avocado oil, 1 tablespoon	✓ Mixed salad, 1 c.
✓ Bite-sized cauliflower florets, 2 c.	
✓ Sauce -	
✓ Sea Salt	

❖ Start by setting your kitchen appliance to three hundred and fifty degrees then place some paper on a kitchen wrap.	❖ Cook thirty to thirty-five minutes, or until cauliflower is soft.
❖ To prepare the cauliflower, toss it in the avocado oil and make sure it's evenly coated.	❖ While the cauliflower is cooking, add the salt, vinegar, garlic, habanero and mango to your blender and blend until well combined. Be sure to use gloves or wash your hands thoroughly when you need to handle the habanero.
❖ In a container, combine together all the seasonings: pepper, salt, garlic powder, healthy mushrooms, along with almond flour.	❖ To assemble, divide the salad mix between the collard leaves, top with the cauliflower and pour the sauce over it. Wrap the whole thing like a burrito and enjoy.
❖ Sprinkle the breading over the cauliflower and toss, making sure the cauliflower is well coated. Spread on the baking sheet.	

171) SLICED SWEET POTATO WITH ARTICHOKE AND BELL PEPPER SPREAD

		Servings: 4

✓ Pepper, .25 tsp	✓ Unpeeled sweet potatoes, 2 cut into 4 slices lengthwise
✓ Salt, .5 tsp	✓ Garlic, 2 cloves
✓ Avocado oil, 6 tablespoons - divided	✓ Artichoke hearts, 14 oz can
✓ Red bell pepper cut into quarters	

❖ Start by setting the oven to 350. Place some parchment on a tray and set aside.	❖ Bake for 30 minutes. Turn them over and bake for another 15 minutes.
❖ Lay the bell bell pepper and sweet potato on the sheet tray and cover with two teaspoons of avocado oil, a pinch of pepper and a pinch of salt.	❖ Add the roasted red bell pepper to a food processor along with the garlic, artichoke hearts, pepper, salt and remaining avocado oil. Pulse until combined but still somewhat chunky. Adjust seasonings as needed.
	❖ Top the sweet potato slices with the cream and enjoy.

172) COOKING SCALLOPS, ONIONS AND POTATOES

		Servings: 4

✓ Cashew cheese sauce -	✓ Pepper, 1 teaspoon
✓ Sea salt, 0.5 teaspoons	✓ Sea salt, one teaspoon
✓ Nutritional yeast, .5 c.	✓ Oil - Avocado, one tablespoon
✓ Almond milk, 1 c.	✓ Chopped small onion bulbs, 1.5
✓ Raw cashews, 1 c.	✓ New potatoes, thinly sliced, 8
✓ Scallop Bake -	
✓ Chopped tarragon, 1 tablespoon	

❖ To make the cheese sauce, add the cashews to a bowl and cover them with room temperature water. Let them soak for 15-20 minutes and then drain and rinse them.	❖ Using an 8-inch square baking dish, place the potato and onion mixture in the dish. Do your best to arrange them in nice rows. It doesn't have to be perfect.
❖ Blend together cashews with remaining cheese sauce ingredients until smooth and creamy. Set aside until later.	❖ Bake for 45 minutes, or until potatoes are soft
❖ Start by heating the oven to 375.	❖ Remove from oven and top with cheese sauce. Divide among four plates and enjoy. You can also slide this on, and bake inside the cooking appliance on about 5 minutes in order to warm the cheese sauce through before serving.
❖ Combine the onions and potatoes in a bowl with the avocado oil. Add the tarragon, pepper and salt, making sure everything is well coated.	

173) SPICY CILANTRO AND COCONUT SOUP

		Servings: 2

Ingredients:

- ✓ Cilantro leaves, 2 tablespoons
- ✓ Jalapeno
- ✓ Lime juice, 1 tablespoon
- ✓ Whole Coconut Milk, 13.5 oz. can

Ingredients:

- ✓ Sea salt, .25 tsp
- ✓ Crushed garlic, 3 cloves
- ✓ Diced onion, .5 c.
- ✓ Avocado oil, 2 tablespoons

Directions:

- ❖ Add the avocado oil to a medium skillet and heat. Add the salt, garlic and onion, cooking three to five minutes, or until the onion bulbs become smooth.

- ❖ Place the onion mixture, cilantro, jalapeno, lime juice and coconut milk in a blender and blend until creamy.
- ❖ Pour into a bowl and enjoy.

174) TARRAGON SOUP

		Servings: 2

Ingredients:

- ✓ Chopped fresh tarragon, 2 tablespoons
- ✓ Celery stalk
- ✓ Raw cashews, .5 c.
- ✓ Lemon juice, 1 tablespoon
- ✓ Whole Coconut Milk, 13.5 oz. can

Ingredients:

- ✓ Pepper, .5 tsp - divided
- ✓ Sea salt, .5 tsp - divided
- ✓ Crushed garlic, 3 cloves
- ✓ Diced onion, .5 c.
- ✓ Avocado oil, 1 tablespoon

Directions:

- ❖ Add the oil to a medium skillet and heat it up. Put all the seasonings: pepper, salt, garlic bulbs, along with the onion bulbs then prepare about three to five minutes, or until the onions become soft.

- ❖ Using a high-speed blender, add the onion mixture, tarragon, celery, cashews, lemon juice, and coconut milk. Blend everything until smooth. Taste and adjust seasonings if needed.
- ❖ Divide between two bowls and enjoy. You can also add back into a pot and reheat before serving.

175) ASPARAGUS AND ARTICHOKE SOUP

		Servings: 4

Ingredients:

- ✓ Artichoke hearts halved and chopped, 1 can
- ✓ Almond milk, 2 c.
- ✓ Pepper, .5 tsp
- ✓ Sea Salt, .5 - .75 tsp
- ✓ Vegetable broth, 2 c.
- ✓ Asparagus diced, 8 stalks

Ingredients:

- ✓ Cubed potatoes, 1 c.
- ✓ Crushed garlic, 2 cloves
- ✓ Avocado oil, 1 tablespoon
- ✓ Diced onion, .5 c.

Directions:

- ❖ Add the garlic, avocado oil and onion to a skillet and cook for a few minutes, or until the onion bulbs have softened and weakened.
- ❖ Place the cooked vegetables in a pot and add the pepper, salt, vegetable stock, asparagus and potatoes. Stir everything together and let it simmer. Lower the heat and simmer gently eighteen to twenty minutes, or until the potatoes have become soft.

- ❖ Add a little more broth if you find you need it, so that the liquid remains about an inch above the vegetables.
- ❖ Place the pot away from the heat and let it cool.
- ❖ Using a blender, blend the cooled soup with the artichokes and almond milk until everything is well combined and smooth. Adjust seasonings as needed. You can add more broth or milk to thicken everything if needed.
- ❖ Pour back into the pot and allow to heat over low heat until ready to serve.

176) MINT AND BERRY SOUP

		Servings: 1

Ingredients:

- ✓ Sweetener -
- ✓ Water, .25 c - more if needed
- ✓ Unrefined whole cane sugar, .25 c.
- Soup -
- ✓ Water, .5 c.

Ingredients:

- ✓ Mixed berries, 1 c.
- ✓ Mint leaves, 8
- ✓ Lemon juice, 1 teaspoon

Directions:

- ❖ Add the water and sugar to a small saucepan and cook, stirring constantly, until the sugar has dissolved. Allow to cool.
- ❖ Add the mint leaves, lemon juice, water, berries and cooled sugar mixture to a blender. Blend everything together until smooth.

- ❖ Pour into a bowl and then refrigerate until the broth is completely cooled. This will take about 20 minutes.
- ❖ Enjoy.

177) MUSHROOM SOUP

		Servings: 2

Ingredients:

- ✓ Whole Coconut Milk, 13.5 oz. can
- ✓ Vegetable stock, 1 c.
- ✓ Pepper, .5 tsp
- ✓ Sea salt, .75 tsp
- ✓ Crush the garlic clove
- ✓ Diced onion, 1 cup

Ingredients:

- ✓ Cut cremini mushrooms, 1 cup
- ✓ Chinese black mushrooms cut into pieces, one cup
- ✓ Avocado oil, 1 tablespoon
- ✓ Coconut amino acids, 1 tablespoon
- ✓ Dried thyme, .5 tsp

Directions:

- ❖ Heat the fat in a very massive pan, then put in all the seasonings: pepper, salt, garlic, onion bulb and mushrooms. Boil and prepare for a few minutes, or until onions become soft.
- ❖ Stir in the coconut amino acid, thyme, coconut milk and vegetable broth.

- ❖ Lower the heat and let the broth simmer for about fifteen minutes. Stir the broth occasionally.
- ❖ Taste and adjust any seasoning you need. Divide between two bowls and enjoy.

178) POTATO AND LENTIL STEW

		Servings: 4

Ingredients:

- ✓ Chopped oregano sprigs, 2 sprigs
- ✓ Diced celery stalk
- ✓ Diced and peeled potato, 1 c.
- ✓ Sliced carrots, 2
- ✓ Dried lentils, 1 c.
- ✓ Spicy seasoning / Pepper, one teaspoon
- ✓ Sea salt, one to 1.5 teaspoons

Ingredients:

- ✓ Crushed garlic bulbs, two buds
- ✓ Diced onion, .5 c.
- ✓ Avocado oil, 2 tablespoons
- ✓ Whole Coconut Milk, 13.5 oz. can
- ✓ Vegetable broth, 5 c - divided
- ✓ Chopped tarragon, 2 sprigs

Directions:

- ❖ Using a large cooking utensil, heat the avocado fat along with the inclusion of seasonings: pepper, salt, garlic bulbs, along with the onion. Cook for three to five minutes, or until onion is soft.
- ❖ Add the tarragon, oregano, celery, potato, carrots, lentils and 2 ½ cups of vegetable stock. Stir everything together.

- ❖ Allow the saucepan to return to heat and then lower the heat. Allow to cook, stirring frequently. Add more vegetable broth in half-cup portions, if necessary, to make sure the lentils have enough liquid to cook. Let the stew cook for 20-25 minutes, or until the lentils and potatoes are soft.
- ❖ Remove the stew from the heat and stir in the coconut milk. Divide among four bowls and enjoy.

179) MIXED MUSHROOM STEW

Preparation Time: 15 minutes	Cooking Timw: 15 minutes	Servings: 4

Ingredients:

- ✓ 2 tablespoons of olive oil
- ✓ 2 onions, chopped
- ✓ 3 cloves of garlic, minced
- ✓ ½ lb. fresh mushrooms, chopped
- ✓ ¼ pound of fresh shiitake mushrooms, chopped

Directions:

- ❖ In a large skillet, heat the oil over medium heat and sauté the onion and garlic for 4-5 minutes.
- ❖ Add the mushrooms, salt and black pepper and cook for 4-5 minutes.

Ingredients:

- ✓ ¼ pound fresh Portobello mushrooms, chopped
- ✓ Sea salt and freshly ground black pepper, to taste
- ✓ ¼ cup of homemade vegetable broth
- ✓ ½ cup unsweetened coconut milk
- ✓ 2 tablespoons fresh parsley, chopped

- ❖ Add the broth and coconut milk and bring to a gentle boil.
- ❖ Simmer for 4-5 minutes or until desired doneness.
- ❖ Add the parsley and remove from heat.
- ❖ Serve hot.

180) MIXED STEW OF SPICY VEGETABLES

Preparation Time: 20 minutes	Cooking Time: 35 minutes	Servings: 8

Ingredients:

- ✓ 2 tablespoons of coconut oil
- ✓ 1 large sweet onion, chopped
- ✓ 1 medium parsnip, peeled and chopped
- ✓ 3 tablespoons of homemade tomato paste
- ✓ 2 large cloves of garlic, minced
- ✓ ½ teaspoon of cinnamon powder
- ✓ ½ teaspoon of ground ginger
- ✓ 1 teaspoon of ground cumin
- ✓ ¼ teaspoon cayenne pepper

- ❖ In a large soup pot, melt the coconut oil over medium-high heat and sauté the onion for about 5 minutes.
- ❖ Add the parsnips and sauté for about 3 minutes.
- ❖ Stir in the tomato paste, garlic and spices and sauté for 2 minutes.

Ingredients:

- ✓ 2 medium carrots, peeled and chopped
- ✓ 2 medium purple potatoes, peeled and cut into pieces
- ✓ 2 medium sweet potatoes, peeled and cut into pieces
- ✓ 4 cups of homemade vegetable broth
- ✓ 2 tablespoons fresh lemon juice
- ✓ 2 cups fresh cabbage, hard ribs removed and chopped
- ✓ ¼ cup fresh parsley leaves, chopped

- ❖ Stir in the carrots, potatoes, sweet potatoes and broth and bring to a boil.
- ❖ Reduce heat to medium-low and simmer, covered for about 20 minutes.
- ❖ Add the lemon juice and cabbage and simmer for 5 minutes.
- ❖ Serve with a garnish of parsley.

181) MIXED VEGETABLE STEW WITH HERBS

Preparation Time: 15 minutes	Cooking Time: 2¼ hours	Servings: 8

Ingredients:

- ✓ 2 tablespoons of coconut oil
- ✓ 1 medium yellow onion, chopped
- ✓ 2 cups celery, chopped
- ✓ ½ teaspoon of minced garlic
- ✓ 3 cups fresh cabbage, hard ribs removed and chopped
- ✓ ½ cup fresh mushrooms, sliced
- ✓ 2½ cups tomatoes, finely chopped
- ✓ 1 teaspoon dried rosemary, crushed

- ❖ In a large skillet, melt the coconut oil over medium heat and sauté the onion, celery and garlic for about 5 minutes.
- ❖ Add the rest of all ingredients and stir to combine.
- ❖ Increase heat to high and bring to a boil.
- ❖ Cook for about 10 minutes.

Ingredients:

- ✓ 1 teaspoon dried sage, crushed
- ✓ 1 teaspoon dried oregano, crushed
- ✓ Sea salt and freshly ground black pepper, to taste
- ✓ 2 cups of homemade vegetable broth
- ✓ 3-4 cups of alkaline water
- ✓ ¼ cup fresh parsley, chopped

- ❖ Reduce heat to medium and cook, covered for about 15 minutes.
- ❖ Uncover the pan and cook for about 15 minutes, stirring occasionally.
- ❖ Now, reduce the heat to low and simmer, covered for about 1 1/2 hours.
- ❖ Serve warm with the parsley garnish.

182) TOFU AND BELL PEPPER STEW

Preparation Time: 15 minutes	Cooking Time: 15 minutes	Servings: 6

- ✓ 2 tablespoons of garlic
- ✓ 1 jalapeño bell pepper, seeded and chopped
- ✓ 1 (16-ounce) jar of roasted red peppers, rinsed, drained and chopped
- ✓ 2 cups of homemade vegetable broth
- ✓ 2 cups of alkaline water

- ✓ 1 medium green bell pepper, seeded and thinly sliced
- ✓ 1 medium red bell pepper, seeded and thinly sliced
- ✓ 1 (16-ounce) package of extra-firm tofu, drained and diced
- ✓ 10 ounces of frozen sprouts, thawed
- ✓ Sea salt and freshly ground black pepper, to taste

Directions:

- ❖ In a food processor, add the garlic, jalapeño bell pepper and roasted red peppers and pulse until smooth.
- ❖ In a large skillet, add the pepper puree, broth and water over medium-high heat and bring to a boil.
- ❖ Add the peppers and tofu and stir to combine.

- ❖ Reduce the heat to medium and cook for about 5 minutes.
- ❖ Stir in the cabbage and cook for about 5 minutes.
- ❖ Add the salt and black pepper and remove from heat.
- ❖ Serve hot.

183) ROASTED PUMPKIN CURRY

Preparation Time: 15 minutes	Cooking Time: 35 minutes	Servings: 4

- For the roasted squash:
- ✓ 1 medium-sized sugar pumpkin, peeled and cut into cubes
- ✓ Sea salt, to taste
- ✓ 1 teaspoon of olive oil
- For Curry:
- ✓ 1 teaspoon of olive oil
- ✓ 1 onion, chopped
- ✓ 1 tablespoon fresh ginger root, peeled and chopped

- ✓ 1 tablespoon chopped garlic
- ✓ 1 cup unsweetened coconut milk
- ✓ 2 cups of vegetable broth
- ✓ 1 teaspoon of ground cumin
- ✓ ½ teaspoon ground turmeric
- ✓ Sea salt and freshly ground black pepper, to taste
- ✓ 1 tablespoon fresh lime juice
- ✓ 2 tablespoons fresh parsley, chopped

Directions:

- ❖ Preheat oven to 400 degrees F. Line a large baking sheet with baking paper.
- ❖ In a large bowl, add all the ingredients for the roasted squash and stir to coat well.
- ❖ Place the squash on the prepared baking sheet in a single layer.
- ❖ Roast for about 20-25 minutes, turning once halfway through.

- ❖ Meanwhile, for the curry: in a large skillet, heat the oil over medium-high heat and sauté the onion for about 4-5 minutes.
- ❖ Add the ginger and garlic and sauté for about 1 minute.
- ❖ Add the coconut milk, broth, spices, salt and black pepper and bring to a boil.
- ❖ Reduce the heat to low and simmer for about 10 minutes.
- ❖ Add the roasted squash and simmer for another 10 minutes.
- ❖ Serve warm with a garnish of parsley.

184) LENTILS, VEGETABLES AND APPLE CURRY

Preparation Time: 20 minutes	Cooking Time: 1 hour and a half	Servings: 6

- ✓ 8 cups of alkaline water
- ✓ ½ teaspoon ground turmeric
- ✓ 1 cup brown lentils
- ✓ 1 cup of red lentils
- ✓ 1 tablespoon of olive oil
- ✓ 1 large white onion, chopped
- ✓ 3 cloves of garlic, minced
- ✓ 2 tomatoes, seeded and chopped

- ✓ ¼ teaspoon ground cloves
- ✓ 2 teaspoons of ground cumin
- ✓ 2 carrots, peeled and cut into pieces
- ✓ 2 potatoes, hulled and cut into pieces
- ✓ 2 cups of squash, peeled, seeded and cut into 1-inch cubes
- ✓ 1 granny smith apple, cored and chopped
- ✓ 2 cups fresh cabbage, hard ribs removed and chopped
- ✓ Sea salt and freshly ground black pepper, to taste

Directions:

- ❖ In a large skillet, add the water, turmeric and lentils over high heat and bring to a boil.
- ❖ Reduce heat to medium-low and simmer, covered for about 30 minutes.
- ❖ Drain the lentils, reserving 2½ cups of the cooking liquid.
- ❖ Meanwhile, in another large skillet, heat the oil over medium heat and sauté the onion for about 2-3 minutes.
- ❖ Add the garlic and sauté for about 1 minute.
- ❖ Add the tomatoes and cook for about 5 minutes.

- ❖ Stir in the spices and cook for about 1 minute.
- ❖ Add the carrots, potatoes, squash, cooked lentils and reserved cooking liquid and bring to a gentle boil.
- ❖ Reduce heat to medium-low and simmer, covered for about 40-45 minutes or until desired doneness of vegetables.
- ❖ Add the apple and cabbage and simmer for about 15 minutes.
- ❖ Add the salt and black pepper and remove from heat.
- ❖ Serve hot.

185) CURRIED RED BEANS

Preparation Time: 15 minutes	Cooking Time: 25 minutes	Servings: 4

Ingredients:

- ✓ 4 tablespoons of olive oil
- ✓ 1 medium onion, finely chopped
- ✓ 2 cloves of garlic, minced
- ✓ 2 tablespoons fresh ginger root, peeled and chopped
- ✓ 1 teaspoon of ground coriander
- ✓ 1 teaspoon of ground cumin
- ✓ ½ teaspoon ground turmeric

Ingredients:

- ✓ ¼ teaspoon cayenne pepper
- ✓ Sea salt and freshly ground black pepper, to taste
- ✓ 2 large plum tomatoes, finely chopped
- ✓ 3 cups of cooked red beans
- ✓ 2 cups of alkaline water
- ✓ ¼ cup fresh parsley, chopped

Directions:

- ❖ In a large skillet, heat the oil over medium heat and sauté the onion, garlic and ginger for about 6-8 minutes.
- ❖ Stir in the spices and cook for about 1-2 minutes.

- ❖ Add the tomatoes, beans and water and bring to a boil over high heat.
- ❖ Reduce heat to medium and simmer for 10-15 minutes or until desired thickness.
- ❖ Serve warm with a garnish of parsley.

186) LENTIL AND CARROT CHILI

Preparation Time: 15 minutes	Cooking Time: 2 hours and 40 minutes	Servings: 8

Ingredients:

- ✓ 2 teaspoons of olive oil
- ✓ 1 large onion, chopped
- ✓ 3 medium carrots, peeled and chopped
- ✓ 4 celery stalks, chopped
- ✓ 2 cloves of garlic, minced
- ● 1 jalapeño bell pepper, seeded and chopped
- ✓ ½ tablespoon dried thyme, crushed
- ✓ 1 tablespoon of chipotle chili powder

Ingredients:

- ✓ ½ tablespoon of cayenne pepper
- ✓ 1½ tablespoons ground coriander
- ✓ 1½ tablespoons of ground cumin
- ✓ 1 teaspoon ground turmeric
- ✓ Sea salt and freshly ground black pepper, to taste
- ✓ 1 pound of red lentils, rinsed
- ✓ 8 cups of homemade vegetable broth
- ✓ ½ cup shallots, chopped

Directions:

- ❖ In a large skillet, heat the oil over medium heat and sauté the onion, carrot and celery for about 5 minutes.
- ❖ Add the garlic, jalapeño pepper, thyme and spices and sauté for about 1 minute.

- ❖ Add the lentils and broth and bring to a boil.
- ❖ Reduce heat to low and simmer, covered for about 2-2½ hours.
- ❖ Remove from heat and serve hot with a scallion garnish.

187) CHILI BLACK BEANS

15 minutes	2 hours and 5 minutes	5

Ingredients:

- ✓ 2 tablespoons of olive oil
- ✓ 1 onion, chopped
- ✓ 1 large green bell pepper, seeded and sliced
- ✓ 4 cloves of garlic, minced
- ✓ 2 jalapeño peppers, sliced
- ✓ 1 teaspoon of ground cumin
- ✓ 1 teaspoon of cayenne pepper

Ingredients:

- ✓ 1 tablespoon of red chili powder
- ✓ 1 teaspoon of paprika
- ✓ 2 cups of tomatoes, finely chopped
- ✓ 4 cups of cooked black beans
- ✓ 2 cups of homemade vegetable broth
- ✓ Sea salt and freshly ground black pepper, to taste
- ✓ ¼ cup fresh parsley, chopped

- ❖ In a large skillet, heat the oil over medium-high heat and sauté the onion and peppers for 3-4 minutes.
- ❖ Add the garlic, jalapeño peppers and spices and sauté for about 1 minute.
- ❖ Add the remaining ingredients and bring to a boil.

- ❖ Reduce heat to medium-low and simmer, covered for about 1½-2 hours.
- ❖ Season with the salt and black pepper and remove from heat.
- ❖ Serve warm with the parsley garnish.

188) COOK MIXED VEGETABLES

Preparation Time: 15 minutes	Cooking Time: 20 minutes	Servings: 4

✓ 1 small zucchini, chopped ✓ 1 small summer squash, chopped ✓ 1 diced eggplant ✓ 1 red bell pepper, seeded and diced ✓ 1 green bell pepper, seeded and diced	✓ 1 onion, thinly sliced ✓ 1 tablespoon of pure maple syrup ✓ 2 tablespoons of olive oil ✓ Sea salt and freshly ground black pepper, to taste

Directions:

❖ Preheat oven to 375 degrees F. Lightly grease a large baking dish.
❖ In a large bowl, add all ingredients and mix well.

❖ Transfer the vegetable mixture to the prepared baking dish.
❖ Bake for about 15-20 minutes.
❖ Remove from oven and serve immediately.

189) VEGETARIAN RATATOUILLE

Preparation Time: 20 minutes	Cooking Time 45 minutes	Servings: 4

✓ 6 ounces of homemade tomato paste ✓ 3 tablespoons of olive oil, divided by ✓ ½ onion, chopped ✓ 3 tablespoons minced garlic ✓ Sea salt and freshly ground black pepper, to taste ✓ 1 zucchini, cut into thin circles	✓ 1 yellow pumpkin, cut into thin circles ✓ 1 eggplant, cut into thin circles ✓ 1 red bell pepper, with seeds and cut into thin rounds ✓ 1 yellow bell pepper, seeded and cut into thin rounds ✓ 1 tablespoon fresh thyme leaves, chopped ✓ 1 tablespoon fresh lemon juice

Directions:

❖ Preheat the oven to 375 degrees F.
❖ In a bowl, add the tomato paste, 1 tablespoon oil, onion, garlic, salt and black pepper and mix well.
❖ In the bottom of a 10x10-inch baking dish, spread tomato paste mixture evenly.
❖ Arrange the vegetable slices alternately, starting at the outer edge of the pan and working concentrically toward the center.

❖ Drizzle the vegetables with the remaining oil and sprinkle with salt and black pepper, followed by the thyme.
❖ Arrange a piece of parchment paper over the vegetables.
❖ Bake for about 45 minutes.
❖ Remove from oven and serve hot.

190) QUINOA WITH VEGETABLES

Preparation Time: 15 minutes	Cooking Time: 26 minutes	Servings: 4

For roasted mushrooms: ✓ 2 cups of small fresh Baby Bella mushrooms ✓ 1 tablespoon of olive oil ✓ Sea salt, to taste For the quinoa: ✓ 2 cups of alkaline water ✓ 1 cup red quinoa, rinsed ✓ 2 tablespoons fresh parsley, chopped	✓ 1 garlic clove chopped ✓ 1 tablespoon of olive oil ✓ 2 teaspoons of fresh lemon juice ✓ Sea salt and freshly ground black pepper, to taste For the broccoli: ✓ 1 cup of broccoli florets ✓ 2 tablespoons of olive oil

Directions:

❖ Preheat oven to 425 degrees F. Line a large rimmed baking sheet with parchment paper.
❖ In a bowl, add the mushrooms, oil and salt and stir to coat well.
❖ Arrange the mushrooms on the prepared baking sheet in a single layer.
❖ Roast for about 15-18 minutes, tossing once halfway through cooking.
❖ Meanwhile, for the quinoa: in a skillet, add the water and quinoa over medium-high heat and bring to a boil.
❖ Reduce the heat to low and simmer, covered for about 15-20 minutes or until all the liquid is absorbed.
❖ Remove from heat and set pan aside, covered for about 5 minutes.
❖ Uncover the pan and with a fork, stir in the quinoa.

❖ Stir in the parsley, garlic, oil, lemon juice, salt and black pepper and set aside to cool completely.
❖ Meanwhile, for the broccoli: in a pot of water, arrange a steamer basket and bring to a boil.
❖ Place the broccoli florets in the basket of the steamer and steam, covered for about 5-6 minutes.
❖ Drain broccoli florets well.
❖ Transfer the broccoli florets to the bowl with the quinoa and mushrooms and stir to combine.
❖ Drizzle with the oil and serve immediately.

191) LENTILS WITH CABBAGE

Preparation Time: 15 minutes	Cooking Time: 20 minutes	Servings: 6

Ingredients:

- ✓ 1½ cups of red lentils
- ✓ 1½ cups of homemade vegetable broth
- ✓ 1½ tablespoons of olive oil
- ✓ ½ cup onion, chopped
- ✓ 1 teaspoon fresh ginger, minced

Ingredients:

- ✓ 2 cloves of garlic, minced
- ✓ 1½ cups tomato, chopped
- ✓ 6 cups fresh cabbage, hard ribs removed and chopped
- ✓ Sea salt and ground black pepper, to taste

Directions:

- ❖ In a skillet, add the broth and lentils over medium-high heat and bring to a boil.
- ❖ Reduce heat and simmer, covered for about 20 minutes or until almost all liquid is absorbed.
- ❖ Remove from heat and set aside covered.

- ❖ Meanwhile, in a large skillet, heat the oil over medium heat and sauté the onion for about 5-6 minutes.
- ❖ Add the ginger and garlic and sauté for about 1 minute.
- ❖ Add the tomatoes and cabbage and cook for about 4-5 minutes.
- ❖ Add the lentils, salt and black pepper and remove from heat.
- ❖ Remove from heat and serve hot.

192) LENTILS WITH TOMATOES

Preparation Time: 15 minutes	Cooking Time: 55 minutes	Servings: 4

- ✓ For the tomato puree:
- ✓ 1 cup tomatoes, chopped
- ✓ 1 garlic clove, minced
- ✓ 1 green chilli chopped
- ✓ ¼ cup of alkaline water
- For the lentils:
- ✓ 1 cup of red lentils
- ✓ 3 cups of alkaline water

- ✓ 1 tablespoon of olive oil
- ✓ ½ medium white onion, chopped
- ✓ ½ teaspoon of ground cumin
- ✓ ½ teaspoon of cayenne pepper
- ✓ ¼ teaspoon ground turmeric
- ✓ ¼ cup of tomato, chopped
- ✓ ¼ cup fresh parsley leaves, chopped

Directions:

- ❖ To tomato paste in a blender, add all ingredients and pulse until it forms a smooth puree. Set aside.
- ❖ In a large skillet, add 3 cups of water and the lentils over high heat and bring to a boil.
- ❖ Reduce heat to medium-low and simmer, covered for about 15-20 minutes or until quite tender.
- ❖ Drain lentils well.

- ❖ In a large skillet, heat the oil over medium heat and sauté the onion for about 6-7 minutes.
- ❖ Add the spices and sauté for about 1 minute.
- ❖ Add the tomato puree and cook, stirring for about 5-7 minutes.
- ❖ Stir in the lentils and cook for about 4-5 minutes or until desired degree of doneness.
- ❖ Stir in chopped tomato and immediately remove from heat.
- ❖ Serve warm with the parsley garnish.

193) SPICY BAKED BEANS

Preparation Time: 15 minutes	Cooking Time: 2 hours and 5 minutes	Servings: 4

- ✓ ½ pound of dried red beans, soaked overnight and drained
- ✓ 1¼ tablespoons of olive oil
- ✓ 1 small yellow onion, chopped
- ✓ 4 cloves of garlic, minced
- ✓ 1 teaspoon dried thyme, crushed
- ✓ ½ teaspoon of ground cumin
- ✓ ½ teaspoon of red pepper flakes, crushed

- ✓ ¼ teaspoon of smoked paprika
- ✓ 1 tablespoon fresh lemon juice
- ✓ 1 cup of homemade tomato sauce
- ✓ 1 cup homemade vegetable broth
- ✓ Sea salt and freshly ground black pepper, to taste

Directions:

- ❖ In a large pot of boiling water, add the beans and bring to a boil.
- ❖ Reduce heat to low and cook, covered for about 1 hour.
- ❖ Remove from heat and drain beans well.
- ❖ Preheat the oven to 325 degrees F.
- ❖ In a large ovenproof skillet, heat the oil over medium heat and sauté the onion for about 4 minutes.

- ❖ Add the garlic, thyme and spices and sauté for about 1 minute.
- ❖ Stir in cooked beans and remaining ingredients and immediately remove from heat.
- ❖ Cover the pan and bake for about 1 hour.
- ❖ Remove from oven and serve hot.

194) CHICKPEAS WITH PUMPKIN

Preparation Time: 20 minutes	Cooking Time: 35 minutes	Servings: 4

✓ 1 tablespoon of olive oil ✓ 1 onion, chopped ✓ 2 cloves of garlic, minced ✓ 1 green chili pepper, seedless and finely chopped ✓ 1 teaspoon of ground cumin ✓ ½ teaspoon of ground coriander ✓ 1 teaspoon of red chili powder	✓ 2 cups fresh tomatoes, finely chopped ✓ 2 pounds of pumpkin, peeled and diced ✓ 2 cups of homemade vegetable broth ✓ 2 cups of cooked chickpeas ✓ 2 tablespoons fresh lemon juice ✓ Sea salt and freshly ground black pepper, to taste ✓ 2 tablespoons fresh parsley leaves, chopped
❖ In a large skillet, heat the oil over medium-high heat and sauté the onion for about 5-7 minutes. ❖ Add the garlic, green chiles and spices and sauté for about 1 minute. ❖ Add tomatoes and cook for 2-3 minutes, mashing with the back of a spoon.	❖ Add the squash and cook for about 3-4 minutes, stirring occasionally. ❖ Add the broth and bring to a boil. ❖ Reduce the heat to low and simmer for about 10 minutes. ❖ Stir in the chickpeas and simmer for about 10 minutes. ❖ Add the lemon juice, salt, and black pepper and remove from heat. ❖ Serve warm with the parsley garnish.

195) CHICKPEAS WITH KALE

Preparation Time: 15 minutes	Cooking Time: 18 minutes	Servings: 6

✓ 2 tablespoons of olive oil ✓ 1 medium onion, chopped ✓ 4 cloves of garlic, minced ✓ 1 teaspoon dried thyme, crushed ✓ 1 teaspoon dried oregano, crushed ✓ ½ teaspoon of paprika ✓ 1 cup of tomato, finely chopped	✓ 2½ cups of cooked chickpeas ✓ 4 cups fresh cabbage, hard ribs removed and chopped ✓ 2 tablespoons of alkaline water ✓ 2 tablespoons fresh lemon juice ✓ Sea salt and freshly ground black pepper, to taste ✓ 3 tablespoons fresh basil, chopped
❖ In a large skillet, heat the oil over medium heat and sauté the onion for about 8-9 minutes. ❖ Add the garlic, herbs and paprika and sauté for about 1 minute. ❖ Add the cabbage and water and cook for about 2-3 minutes.	❖ Add the tomatoes and chickpeas and cook for about 3-5 minutes. ❖ Add the lemon juice, salt and black pepper and remove from heat. ❖ Serve warm with the basil garnish.

196) STUFFED CABBAGE ROLLS

Preparation Time: 15 minutes	Cooking Time: 15 minutes	Servings: 4

For filling: ✓ 1½ cups fresh button mushrooms, chopped ✓ 3¼ cups zucchini, chopped ✓ 1 cup red bell bell pepper, seeded and chopped ✓ 1 cup green bell bell pepper, seeded and chopped ✓ ½ teaspoon dried thyme, crushed ✓ ½ teaspoon dried marjoram, crushed ✓ ½ teaspoon dried basil, crushed	✓ Sea salt and freshly ground black pepper, to taste ✓ ½ cup of homemade vegetable broth ✓ 2 teaspoons of fresh lemon juice For rolls: ✓ 8 large cabbage leaves, rinsed ✓ 8 ounces of homemade tomato sauce ✓ 3 tablespoons fresh parsley, chopped
❖ Preheat oven to 400 degrees F. Lightly grease a 13x9-inch casserole dish. ❖ For the filling: in a large skillet, add all ingredients except lemon juice over medium heat and bring to a boil. ❖ Reduce heat to low and simmer, covered for about 5 minutes. ❖ Remove from heat and set aside for about 5 minutes. ❖ Add the lemon juice and stir to combine. ❖ Meanwhile, for the rolls: in a large pot of boiling water, add the cabbage leaves and boil for about 2-4 minutes. ❖ Drain the cabbage leaves well. ❖ Carefully pat each cabbage leaf dry with paper towels. ❖ Arrange the cabbage leaves on a smooth surface. ❖ Using a knife, make a V-shaped cut in each leaf by cutting through the thick vein.	❖ Carefully overlap the cut ends of each leaf. ❖ Place the filling mixture evenly on each leaf and fold in the sides. ❖ Then, roll up each leaf to seal in the filling and then, secure each leaf with toothpicks. ❖ In the bottom of the prepared casserole dish, place 1/3 cup of the tomato sauce evenly. ❖ Arrange the cabbage rolls over the sauce in a single layer and top with the remaining sauce evenly. ❖ Cover the casserole dish and cook for about 15 minutes. ❖ Remove from oven and set aside, uncovered for about 5 minutes. ❖ Serve warm with the parsley garnish.

197) GREEN BEANS AND MUSHROOM CASSEROLE

Preparation Time: 20 minutes	Cooking Time: 20 minutes	Servings: 6

Ingredients:

For the onion slices:
- ✓ ½ cup yellow onion, cut very thinly
- ✓ ¼ cup of almond flour
- ✓ 1/8 teaspoon of garlic powder
- ✓ Sea salt and freshly ground black pepper, to taste

For the casserole:
- ✓ 1 lb. fresh green beans, chopped
- ✓ 1 tablespoon of olive oil

Ingredients:
- ✓ 8 ounces of fresh cremini mushrooms, sliced
- ✓ ½ cup yellow onion, thinly sliced
- ✓ 1/8 teaspoon of garlic powder
- ✓ Sea salt and freshly ground black pepper, to taste
- ✓ 1 teaspoon fresh thyme, chopped
- ✓ ½ cup of homemade vegetable broth
- ✓ ½ cup of coconut cream

Directions:

- ❖ Preheat the oven to 350 degrees F.
- ❖ For the onion slices: in a bowl, place all ingredients and mix to coat well.
- ❖ Arrange the onion slices on a large baking sheet in a single layer and set aside.
- ❖ For the casserole: in a pot of boiling salted water, add the green beans and cook for about 5 minutes.
- ❖ Drain green beans and transfer to a bowl of ice water.
- ❖ Again, drain them well and transfer them back to a large bowl. Set aside.
- ❖ In a large skillet, heat the oil over medium-high heat and sauté the mushrooms, onion, garlic powder, salt and black pepper for about 2-3 minutes.

- ❖ Stir in the thyme and broth and cook for about 3-5 minutes or until all the liquid is absorbed.
- ❖ Remove from heat and transfer the mushroom mixture to the bowl with the green beans.
- ❖ Add the coconut cream and stir to combine well.
- ❖ Transfer the mixture to a 10-inch casserole dish.
- ❖ Place the casserole dish and pan of onion slices in the oven.
- ❖ Bake for about 15-17 minutes.
- ❖ Remove the pan and sheet from the oven and let cool for about 5 minutes before serving.
- ❖ Top the casserole with the crispy onion slices evenly.
- ❖ Cut into 6 equal-sized portions and serve.

198) MEATLOAF OF WILD RICE AND LENTILS

Preparation Time: 20 minutes	Cooking Time: 1 hour and 50 minutes	Servings: 8

Ingredients:
- ✓ 1¾ cups plus 2 tablespoons of alkaline water, divided
- ✓ ½ cup of wild rice
- ✓ ½ cup of brown lentils
- ✓ Pinch of sea salt
- ✓ ½ teaspoon of sodium-free Italian seasoning
- ✓ 1 medium yellow onion, chopped
- ✓ 1 celery stalk, chopped
- ✓ 6 cremini mushrooms, chopped

Ingredients:
- ✓ 4 cloves of garlic, minced
- ✓ ¾ cup rolled oats
- ✓ ½ cup pecans, finely chopped
- ✓ ¾ cup of homemade tomato sauce
- ✓ ½ teaspoon of red pepper flakes, crushed
- ✓ 1 teaspoon fresh rosemary, chopped
- ✓ 2 teaspoons fresh thyme, chopped

Directions:

- ❖ In a saucepan, add 1¾ cups water, the rice, lentils, salt and Italian seasoning and bring to a boil over medium-high heat.
- ❖ Reduce the heat to low and simmer covered for about 45 minutes.
- ❖ Remove from heat and set aside, covered for at least 10 minutes.
- ❖ Preheat oven to 350 degrees F. Line a 9x5-inch baking pan with parchment paper.
- ❖ In a skillet, heat the remaining water over medium heat and sauté the onion, celery, mushrooms and garlic for about 4-5 minutes.
- ❖ Remove from heat and allow to cool slightly.
- ❖ In a large bowl, add the oats, pecans, tomato sauce and fresh herbs and stir until well combined.

- ❖ Combine the rice mixture and vegetable mixture with the oat mixture and mix well.
- ❖ In a blender, add the mixture and pulse until it forms a chunky mixture.
- ❖ Transfer the mixture to the prepared baking dish evenly.
- ❖ With a piece of foil, cover the pan and bake for about 40 minutes.
- ❖ Uncover and bake for about 15-20 minutes more or until the top turns golden brown.
- ❖ Remove from oven and set aside for about 5-10 minutes before slicing.
- ❖ Cut into slices of desired size and serve

199) VEGETABLE SOUP AND SPELT NOODLES

Preparation Time: 5 minutes	Cooking Time: 12 minutes	Servings: 2

Ingredients:

- ✓ ½ onion, peeled, cut into cubes
- ✓ ½ green bell pepper, chopped
- ✓ ½ zucchini, grated
- ✓ 4 ounces (113 g) sliced mushrooms, chopped
- ✓ ½ cup of cherry tomatoes
- ✓ ¼ cup of basil leaves

Ingredients:

- ✓ 1 package of spelt tagliatelle, cooked
- ✓ ¼ teaspoon salt
- ✓ ⅛ teaspoon of cayenne pepper
- ✓ ½ key lime, squeezed
- ✓ 1 tablespoon of grape oil
- ✓ 2 cups of spring water

❖ Then, turn the heat to low, add the cooked noodles and then simmer the soup for 5 minutes.

❖ When finished, pour soup into two bowls, top with basil leaves, drizzle with lime juice and serve.

Directions:

❖ Take a medium saucepan, put it over medium heat, add the oil and when hot, add the onion and then cook for 3 minutes or more until tender.

❖ Add the cherry tomatoes, bell bell pepper and mushrooms, stir until combined and continue cooking for 3 minutes until soft.

❖ Add the grated zucchini, season with salt, cayenne pepper, pour in the water, and then bring the mixture to a boil.

200) AVOCADO AND CUCUMBER GAZPACHO

Preparation Time: 5 minutes	Cooking Time: 0 minutes	Servings: 2

Ingredients:

- ✓ 1 avocado, peeled, pitted, cold
- ✓ 1 cucumber, seedless, unpeeled, cold
- ✓ ½ cup basil leaves, cold

Ingredients:

- ✓ ½ of key lime, squeezed
- ✓ 2 cups of spring water, chilled
- ✓ 1½ teaspoon of sea salt

❖ Divide the soup evenly between two bowls, top with more basil and serve.

Directions:

❖ Place all ingredients in the jar of a high-speed food processor or blender and then pulse until smooth.

❖ Pour the soup into a medium bowl and then chill for a minimum of 1 hour.

201) CABBAGE, SOURSOP AND ZUCCHINI SOUP

Preparation Time: 5 minutes	Cooking Time: 45 minutes	Servings: 2

Ingredients:

- ✓ 1 cup chopped cabbage
- ✓ 2 soursop leaves, rinsed, torn in half
- ✓ ½ cup summer squash cubes
- ✓ 1 cup chayote pumpkin cubes
- ✓ ½ cup of zucchini cubes
- ✓ ½ cup wild rice
- ✓ ½ cup diced white onions

Ingredients:

- ✓ 1 cup diced green peppers
- ✓ 2 teaspoons of sea salt
- ✓ ½ tablespoon of basil
- ✓ ¼ teaspoon cayenne pepper
- ✓ ½ tablespoon of oregano
- ✓ 6 cups of spring water

❖ Once done, remove the gutters from the broth, turn the heat to medium, add the remaining ingredients to the pot, stir until combined, and then cook for 30 minutes or more until cooked through.

❖ Serve immediately.

Directions:

❖ Take a medium saucepan, place it over medium-high heat, add the soursop leaves, pour in 1½ cups of water and boil for 15 minutes, covering the pan with a lid.

202) GREEN CHICKPEA SOUP

Preparation Time: 5 minutes	Cooking Time: 25 minutes	Servings: 2

Ingredients:

- ✓ ½ cup of cooked chickpeas
- ✓ ½ of a medium white onion, peeled, diced
- ✓ ½ of a large zucchini, chopped
- ✓ 1 cup of kale leaves
- ✓ 1 cup of pumpkin cubes

Ingredients:

- ✓ ¾ teaspoon salt
- ✓ ¾ tablespoon chopped thyme, fresh
- ✓ ¾ tablespoon tarragon, fresh
- ✓ 2 cups of vegetable broth, homemade
- ✓ 1½ cups of spring water

Directions:

- ❖ Take a saucepan, place it over medium-high heat, pour in the ¼ cup of broth, add the zucchini, onion and thyme and cook for 4 minutes.

- ❖ Pour in the remaining broth and water, bring to a boil, turn the heat to low, and then simmer for 10-15 minutes until tender.
- ❖ Add the remaining ingredients, stir until combined, and then continue cooking for 10 minutes or more, until cooked through.
- ❖ Serve immediately.

203) GREEN ZUCCHINI SOUP

Preparation Time: 10 minutes	Cooking Time: 10 minutes	Servings: 2

Ingredients:

- ✓ 2 cups of leafy greens
- ✓ 1 small zucchini, sliced
- ✓ 1 small white onion, peeled, sliced
- ✓ 1 medium green bell pepper, with core, cut into slices

Ingredients:

- ✓ 2 ½ cups of spring water
- ✓ ¾ teaspoon salt
- ✓ ¼ teaspoon cayenne pepper
- ✓ 1 teaspoon of dried basil

Directions:

- ❖ Take a medium saucepan, place it over medium heat, add all the ingredients, stir until mixed, and then cook for 5-10 minutes until the vegetables become tender-crisp.

- ❖ Remove the pot from the heat, puree the soup with an immersion blender and then serve.

204) KAMUT VEGETABLE SOUP WITH TARRAGON

Preparation Time: 5 minutes	Cooking Time: 32 minutes	Servings: 2

Ingredients:

- ✓ 6 tablespoons of kamut berries
- ✓ 1 cup chopped white onion
- ✓ ½ cup chopped pumpkin
- ✓ ½ cup of cooked chickpeas
- ✓ 1 cup homemade vegetable broth
- ✓ ¼ teaspoon cayenne pepper

Ingredients:

- ✓ ½ tablespoon of chopped tarragon
- ✓ 1 bay leaf
- ✓ 1 teaspoon of chopped thyme
- ✓ 1 tablespoon of olive oil
- ✓ 1 cup of spring water, boiling

Directions:

- ❖ Place the kamut in a small bowl, pour in the boiling water and let it sit for 30 minutes.
- ❖ Then take a medium saucepan, put it over medium heat, add the oil and when hot, add the onion, stir in the thyme and tarragon and then cook for 5 minutes until tender.

- ❖ Drain the kamut, add it to the pot, add the bay leaf, pour in the vegetable stock and bring to a boil.
- ❖ Cover the pot with its lid, simmer for 20-30 minutes, then stir in the cayenne pepper and cook for 5 minutes.
- ❖ Remove the bay leaf, add the chickpeas and cook for 2 minutes.
- ❖ Serve immediately.

205)   PUMPKIN SOUP WITH BASIL

Preparation Time: 5 minutes	Cooking Time: 25 minutes	Servings: 2

Ingredients:

- ✓ ½ of a medium white onion, peeled, cut into cubes
- ✓ 2 cups cubed pumpkin
- ✓ ¼ cup of basil leaves
- ✓ ½ cup coconut cream jelly softener

Ingredients:

- ✓ ⅛ teaspoon sea salt
- ✓ ⅛ teaspoon of cayenne pepper
- ✓ 1 tablespoon of grape oil
- ✓ 1 cup homemade vegetable broth

Directions:

- ❖ Take a medium saucepan, put it over medium heat, add the oil and when hot, add the onion, and then cook for 5 minutes or until softened.
- ❖ Add the squash, cook for 10 minutes until golden brown and beginning to soften, pour in the vegetable broth, season with salt and pepper and then bring the soup to a boil.
- ❖ Turn the heat to medium and then simmer the soup for 10 minutes until the squash becomes very soft.
- ❖ Remove pan from heat, puree with an immersion blender until smooth, and then garnish with basil.
- ❖ Serve immediately.

206)   COCONUT MUSHROOM SOUP

Preparation Time: 5 minutes	Cooking Time: 20 minutes	Servings: 2

Ingredients:

- ✓ 2 cups of baby Bella mushrooms, diced
- ✓ ½ cup diced red onions
- ✓ 1 cup of vegetable broth
- ✓ 1½ cups of coconut milk soft jelly

Ingredients:

- ✓ ½ teaspoon of sea salt
- ✓ ¼ teaspoon cayenne pepper
- ✓ 2 teaspoons of grape oil

Directions:

- ❖ Take a medium saucepan, put it over medium-high heat, add the oil and when hot, add the onion, mushrooms, season with salt and pepper, and then cook for 3 to 4 minutes until the vegetables become tender.
- ❖ Then add the soy sauce, pour in the milk and broth, stir until combined and bring to a boil.
- ❖ Turn the heat to medium-low and then simmer the soup for 15 minutes until it has thickened to the desired level.
- ❖ Serve immediately.

207)   ONION AND PUMPKIN SOUP

Preparation Time: 5 minutes	Cooking Time: 35 minutes	Servings: 2

Ingredients:

- ✓ 2 large white onions, peeled, sliced
- ✓ ½ cup diced pumpkin
- ✓ 1 sprig of thyme
- ✓ 1 tablespoon of grape oil

Ingredients:

- ✓ 2 cups of spring water
- ✓ ½ teaspoon salt
- ✓ ¼ teaspoon cayenne pepper

Directions:

- ❖ Take a medium saucepan, place it over medium heat, add the oil and when hot, add the onion and cook for 10 minutes.
- ❖ Add the sprig of thyme, turn the heat to low and then cook the onions for 15-20 minutes until soft, covering the pan with its lid.
- ❖ Add remaining ingredients, stir until combined and simmer for 5 minutes.
- ❖ Pour the soup into bowls and then serve.

208) CHAYOTE MUSHROOM AND HEMP MILK STEW

Preparation Time: 10 minutes	Cooking Time: 40 minutes	Servings: 2

Ingredients:

- ✓ ⅔ cup of chayote pumpkin cubes
- ✓ 1 cup sliced mushrooms
- ✓ ⅓ cup of diced white onions
- ✓ ½ cup of chickpea flour
- ✓ ⅓ cup of vegetable broth, homemade
- ✓ ⅓ tablespoon of onion powder
- ✓ ⅔ teaspoon of sea salt

Ingredients:

- ✓ ⅔ teaspoon dried basil
- ✓ ⅓ teaspoon crushed red pepper
- ✓ 2 cups of spring water
- ✓ ½ tablespoon of grape oil
- ✓ ⅓ cup of hemp milk, homemade

Directions:

- ❖ Take a medium saucepan, put it over medium-high heat, add the oil and when it's hot, add the onion and mushrooms, and then cook for 5 minutes.
- ❖ Turn the heat to medium, pour in 1 cup of the water, milk and broth, add the chayote and all the seasonings, stir until blended, and then bring everything to a boil, covering the pot with the lid.

- ❖ Pour the remaining water into a food processor, add the chickpea flour, pulse until combined, add to the pot and then blend until combined.
- ❖ Turn the heat to low, simmer for 30 minutes and then serve.

209) COCONUT SOUP WITH BUTTERNUT SQUASH

Preparation Time: 5 minutes	Cooking Time: 15 minutes	Servings: 2

Ingredients:

- ✓ 2 medium-sized pumpkins, peeled, seeds removed and cut into pieces
- ✓ 1 medium white onion, peeled, chopped
- ✓ 2 cups of coconut milk soft jelly

Ingredients:

- ✓ ⅔ teaspoon of sea salt
- ✓ 1 cup of spring water

Directions:

- ❖ Take a large saucepan, place it over medium-high heat, pour in the water and bring it to a boil.
- ❖ Stir in salt and add the vegetables and then cook for 5-10 minutes until the vegetables become tender.

- ❖ Remove the pan from the heat, add the milk and then puree with an immersion blender until smooth.
- ❖ Serve immediately

210) MUSHROOM AND TOMATO COCONUT SOUP

Preparation Time: 5 minutes	Cooking Time: 10 minutes	Servings: 2

Ingredients:

- ✓ 1½ cups sliced mushrooms
- ✓ 8 cherry tomatoes, chopped
- ✓ 1 medium onion, peeled, sliced
- ✓ ¾ cup of vegetable broth, homemade
- ✓ 6 teaspoons of spice mixture

Ingredients:

- ✓ ¼ teaspoon salt
- ✓ ½ tablespoon of grape oil
- ✓ ¼ teaspoon cayenne pepper
- ✓ ¾ cup tomato sauce, alkaline
- ✓ 6 tablespoons of coconut milk soft jelly

Directions:

- ❖ Take a large skillet, put it over medium heat, add the oil and heat, add the onion, and then cook for 5 minutes until golden brown.
- ❖ Add the spice mix, add the remaining ingredients to the pan except the okra, stir until combined, and then bring the mixture to a simmer.

- ❖ Add mushrooms, stir until combined and cook for 10-15 minutes over medium-low heat until cooked through.
- ❖ Serve immediately

211) CABBAGE AND CHICKPEA CURRY

Preparation Time: 5 minutes	**Cooking Time**: 10 minutes	**Servings**: 2

Ingredients:

- ✓ 2 cups of cooked chickpeas
- ✓ ⅔ teaspoon of salt
- ✓ 1 cup of kale leaves

Ingredients:

- ✓ ⅔ cup of coconut cream in soft jelly
- ✓ 2 tablespoons of grape oil
- ✓ ⅓ teaspoon cayenne pepper

Directions:

- ❖ Turn on the oven, then set it to 425ºF (220ºC) and let it preheat.
- ❖ Then take a medium baking dish, spread the chickpeas on it, drizzle with 1 tablespoon of oil, sprinkle with all the seasonings and then bake for 15 minutes until roasted.

- ❖ Then take a skillet, put it over medium heat, add the remaining oil and when hot, add the cabbage and cook for 5 minutes.
- ❖ Add the roasted chickpeas, pour in the cream, stir until combined and then simmer for 4 minutes, mashing the chickpeas slightly.
- ❖ Serve immediately.

212) COCONUT AND CASHEW SOUP WITH TARRAGON

Preparation Time: 10 minutes	**Cooking Time**: 10 minutes	**Servings**: 1 to 2

Ingredients:

- ✓ 1 tablespoon avocado oil
- ✓ ½ cup diced onion
- ✓ 3 garlic cloves, crushed
- ✓ ¼ plus ⅛ teaspoon sea salt
- ✓ ¼ plus ⅛ teaspoon freshly ground black pepper

Ingredients:

- ✓ 1 (13.5-ounce / 383-g) can of whole coconut milk
- ✓ 1 tablespoon freshly squeezed lemon juice
- ✓ ½ cup raw cashews
- ✓ 1 celery stalk
- ✓ 2 tablespoons fresh tarragon chopped

Directions:

- ❖ In a medium skillet over medium-high heat, heat the avocado oil. Add the onion, garlic, salt and pepper and sauté for 3-5 minutes, or until the onion is soft.
- ❖ In a high-speed blender, blend together the coconut milk, lemon juice, cashews, celery, and tarragon with the onion mixture until smooth. Adjust seasonings as needed.

- ❖ Pour into 1 large or 2 small bowls and enjoy immediately, or transfer to a medium saucepan and heat over low heat for 3-5 minutes before serving.

213) CUCUMBER AND ZUCCHINI SOUP

Preparation Time: 5 minutes	**Cooking Time**: 0 minutes	**Servings**: 1 to 2

Ingredients:

- ✓ 1 cucumber, peeled
- ✓ ½ zucchini, peeled
- ✓ 1 tablespoon freshly squeezed lime juice

Ingredients:

- ✓ 1 tablespoon of fresh coriander leaves
- ✓ 1 garlic clove, crushed
- ✓ ¼ teaspoon of sea salt

- ❖ Pour into 1 large or 2 small bowls and enjoy immediately, or refrigerate for 15-20 minutes to chill before serving.

Directions:

- ❖ In a blender, blend together the cucumber, zucchini, lime juice, cilantro, garlic and salt until well combined. Add more salt, if needed.

214) COCONUT SOUP WITH JALAPENO AND LIME

Preparation Time: 5 minutes	Cooking Time: 5 minutes	Servings: 2

Ingredients:

- ✓ 2 tablespoons of avocado oil
- ✓ ½ cup diced onions
- ✓ 3 garlic cloves, crushed
- ✓ ¼ teaspoon of sea salt

Ingredients:

- ✓ 1 (13.5-ounce / 383-g) can of whole coconut milk
- ✓ 1 tablespoon freshly squeezed lime juice
- ✓ ½ to 1 jalapeño
- ✓ 2 tablespoons of fresh coriander leaves

❖ In a blender, blend together the coconut milk, lime juice, jalapeño and cilantro with the onion mixture until creamy.
❖ Pour into 1 large or 2 small bowls and enjoy.

Directions:

❖ In a medium skillet over medium-high heat, heat the avocado oil. Add the onion, garlic and salt, and sauté for 3-5 minutes, or until the onions are soft.

215) WATERMELON AND JALAPENO GAZPACHO

Preparation Time: 5 minutes	Cooking Time: 0 minutes	Servings: 1 to 2

Ingredients:

- ✓ 2 cups of diced watermelon
- ✓ ¼ cup diced onion
- ✓ ¼ cup of packed coriander leaves

Ingredients:

- ✓ ½ to 1 jalapeño
- ✓ 2 tablespoons of freshly squeezed lime juice

❖ Pour into 1 large or 2 small bowls and enjoy.
❖ Per serving

Directions:

❖ In a blender or food processor, give a pulse to combine the watermelon, onion, cilantro, jalapeño and lime juice just long enough to break down the ingredients, leaving them chopped very finely and being careful not to over process them.

57 | fat: 0.3g | protein: 1.2g | carbohydrates: 14.4g | fiber: 1.1g

216) CARROT AND FENNEL SOUP

Preparation Time: 10 minutes	Cooking Time: 30 minutes	Servings: 2 to 1

Ingredients:

- ✓ 6 carrots
- ✓ 1 cup chopped onion
- ✓ 1 fennel bulb, diced
- ✓ 2 garlic cloves, crushed

Ingredients:

- ✓ 2 tablespoons of avocado oil
- ✓ 1 teaspoon of sea salt
- ✓ 1 teaspoon of freshly ground black pepper
- ✓ 2 cups almond milk, more if desired

❖ Transfer the vegetables to the prepared baking sheet and roast for 30 minutes.
❖ Remove from oven and allow vegetables to cool.
❖ In a high-speed blender, blend together the almond milk and roasted vegetables until creamy and smooth. Adjust seasonings, if necessary, and add more milk if you prefer a thinner consistency.
❖ Pour into 2 large or 4 small bowls and enjoy.

Directions:

❖ Preheat the oven to 400ºF (205ºC). Line a baking sheet with baking paper.
❖ Cut carrots into thirds and then cut each third in half. Transfer to a medium bowl.
❖ Add the onion, fennel, garlic and avocado oil and toss to coat. Season with the salt and pepper and toss again.

217) COCONUT STEW WITH LENTILS AND HERB POTATOES

Preparation Time: 10 minutes	Cooking Time: 30 minutes	Servings: 4

✓ 2 tablespoons of avocado oil ✓ ½ cup diced onion ✓ 2 garlic cloves, crushed ✓ 1 to 1½ teaspoons of sea salt ✓ 1 teaspoon of freshly ground black pepper ✓ 1 cup of dried lentils ✓ 2 carrots, sliced	✓ 1 cup of potatoes peeled and diced ✓ 1 celery stalk, diced ✓ 2 sprigs of fresh oregano, chopped ✓ 2 sprigs fresh tarragon, chopped ✓ 5 cups vegetable stock, divided ✓ 1 (13.5-ounce / 383-g) can of whole coconut milk

Directions:

❖ In a large soup pot over medium-high heat, heat the avocado oil. Add the onion, garlic, salt and pepper, and sauté for 3-5 minutes, or until the onion is soft.
❖ Add the lentils, carrots, potato, celery, oregano, tarragon and 2½ cups of vegetable stock and stir.

❖ Bring to a boil, reduce the heat to medium-low and cook, stirring often and adding more vegetable stock a half cup at a time to make sure there is enough liquid to cook the lentils and potatoes, for 20-25 minutes, or until the potatoes and lentils are soft.
❖ Remove from heat and stir in coconut milk. Pour into 4 soup bowls and enjoy.

218) CAULIFLOWER AND ROASTED GARLIC SOUP

Preparation Time: 10 minutes	Cooking Time: 35 minutes	Servings: 1 to 2

✓ 4 cups of chopped cauliflower florets ✓ 5 garlic cloves ✓ 1½ tablespoons of avocado oil ✓ ¾ teaspoon of sea salt	✓ ½ teaspoon of freshly ground black pepper ✓ 1 cup of almond milk ✓ 1 cup vegetable stock, more if desired

Directions:

❖ Preheat the oven to 450°F (235°C). Line a baking sheet with baking paper.
❖ In a medium bowl, toss the cauliflower and garlic with the avocado oil. Season with the salt and pepper and toss again.
❖ Transfer to prepared baking sheet and roast for 30 minutes. Cool before adding to blender.

❖ In a high-speed blender, blend together the cooled vegetables, almond milk, and vegetable broth until smooth. Adjust the salt and pepper, if necessary, and add more vegetable broth if you prefer a thinner consistency.
❖ Transfer to a medium saucepan and heat slightly over medium-low heat for 3-5 minutes.
❖ Pour into 1 large or 2 small bowls and enjoy.

219) CARROT AND POTATO STEW WITH HERBS

Preparation Time: 10 minutes	Cooking Time: 50 minutes	Servings: 4 people

✓ 1 tablespoon avocado oil ✓ 1 cup onion, diced ✓ 2 garlic cloves, crushed ✓ 1 teaspoon of sea salt ✓ 1 teaspoon of freshly ground black pepper ✓ 3 cups vegetable stock, more if desired	✓ 2 cups of water, plus more if desired ✓ 3 cups of sliced carrots ✓ 1 large potato, cubed ✓ 2 stalks of celery, diced ✓ 1 teaspoon of dried oregano ✓ 1 dried bay leaf

Directions:

❖ In a medium saucepan over medium heat, heat the avocado oil. Add the onion, garlic, salt and pepper, and sauté for 2 to 3 minutes, or until the onion is soft.
❖ Add the vegetable stock, water, carrot, potato, celery, oregano, and bay leaf and stir. Bring to a boil, reduce heat to medium-low and cook for 30-45 minutes, or until potatoes and carrots are soft.

❖ Adjust seasonings, if necessary, and add more water or vegetable broth if you prefer a softer consistency, in half-cup increments.
❖ Pour into 4 soup bowls and enjoy.

220)   BERRY AND MINT SOUP

Preparation Time: 5 minutes	Cooking Time: 0 minutes	Servings: 1 to 2

Ingredients:

- ✓ ¼ cup unrefined whole cane sugar, such as Sucanat
- ✓ ¼ cup water, more if desired
- ✓ 1 cup mixed berries (raspberries, blackberries, blueberries)

Directions:

- ❖ In a small saucepan over medium-low heat, heat sugar and water, stirring constantly for 1 to 2 minutes, until sugar is dissolved. Cool.
- ❖ In a blender, blend together the cooled sugar water with the berries, water, lemon juice and mint leaves until well combined.

Ingredients:

- ✓ ½ cup of water
- ✓ 1 teaspoon of freshly squeezed lemon juice
- ✓ 8 fresh mint leaves

- ❖ Transfer the mixture to the refrigerator and let it cool completely, about 20 minutes.
- ❖ Pour into 1 large or 2 small bowls and enjoy.

---

221)   POTATO AND BROCCOLI SOUP

Preparation Time: 10 minutes	Cooking Time: 25 minutes	Servings: 2 to 1

Ingredients:

- ✓ 1 tablespoon avocado oil
- ✓ ½ cup diced onion
- ✓ 2 garlic cloves, crushed
- ✓ 3 cups of vegetable broth
- ✓ 1 (13.5-ounce / 383-g) can of whole coconut milk

Directions:

- ❖ In a large skillet over medium-high heat, heat the avocado oil. Add the onion and garlic and sauté for 2 to 3 minutes, or until the onions are soft.
- ❖ Add the vegetable broth, coconut milk, potatoes, broccoli, salt and pepper, and continue to cook for 18-20 minutes, or until the potatoes are soft. Remove from heat and cool.

Ingredients:

- ✓ 2 cups of potatoes peeled and cut into cubes
- ✓ 3 cups of chopped broccoli florets
- ✓ 1 teaspoon of sea salt
- ✓ 1½ teaspoons of freshly ground black pepper

- ❖ In a blender, blend the cooled soup until smooth.
- ❖ Adjust seasonings as needed. Pour into 2 large or 4 small bowls and enjoy.

222)   LUSH PEPPER SOUP

Preparation Time: 5 minutes	Cooking Time: 10 minutes	Servings: 2 to 4

Ingredients:

- ✓ 1 teaspoon of avocado oil
- ✓ ¼ cup diced onions
- ✓ 2 garlic cloves, crushed
- ✓ 2 cups of diced red peppers
- ✓ 2 cups of vegetable broth

Directions:

- ❖ In a skillet over medium-high heat, add avocado oil, onions, garlic, and red peppers, and sauté for 2 to 3 minutes, or until onions are soft; let cool.
- ❖ In a blender, whisk together the soffritto, vegetable broth, jalapeño and salt until well combined and completely liquid; adjust seasonings according to your preference.

Ingredients:

- ✓ ½ to 1 jalapeño, seeded and diced
- ✓ 1 teaspoon of sea salt
- ✓ ½ cup of red peppers cut into small cubes
- ✓ ½ cup yellow peppers cut into small cubes

- ❖ Transfer the soup to a medium bowl and toss with the diced red and yellow peppers.
- ❖ Cover and refrigerate for 20-30 minutes to chill or chill overnight.
- ❖ Pour into 2 large or 4 small bowls and enjoy.

223)   CABBAGE AND YELLOW ONION SOUP

Preparation Time: 10 minutes	**Cooking Time**: 20 minutes	**Servings: 2 to 4**

Ingredients:

- ✓ 1 tablespoon avocado oil
- ✓ 2 cups thinly sliced yellow onions (3 medium)
- ✓ 1 teaspoon of unrefined whole cane sugar, such as Sucanat
- ✓ 1 cup of vegetable broth
- ✓ 2 cups of water

Directions:

- ❖ In a medium saucepan over medium-high heat, heat the avocado oil. Add onions and sauté for 3 to 5 minutes, or until onions begin to get soft.
- ❖ Add the sugar and continue to sauté, stirring constantly, for 8-10 minutes, or until the onions are slightly caramelized.

Ingredients:

- ✓ 2 tablespoons of coconut amino acids
- ✓ 2 garlic cloves, crushed
- ✓ ½ teaspoon of dried thyme
- ✓ ½ teaspoon of sea salt
- ✓ 3 stalks of kale, shredded and cut into ribbons (about 2 cups)

- ❖ Add the vegetable broth, water, coconut amino acid, garlic, thyme, and salt. Reduce heat to medium-low and simmer for 5-7 minutes. Adjust seasonings as needed.
- ❖ Add the cabbage and leave on the heat just long enough for it to wilt.
- ❖ Remove from heat, pour into 2 large or 4 small bowls and serve.

224)   WILD RICE, MUSHROOM AND LEEK SOUP

Preparation Time: 10 minutes	**Cooking Time**: 55 minutes	**Servings: 1 to 2**

Ingredients:

- ✓ ⅓ cup of wild rice
- ✓ 1 cup sliced cremini mushrooms
- ✓ ½ cup sliced leeks, white part only
- ✓ 3 cups of water

Directions:

- ❖ Prepare wild rice according to package directions.
- ❖ In a medium saucepan over high heat, bring sliced mushrooms, leeks and water to a boil. Boil for 8-10 minutes, or until mushrooms are soft.

Ingredients:

- ✓ 2 tablespoons of organic white miso
- ✓ ¼ to ½ teaspoon freshly ground black pepper
- ✓ Sliced shallots, for garnish

- ❖ Add the cooked wild rice, miso, and black pepper. Using the back side of a spoon, mash the miso on the side of the pot to break it up, then stir it in.
- ❖ Remove from heat. Pour into 1 large or 2 small bowls, garnish with chopped shallots and enjoy.

225)   PEAR AND GINGER SOUP

Preparation Time: 10 minutes	**Cooking Time**: 15 minutes	**Servings: 1 to 2**

Ingredients:

- ✓ 2 teaspoons of avocado oil
- ✓ ½ cup diced onions
- ✓ 2 garlic cloves, crushed
- ✓ 1 cup of vegetable broth
- ✓ 2 cups of water
- ✓ ¼ cup coconut milk (canned)

Directions:

- ❖ In a large skillet over medium-high heat, heat the avocado oil. Add the onion and garlic and sauté for 2 to 3 minutes, or until the onions are soft.
- ❖ Add the vegetable broth, water, coconut milk, pears, ginger and salt, and cook over medium-high heat for 8-10 minutes, or until the pears are soft. Remove from heat and cool.

Ingredients:

- ✓ 2 pears peeled and cut into cubes
- ✓ 1 inch fresh ginger root, chopped
- ✓ ¼ teaspoon of sea salt
- ✓ Sliced radishes, for garnish (optional)
- ✓ Chopped shallots, for garnish (optional)

- ❖ Transfer the soup to a blender and blend until well combined. Adjust seasonings as needed.
- ❖ Pour immediately into 1 large or 2 small bowls, garnish with the radishes and scallions (if using), and enjoy, or return the soup to the stove to warm slightly over low heat before serving.

226) ASPARAGUS AND ARTICHOKE SOUP

Preparation Time: 5 minutes	Cooking Time: 20 minutes	Servings: 4 cups

✓ ½ cup diced onion ✓ 1 tablespoon avocado oil ✓ 2 garlic cloves, crushed ✓ 1 cup of diced potatoes ✓ 8 asparagus stalks, cut into small pieces	✓ 2 cups of vegetable broth ✓ ½ to ¾ teaspoon sea salt ✓ ½ teaspoon of ground black pepper ✓ 2 cups of almond milk ✓ 1 can of artichoke hearts, cut in half and with stem

Directions:

❖ In a medium skillet, sauté onion, avocado oil and garlic over medium-high heat for 2 to 3 minutes, or until onion is soft.

❖ Transfer the sauté to a medium-sized saucepan and add the potatoes, asparagus, vegetable broth, salt and pepper; cook over medium-high heat for 18 to 20 minutes, or until the potatoes are soft. Add more vegetable broth, if necessary, to keep the liquid level between ½ and 1 inch above the contents of the saucepan. Remove from heat and allow to cool.

❖ In a blender, blend the cooled soup mixture, almond milk and artichokes until everything is well combined and the soup is smooth. Adjust the seasonings to your liking and add more almond milk or vegetable broth to thin it out, if you prefer.

❖ Return the soup to the casserole dish and heat slightly over low heat before serving.

227) CARROT AND CELERY SOUP

Preparation Time: 15 minutes	Cooking Time: 1 hour and 10 minutes	Servings: 4 people

✓ Kitchen spray ✓ 1 large onion, coarsely chopped ✓ 2 large carrots, peeled and coarsely chopped ✓ 2 large celery stalks (with leaves), roughly chopped ✓ 1 parsnip, peeled and coarsely chopped	✓ 5 cloves of garlic, crushed ✓ 1 leek, well cleaned and coarsely chopped ✓ 9 cups of water ✓ 2 bay leaves ✓ 2 teaspoons of sea salt

Directions:

❖ Spray the bottom of a large pot with cooking spray. Place the pot over medium-low heat, add the onion and sauté for about 5 minutes, stirring constantly.

❖ Add the carrots, celery, parsnips, garlic and leek to the pot. Sauté for an additional 3 minutes.

❖ Add the water, bay leaf and salt. Simmer for 1 hour.

❖ Remove from heat and cool slightly. Drain the vegetables, leaving only the broth.

❖ To serve, add back some of the vegetables if you like and heat the soup to your desired temperature.

228) CREAMY MUSHROOM CLAM CHOWDER

Preparation Time: 15 minutes	Cooking Time: 30 minutes	Servings: 4

For the mushroom clams: ✓ ½ cup coarsely chopped shiitake mushrooms ✓ 1 teaspoon of coconut oil ✓ ¼ cup of water ✓ ½ teaspoon celery seeds For the soup base: ✓ ½ medium onion, chopped ✓ 3 medium carrots, peeled and chopped ✓ 2 stalks of celery, finely chopped	✓ 1 teaspoon of dried thyme ✓ 3 cups of vegetable broth ✓ 1 sheet of nori, finely crumbled ✓ For the cream base: ✓ 1 cup lightly steamed cauliflower ✓ ¾ cup unsweetened almond milk ✓ ¼ teaspoon of sea salt

Directions:

❖ To make clams with mushrooms

❖ In a large pot over medium-high heat, add mushrooms and coconut oil. Sauté for 3 minutes. Add the water and celery seeds, stirring until the water is absorbed.

❖ Remove from heat and transfer mushrooms to a plate.

❖ To make the soup base

❖ In the same pot, over medium heat, sauté the onion, carrots, celery and thyme for about 5 minutes, or until the onion is softened. Add a little broth, if needed.

❖ Then, add the remaining broth and nori and bring to a boil.

❖ To make the cream base

❖ In a blender or food processor, add the cauliflower, almond milk and salt. Blend to combine. If the mixture is too thick, add a little soup base to thin it out. Blend until the mixture is smooth.

❖ To assemble the fish soup

❖ Add the mushroom mix and cream base to the soup base. Stir well to combine.

❖ Reheat for 5 minutes, or until hot, and serve.

229) SOUP OF BOK CHOY, BROCCOLINI AND BROWN RICE

Preparation Time: 5 minutes	Cooking Time: 10 minutes	Servings: 2

Ingredients:

- ✓ 3 cups of vegetable broth
- ✓ 1 cup of chopped bok choy

Ingredients:

- ✓ 1 bunch of broccolini, coarsely chopped
- ✓ ½ cup cooked brown rice

Directions:

- ❖ In a medium saucepan over medium heat, place the broth, bok choy, broccolini and brown rice. Bring to a boil and cook for 10 minutes, or until vegetables are cooked through and tender. Serve.

230) APPLE AND SWEET PUMPKIN SOUP

Preparation Time: 5 minutes	Cooking Time: 25 minutes	Servings: 2 people

Ingredients:

- ✓ 1 medium apple, core and slices
- ✓ ½ cup chopped fennel
- ✓ 1½ cups of water, divided
- ✓ 1 cup unsweetened canned pumpkin puree
- ✓ ¾ cup low-sodium vegetable broth
- ✓ 4 small dates, pitted
- ✓ 2 teaspoons of fresh grated ginger or 2 cubes of frozen ginger

Ingredients:

- ✓ ¼ teaspoon ground cinnamon
- ✓ ¼ teaspoon of curry powder
- ✓ ⅛ teaspoon of dried thyme
- ✓ ⅛ teaspoon sea salt
- ✓ ⅛ teaspoon of ground cumin
- ✓ 4 teaspoons of raisins, for garnish
- ✓ 2 teaspoons fennel seeds, toasted, for garnish

- ❖ Pour soup into two bowls and top each with 2 teaspoons raisins and 1 teaspoon toasted fennel seeds.
- ❖ Serve immediately or let cool and serve at room temperature.

Directions:

- ❖ In a saucepan, combine the apples, fennel and ½ cup water. Cover and simmer for about 25 minutes, until the apples and fennel are softened.
- ❖ In a food processor, combine the apple and fennel mixture, pumpkin, remaining 1 cup water, broth, dates, ginger, cinnamon, curry powder, thyme, salt and cumin. Process until reduced to a puree.

231) TOMATO AND CARROT SOUP WITH LEMON

Preparation Time: 5 minutes	Cooking Time: 35 minutes	Servings: 2

Ingredients:

- ✓ 1 (15-ounce / 425-g) can no sodium added diced tomatoes, drained
- ✓ ¾ cup chopped carrots
- ✓ 1 tablespoon avocado oil
- ✓ ¼ teaspoon of sea salt

Ingredients:

- ✓ 1 cup of water
- ✓ ½ cup low-sodium vegetable broth
- ✓ 2 tablespoons fresh coriander chopped
- ✓ 1 tablespoon freshly squeezed lemon juice

- ❖ Cook tomato and carrot mixture for 35 minutes, or until caramelized, then carefully transfer to a food processor.
- ❖ Add the water and broth and puree until smooth.
- ❖ Garnish with the cilantro and add lemon juice to taste.

Directions:

- ❖ Preheat the oven to 400ºF (205ºC).
- ❖ In a glass baking dish, combine the tomatoes, carrots, oil and salt and mix well.

232) ZUCCHINI AND AVOCADO SOUP WITH BASIL

Preparation Time: 5 minutes	Cooking Time: 0 minutes	Servings: 2 people

Ingredients:

- ✓ 2 large zucchini, chopped
- ✓ 1 medium avocado
- ✓ 1 medium bell pepper
- ✓ ½ cup low-sodium vegetable broth
- ✓ ½ cup of water
- ✓ ¼ cup chopped fennel

Directions:

- ❖ In a high-speed blender or food processor, combine the zucchini, avocado, bell bell pepper, broth, water, fennel, basil, rosemary, garlic and salt and blend until pureed.

Ingredients:

- ✓ 6 fresh basil leaves, plus 2 small leaves for garnish
- ✓ 2 teaspoons fresh rosemary chopped
- ✓ 1 garlic clove, peeled, or 1 frozen garlic cube
- ✓ ⅛ teaspoon sea salt
- ✓ 1½ teaspoons hulled pumpkin seeds, toasted, for garnish

- ❖ Pour the soup into the bowls. Garnish each with a small basil leaf and the pumpkin seeds and serve.

233) ZUCCHINI, SPINACH AND QUINOA SOUP

Preparation Time: 5 minutes	Cooking Time: 25 minutes	Servings: 4 people

Ingredients:

- ✓ 2 tablespoons of avocado oil
- ✓ ¼ teaspoon of dried oregano
- ✓ ¼ teaspoon of dried thyme
- ✓ ⅛ teaspoon sea salt
- ✓ 1 large onion, chopped
- ✓ 2 large zucchini, peeled and cut into pieces

Directions:

- ❖ In a soup pot, heat the oil over medium heat for 1 minute, then add the oregano, thyme and salt and cook for 30 seconds.
- ❖ Add onion, cover and cook for 7-8 minutes, stirring regularly, until softened.
- ❖ Add the zucchini. Cook for an additional 12 minutes, or until zucchini is soft.

Ingredients:

- ✓ 1 cup low-sodium vegetable broth
- ✓ 1 cup of water
- ✓ 1 cup baby spinach
- ✓ 6 large fresh basil leaves
- ✓ ⅓ cup of cooked quinoa (optional)
- ✓ Juice of 1 lemon

- ❖ Add the broth and water and cook for another 3 minutes, until heated through.
- ❖ Add the spinach and basil and cook until just wilted.
- ❖ Transfer the mixture to a food processor and process until pureed.
- ❖ Add the quinoa (if using). Season with lemon juice and serve.

234) EASY CILANTRO LIME QUINOA.

Preparation Time: 5 minutes	Cooking Time: 15 minutes	Servings: 6

Ingredients:

- ✓ 1 cup quinoa, rinsed and draned.
- ✓ ½ cup fresh cilantro, chopped
- ✓ 1 lime zest, grated

- ❖ Add quinoa and water to the instant pot and stir well.
- ❖ Seal with a lid and select manual mode and set the timer for 5 minutes.

Ingredients:

- ✓ 2 tbsp. fresh lime juice
- ✓ 1 ¼ cup of distilled water feed Sea sa sa

- ❖ Once finished, allow pressure naturally release that open thed.
- ❖ Stir in water, let stand and let rest.
- ❖ Season with salt and serve.

235)   SPINACH QUINOA

Preparation Time: 10 minutes	Cooking Time: 25 minutes	Servings: 4

✓ 1 cup quinoa	✓ 1 tsp. fresh ginger, minced
✓ 2 cups fresh spinach, chopped	✓ 2 garlic cloves, chopped
✓ 1 ½ cups filtered alkaline water	✓ 1 onion, cut in half
✓ 1 sweet potato, peeled and cut into pieces	✓ 2 tbsp olive oil
✓ 1 tsp. coriander powder	✓ 1 fresh lime juice
✓ 1 teaspoon of turmandine	✓ Pepper Salt
✓ 1 teaspoon of cumin seds	
❖ Add oil il instant pot and set the sauté mode.	❖ Cook on high pressure for 2 minutes.
❖ Add onion in olive oil and saute for 2 minutes otil onion is softened.	❖ When finished, release the pressure naturally and then open the container. Add the lime juice and mix well.
❖ Add garlic, ginger, spices and quinoa and cook for 3-4 minutes.	❖ Serve and enjoy.
❖ Add spinach, sweet potatoes, and water and stir well.	

236)   HEALTHY BROCCOLI SOUP ASPARAGUS

Preparation Time: 15 minutes.	Cooking Time: 28 minutes.	Servings: 6

✓ 2 cups broccoli florets, chopped	✓ 3 ½ cups filtered alkaline water
✓ 15 asparagus spears, ends cut and chopped	✓ 2 cups cauliflower florets, chopped
✓ 1 tsp. dried oregano	✓ 2 tsp. garlic, chopped 1 cup onion, chopped
✓ 1 tbsp. fresh thyme leaves	✓ 2 tbsp. olive oil
✓ ½ cup unsweetened almond milk	✓ Salt Pepper
❖ Add the oil to the bowl and add the oil to the bowl and stir the bowl.	❖ Seal pot with lid and cook on manual mode for 3 minutes.
❖ Add onion to olive oil and sauté until onion is softened.	❖ Once you are done, you can rinse the pressure off to minimize the pressure and then close the container.
❖ Add the garlic and let sit for 30 minutes.	❖ Puree the soup with an immersion blender until smooth. Add the almond milk, herb, pepper and salt.
❖ Add all the vegetables and salt and dry well.	❖ Serve and enjoy.

237)   CREAMY ASPARAGUS SOUP

Preparation Time: 10 minutes	Cooking Time: 40 minutes	Servings: 6

✓ 2 lbs. fresh asparagus cut off woody stems	✓ 1 ½ cups alkaline water filtered.
✓ ¼ tablespoon of lemon zest	✓ 1 Head of a hunting dog, coming out of the floor.
✓ 2 tbsp. lime juice	✓ 1 tablespoon. garlic, minced
✓ 14 oz. coconut milk	✓ 1 leek, sliced
✓ 1 tsp. tied thyme	✓ 3 tbsp. coconut oil
✓ ½ tsp. oregano	✓ Pinch of Himalayan salt.
✓ ½ tsp. sage	
❖ Preheat the oven to 400°F/ 200°C.	❖ Add the cauliflower florets and water to the bowl and mix well.
❖ The paper tray with waste and scrap paper.	❖ Insert pot with a rod and select steam and let stand for 4 minutes.
❖ Arrange asparagus spears on a baking sheet. Add 2 tablespoons of walnut oil and add salt, seasonings, garlic and sugar.	❖ When finished, release the pressure using the quick-release method.
❖ Kiss it with a dose of 20-25 mnutes.	❖ Add roasted asparagus, lime zest, lime juice, and coco milk and stir well.
❖ Add the remaining oil in the instant pot and set the pot on sauté mode.	❖ Puree the soup with an immersion blender until pureed.
❖ Add the garlic and milk to the pot and saute for 2-3 minutes.	❖ Serve and have fun

238)   SPICY EGGPLANT

Preparation Time: 15 minutes	Cooking Time: 5 minutes	Servings: 4

✓ 1 eggplant, cut into 1inch cubes	✓ ½ tsp. red pepper
✓ ½ cup filtered alkaline water	✓ 1 tsp. garlic powder
✓ 1 life time, in book form.	✓ 2 tbsp. olive oil extra virgin
✓ ½ tsp. Italian seasoning	✓ ¼ teaspoon of sea salt
✓ 1 tsp. paprika	
❖ Add the extract and salt into the instant flour.	❖ Add oil to the Instant Pot and set pot on sauté mode.
❖ Cook on manual high pressure for 5 minutes.	❖ Return the ingredient to the pot with the chopper, garlic, paprika, red, garlic and salt and stir until included.
❖ When done, rinse with peanut butter and then milk. Wet the eggplant well.	❖ Cook on sauté mode for 5 minutes. Stir from time to time.
	❖ Serve enjoy.

239) BRUSSELS SPROUTS AND CARROTS

Preparation Time: 10 minutes	**Cooking Time**: 5 minutes	**Servings: 6**

✓ 1 ½ pounds of Brussels sprouts, trimmed and cut alf ✓ 4 carrots peel and cut slices are knife shaped. ✓ 1 tsp. olive oil ✓ ½ cup alkaline filtered water ✓ 1 tbsp. dried parsley	✓ ¼ tsp. garlic, chopped ✓ ¼ tsp. pepper ✓ ¼ tsp. sea salt
❖ Add all ingredients inside the instant pot and mix well. ❖ Cook the pot with the lid on and cook on high heat for 2 minutes.	❖ When finished, rinse with the quick release button and then the lid. ❖ Stir well all and serve.

240) CAJUN ZUCCHINI SEASONED

Preparation Time: 8 minutes.	**Cooking Time**: 2 minutes.	**Servings: 2**

✓ 4 zucchinis, sliced ✓ 1 tsp. garlic powder ✓ 1 tsp. paprika	✓ 2 tbsp. Cajun seasoning ✓ ½ cup of melted milk water ✓ 1 tablespoon of olive oil
❖ Add all ingredients to the pot and mix well. ❖ Close the pot with the lid and cook on low pressure for 1 minute.	❖ Once finished, release the pressure using the quick-release method then opene the lid. ❖ Mix well and serve.

241) FRIED CABBAGE

Preparation Time: 10 minutes	**Cooking Time**: 3 minutes	**Servings: 6**

✓ 1 head cabbage, chopped ✓ ½ teaspoon of olive oil ✓ ½ onion, diced ✓ ½ tsp. paprika	✓ 1 onion, chopped ✓ 1 fiberglass bathroom basket ✓ 2 tbsp. olive oil ✓ ½ tbsp sea salt
❖ Add olive oil il inside the Instant Pot and set the sauté mode. ❖ Add onion in olive oil and sauté until softened. ❖ Add ingredients for preparation and product for packaging.	❖ Close with lid and cook on high heat for 3 minutes. ❖ When you are finished, release the pressure using the quick-release method then open the lids. ❖ Mix well and serve.

242) TOFU CURRY

Preparation Time: 10 minutes	**Cooking Time**: 4 hours	**Servings: 4**

✓ 1 cup firm tofu, diced ✓ 2 tbsp garlic cloves, minced ✓ 1 onion, chopped ✓ 8 oz. tomato pureed ✓ 2 cups bell pepper, chopped	✓ 1 tablespoon of garm masala ✓ 2 tbsp. olive oil ✓ 1 tablespoon of peanut butter ✓ 10 oz. coconut milk ✓ 1 ½ tsp. sea salt
❖ Add all ingredients except tofu into a blender and blend until smooth. ❖ Place the blended mixture in the Instant Pot.	❖ Add the tofu to a bowl and dry well. ❖ Seal pot with a lid and select slow coook mode and set the timer for 4 hours. ❖ Mix well and serve.

243) CAULIFLOWER WITH SAUCE

Preparation Time: 10 minutes	Cooking Time: 15 minutes	Servings: 5

Ingredients:

- ✓ 1 large bed cauliflower head, cut bottom leaves

  For marinade:
- ✓ 1 tsp. paprika ½ tbsp olive oil
- ✓ Tbsp. fresh parsley, chopped
- ✓ 1 tbsp. thyme fresh
- ✓ 3 garlic cloves
- ✓ Salt Pepper

Ingredients:

- For gravy:
- ✓ ½ tbsp. lime juice
- ✓ ½ teaspoon of thyme
- ✓ 1 ½ cups filtered alkaline water
- ✓ 2 cloves garlic
- ✓ 1 tsp. olive oil
- ✓ 1 onion, diced

Directions:

- ❖ In a full bowl, mix all marinade ingredints.
- ❖ Rub the marinade evenly all over the head of the cauliflower.
- ❖ For gravy: add oil instant pot and set the pot on sauté modeuté.
- ❖ Add the garlic and onion in oil olive oil and sauté until the onion is softened.
- ❖ Add the water, lemon juice and thyme and toss to combine.
- ❖ Place trivet in the Instant Pot. Place cauliflower in trivet.

- ❖ Seal the pot with lid and coook on manual high pressure for 3 minutes.
- ❖ When finished, allow to release naturally pressure for 5 minutes then release using a quick-release method. Transfer the head of cauliflower to a serving dish and salt for 3-4 minutes.
- ❖ Reduce the instant pot to a puree with an immersion blender until it reaches consistency.
- ❖ Place some of the grass on a pan and cook the meat for 3-4 minutes.
- ❖ Serve the cauliflower with the gravy.

244) ZUCCHINI NOODLES

Preparation Time: 8 minutes	Cooking Time: 2 minutes	Servings: 2

Ingredients:

- ✓ 2 large zucchini, spiralized
- ✓ 1 tbsp. fresh mint leaves, sliced
- ✓ 1/3 lime juice
- ✓ ½ lime zest

Ingredients:

- ✓ 2 garlic cloves, chopped
- ✓ 2 tbsp. olive oil
- ✓ ¼ tsp. pepper
- ✓ ½ tsp. sea salt

Directions:

- ❖ Add oil instant pot and set the pot outé.
- ❖ Add the lime zest, garlic, and salt to the olive oil and let dry for 30 minutes.

- ❖ Add the zucchini noodles and lime juice and stir for 30 seconds. Season with pepper and salt. Season with milk.
- ❖ Serve and enjoy.

245) BUCKWHEAT PORRIDGE

Preparation Time: 20 minutes	Cooking Time: 10 minutes	Servings: 4

Ingredients:

- ✓ 1 cup buckwheat groats, rinsed
- ✓ 2 tablespoons almonds, chopped
- ✓ ½ tsp. vanilla

Ingredients:

- ✓ 1 tsp. cinnamon
- ✓ 3 cups of untreated almond milk
- ✓ 4-5 drops liquid stevia.

- ❖ Once finished, let release pressure naturally then open the lid.
- ❖ Top with chopped almonds and serve.

Directions:

- ❖ Add the peanut butter, vanilla, cinnamon, and milk to the instant water and mix well.
- ❖ Close the pot with the lid and cook on manual high pressure for 6 minutes.

246) STUFFED EGGPLANTS

		Servings: 6

Ingredients:

- ✓ Cayenne Pepper
- ✓ Sea Salt
- ✓ 2 spoons of tomato puree
- ✓ 1 teaspoon of ground cumin
- ✓ 1 teaspoon of agave
- ✓ 1 cup chopped cherry tomatoes
- ✓ 1 green bell pepper, seeded and chopped

Ingredients:

- ✓ 2 medium red onions, chopped
- ✓ 3 tablespoons of fresh chopped sage/basilicum
- ✓ 1 fennel bulb, chopped
- ✓ 4 tablespoons of olive oil, divided
- ✓ 6 thin eggplants

Directions:

- ❖ Preheat the oven to 450 degrees F and then place a rack in the center of the oven.
- ❖ Line a baking sheet with parchment paper or aluminum foil and brush with a little olive oil.
- ❖ Then remove the wide strips of the eggplant skin using a peeler. Cut the eggplant lengthwise, but do not slice it completely.
- ❖ Now sprinkle a pinch of salt into each and then place in a colander for about 30 minutes.
- ❖ Place them on the baking sheet and bake until the outer skins begin to wrinkle, about 20 minutes. Remove from oven and cool.
- ❖ Meanwhile, heat 2 tablespoons olive oil in a large skillet over medium heat and add onions.

- ❖ Cook for a few minutes, stirring occasionally, and then add the fennel and bell bell pepper. Cook for about 10 minutes, or until the vegetables are tender and have collapsed.
- ❖ Season the mixture with salt and cayenne pepper then stir in parsley, tomato puree, cumin, sugar and chopped tomato.
- ❖ Bake until fragrant, about 5 minutes. Set aside. Lower oven temperature to 350 degrees F.
- ❖ In a baking dish, arrange eggplant so that each is open with butter. Season with salt and fill with the tomato and onion mixture.
- ❖ Drizzle with the rest of the olive oil, and then add two tablespoons of water to the pan. Bake until the eggplant is flat and the liquid in the pan is caramelized, about 40-45 minutes.
- ❖ Serve the eggplant warm or at room temperature, preferably with the cooking juices poured over the eggplant.

❖

247) QUINOA PASTA WITH TOMATO SAUCE AND ARTICHOKES

		Servings: 2

Ingredients:

- ✓ 2 tablespoons of cold-pressed extra virgin olive oil
- ✓ 1 pinch of cayenne pepper
- ✓ 1/2 teaspoon sea salt, organic
- ✓ 3 tablespoons of fresh basil
- ✓ 1 teaspoon vegetable broth, unleavened
- ✓ 1 ounce of walnuts

Ingredients:

- ✓ 1 fennel bulb
- ✓ 1 medium-sized onion
- ✓ 8 ounces of artichoke hearts, fresh or frozen
- ✓ 5 ounces of cherry tomatoes, fresh
- ✓ 7 ounces of quinoa or spelt pasta

Directions:

- ❖ Cook the artichoke until tender.
- ❖ Then cook the pasta according to the package instructions. While it's cooking, dice the tomatoes, and then chop the basil, fennel, and onion into pieces.
- ❖ In a skillet, heat 2 tablespoons of olive oil and sauté the onions, walnuts and fennel for a few minutes.

- ❖ Then add the cooked artichoke hearts and tomatoes and cook for 2 minutes.
- ❖ Collect about 1/2 cup of water and then dissolve the vegetable broth into the water. Add to a skillet. Let simmer for 2 minutes over low heat, stirring regularly.
- ❖ Finally, add the basil and season with salt and cayenne pepper. To serve, pour sauce over pasta.

❖

248) SAUTEED MUSHROOMS

	Servings: 6

✓ 1 fennel bulb, chopped ✓ ½ lemons ✓ 1 ½ teaspoon of sea salt ✓ 3 tablespoons of extra virgin olive oil	✓ 2 tablespoons sage, chopped ✓ 1/4 teaspoon cayenne pepper ✓ 24 ounces of fresh mushrooms

Directions:

❖ Soak the mushrooms in water and shake them to clean them well, and drain completely. Cut and slice the mushrooms to bite size.

❖ Place the mushrooms in a bowl and squeeze the juice from the half lemon. Stir to combine.

❖ In a large skillet, add the fennel and then pour in the olive oil.

❖ Heat the mixture over medium-high heat until the fennel begins to sizzle; this should take about 30 seconds.

❖ Now add the mushrooms, stir and cover. Continue cooking, stirring occasionally; say in about 4 minute intervals.

❖ Once cooked, remove the lid and add some salt and cayenne pepper, and continue cooking. After about 5 minutes, the mushrooms should start to brown and all the moisture should have evaporated.

❖ Now stir in the sage and then serve the delicious meal. Enjoy!

249) ALKALINE ELECTRIC FLAT BREAD

	Servings: 4

✓ 1/4 teaspoon of cayenne ✓ 2 teaspoons of onion powder ✓ 2 teaspoons of basil ✓ 2 teaspoons of oregano	✓ 1 tablespoon of sea salt ✓ 3/4 cup of spring water ✓ 2 tablespoons of grape oil ✓ 2 cups of spelt flour

Directions:

❖ Start by combining all the seasonings and flour together until well incorporated.

❖ Then add ½ cup water and oil and mix well until the mixture becomes a ball.

❖ Place some flour on the work area and now knead the dough for about 5 minutes. Divide the dough into 6 portions.

❖ Roll individual balls into about 4-inch circles. Place the balls in a skillet and cook over medium heat until cooked through, turning after about 3 minutes.

❖ Serve with curry.

250) ALKALINE DINNER PLATE

	Servings: 4

Ingredients:	Ingredients:
✓ Kale dish ✓ 1/2 cup chopped red onions ✓ 1/4 habanero pepper ✓ 2 tablespoons of agave ✓ Sea Salt ✓ 1/2 cup green onions ✓ 1 cup chopped orange, yellow and sweet red peppers ✓ 2 bunches of green cabbage ✓ Pasta dish ✓ 1/2 teaspoon of grape oil ✓ 1/2 cup chopped yellow squash ✓ 1/4 cup chopped red and green peppers	✓ 1 teaspoon of sea salt ✓ 1/4 cup chopped green and red onions ✓ 1 cup chopped portabella mushrooms ✓ 1 box of Kamut pasta ✓ Fried oyster mushrooms ✓ Sea salt to taste ✓ ½ cup of spelt flour ✓ A pinch of cayenne pepper ✓ ½ teaspoon of onion powder ✓ 1/2 king oyster mushroom, large ✓ Avocado slices, optional

Directions:

❖ Clean the cabbage and cut it into small pieces. Using the grapeseed oil, gently coat the bottom of a pot and add the peppers and onions.

❖ Sauté the vegetables for a few seconds then add the kale and agave. Cook the mixture over medium heat, stirring regularly, for about 30 minutes.

❖ Now bring the water to a boil in a pot and add ½ teaspoon of oil and a teaspoon of salt. Add the kamut pasta

❖ Sauté peppers, onions and portabella mushrooms in a skillet for a few minutes.

❖ Add the cooked kamut pasta to the vegetables along with the shredded squash. Mix well.

❖ At this point, rinse the oyster mushrooms, season with cayenne pepper, onion powder and sea salt.

❖ Coat mushrooms with spelt flour and fry in oil. Once cooked, remove from heat and place on a towel to absorb the extra oil.

❖ Serve while still warm.

251)   BOWL OF ALKALIZING TAHINI NOODLES

		Servings: 2

- ✓ Bowl
- ✓ 1 teaspoon of black sesame seeds
- ✓ 1/2 avocado, sliced
- ✓ 2 green onions, chopped
- ✓ 4 cabbages, chopped
- ✓ 1 parsnip, chopped
- ✓ 4 turbot leaves, chopped

- ✓ 1 yellow zucchini, spiralized
- Seasoning
- ✓ 1 teaspoon of agave or any other liquid sweetener
- ✓ 2 tablespoons of lemon juice
- ✓ 1 tablespoon of tahini
- ✓ A pinch of salt

Directions:

- ❖ Pour the dressing over the vegetables and garnish with the sesame seeds.
- ❖ Slice, chop and shred the vegetables as directed above, add to a bowl.
- ❖ Add all the ingredients for the dressing to another small bowl and whisk until fully combined.

252)   BALANCING ALKALINE SALAD

		Servings: 4

- ✓ 1 tablespoon of sesame seeds
- ✓ 1 tablespoon diced spring onion
- ✓ 1/4 cup chopped culantro
- ✓ 1/2 cup chopped alfalfa sprouts
- ✓ 1/2 cup chopped snow pea shoots
- ✓ 1/2 avocado
- ✓ 5 red radishes
- ✓ 1 cup chopped arugula

- ✓ 10 green beans
- Seasoning
- ✓ 1 teaspoon of green mustard
- ✓ 1 tablespoon of olive oil
- ✓ 1 tablespoon of lemon juice
- ✓ 1/4 teaspoon celtic sea salt
- ✓ Cayenne pepper, to taste

Directions:

- ❖ Now slice the radishes and finely chop the spring onion, culantro and snow pea shoots.
- ❖ Mix all the ingredients for the dressing in a large bowl until combined.
- ❖ Pull the alfafa sprouts by hand and then place all the chopped ingredients in a large bowl along with the dressing.
- ❖ Wash and trim the edges of the green beans.
- ❖ Add the green beans to a saucepan and add enough water to almost completely cover them. Cook over low heat until almost tender, or for about 3 minutes.
- ❖ Serve the salad topped with half of the avocado. Alternatively, you can also chop the avocado and fold it slowly into the salad.
- ❖ Sprinkle with some sesame seeds and serve the salad garnished with lemon juice.
- ❖ Remove the green beans from the heat and let them drain. Then cut the green beans into 1-inch pieces.

253)   ASPARAGUS SALAD WITH CASHEW SAUCE

Preparation Time: 10 minutes	**Cooking Time:** 5 minutes	**Servings:** 1-2

For the salad:
- ✓ 1 teaspoon of avocado oil
- ✓ 24 asparagus stalks, diced
- ✓ 1/2 cup diced onion
- ✓ 3 garlic cloves, crushed
- ✓ 1/2 teaspoon of sea salt
- ✓ 1/4 teaspoon freshly ground black pepper

For the dressing:
- ✓ 1/2 cup raw cashews
- ✓ 1/2 cup of water
- ✓ 2 tablespoons of freshly squeezed lemon juice
- ✓ 1/4 teaspoon of sea salt
- ✓ 1/8 teaspoon of freshly ground black pepper

For assembly:
- ✓ 2 cups of mixed salad
- ✓ To prepare the asparagus mixture

Directions:

- ❖ Prepare the dressing
- ❖ In a high-speed blender, whisk together half of the asparagus mixture with the cashews, water, lemon juice, salt and pepper until smooth.
- ❖ To prepare the asparagus mixture
- ❖ In a large skillet over medium heat, heat the avocado oil. Add the asparagus, onion, garlic, salt and pepper and sauté for 5-7 minutes, or until the onion is soft.
- ❖ To assemble the salad
- ❖ Arrange salad mix on 1 large plate or 2 small plates. Add the rest of the asparagus, drizzle with the dressing and enjoy.
- ❖

254)   SWEET POTATO SALAD WITH JALAPENO SAUCE

Preparation Time: 10 minutes	**Cooking Time**: 25 minutes	**Servings**: 1-2

For sweet potatoes:
- ✓ 3 medium sweet potatoes, peeled and diced
- ✓ 2 tablespoons of avocado oil
- ✓ 2 garlic cloves, crushed
- ✓ 1 teaspoon ground paprika
- ✓ ½ teaspoon of sea salt
- ✓ For Jalapeño Dressing:
- ✓ 1 cup of water
- ✓ 1 cup raw cashews

- ✓ ¼ cup fresh coriander leaves
- ✓ ½ to 1 jalapeño
- ✓ 2 tablespoons of freshly squeezed lime juice
- ✓ ½ teaspoon of sea salt

For assembly:
- ✓ 2 cups of mixed salad

Directions:

- ❖ Preheat the oven to 350ºF (180ºC). Line a baking sheet with baking paper.
- ❖ To prepare sweet potatoes
- ❖ In a medium bowl, mix the sweet potatoes, avocado oil, garlic, paprika and salt.
- ❖ Spread the sweet potato cubes evenly on the prepared baking sheet and bake for 25 minutes, or until soft.
- ❖

- ❖ To prepare the jalapeño dressing
- ❖ Meanwhile, in a high-speed blender, blend together the water, cashews, cilantro, jalapeño, lime juice, and salt until smooth.
- ❖ To assemble
- ❖ Arrange salad mix on 1 large plate or 2 small plates. Add hot sweet potatoes, drizzle with dressing and enjoy.

255)   GREEN PINEAPPLE SALAD

Preparation Time: 10 minutes	**Cooking Time**: 0 minutes	**Servings**: 1-2

For the lime vinaigrette:
- ✓ ¼ cup avocado oil
- ✓ ¼ cup of water
- ✓ 2 tablespoons of freshly squeezed lime juice
- ✓ ½ cup chopped shallots
- ✓ ½ cup chopped fresh cilantro
- ✓ 2 garlic cloves
- ✓ ½ teaspoon of sea salt

For assembly:
- ✓ 2 or 3 cups of mixed salad
- ✓ ½ cup diced pineapple
- ✓ 1 cup chopped purple cabbage
- ✓ Dulse flakes, for garnish (optional)

Directions:

- ❖ To prepare the vinaigrette
- ❖ In a blender, blend together the avocado oil, water, lime juice, onion, cilantro, garlic and salt until well combined. Adjust seasonings as needed.

- ❖ To assemble the salad
- ❖ Arrange salad mix on 1 large plate or 2 small plates. Add pineapple, purple cabbage and dulse flakes (if using); drizzle with dressing and serve.

256)   SWEET PEACH TAHINI SALAD

Preparation Time: 10 minutes	**Cooking Time**: 0 minutes	**Servings**: 1-2

- ✓ 4 tablespoons of tahini
- ✓ 3 to 4 tablespoons of brown rice syrup
- ✓ ¼ cup of water
- ✓ 1 teaspoon of freshly squeezed lemon juice
- ✓ Pinch of sea salt
- ✓ 1 peach, pitted and cut into cubes

- ✓ ¼ cup diced red bell pepper
- ✓ 1 tablespoon fresh coriander chopped
- ✓ 1 tablespoon diced red onion
- ✓ ½ jalapeño, diced
- ✓ 2 or 3 cups of mixed salad

- ❖ In a small bowl, whisk together the tahini, brown rice syrup, water, lemon juice and salt until well combined. Adjust seasonings as needed.

- ❖ In another small bowl, toss together the peach, bell bell pepper, cilantro, onion, and jalapeño.
- ❖ Arrange salad mix on 1 large plate or 2 small plates. Add dressing, drizzle with dressing and enjoy.

257) RED LENTIL PASTA AND VEGETABLE SALAD

Preparation Time: 15 minutes	Cooking Time: 15 minutes	Servings: 2-4

- ✓ 2 cups of red lentil paste
- ✓ ¼ cup avocado oil
- ✓ 2 tablespoons of apple cider vinegar
- ✓ 1 tablespoon freshly squeezed lemon juice
- ✓ 1 teaspoon of dried oregano
- ✓ 2 pinches of sea salt
- ✓ 2 pinches of freshly ground black pepper

- ✓ 1 tablespoon avocado oil
- ✓ 6 asparagus stalks, diced
- ✓ 1 cup diced orange bell bell pepper
- ✓ ⅓ cup of diced red onion
- ✓ ½ zucchini, sliced
- ✓ ½ summer squash, sliced
- ✓ 2 garlic cloves, crushed

Directions:

- ❖ Cook pasta according to package directions.
- ❖ While the pasta is cooking, in a small bowl, whisk together the avocado oil, vinegar, lemon juice, oregano, salt and pepper until well combined. Adjust seasonings as needed.

- ❖ In a skillet over medium-high heat, heat the avocado oil. Add the asparagus, bell bell pepper, onion, zucchini, squash and garlic and sauté for 2 to 3 minutes, or just until soft.
- ❖ In a large bowl, mix cooked pasta, vegetables and dressing until well combined. Transfer to 2 large or 4 small plates and enjoy.

---

258) FENNEL AND CARROT SALAD

Preparation Time: 5 minutes	Cooking Time: 0 minutes	Servings: 4

- ✓ 1 cup chopped fennel
- ✓ 1 cup shredded carrots
- ✓ ¼ cup sliced almonds
- ✓ 3 tablespoons of raisins
- ✓ 1 tablespoon avocado oil

- ✓ 1 tablespoon freshly squeezed lemon juice
- ✓ 1 teaspoon apple cider vinegar
- ✓ 1 teaspoon of Dijon or yellow mustard
- ✓ 1 teaspoon of finely grated fresh ginger or 1 cube of frozen ginger

Directions:

- ❖ In a medium bowl, mix fennel, carrots, almonds and raisins; set aside.
- ❖ In a small bowl, whisk together the oil, lemon juice, vinegar, mustard and ginger until well combined.

- ❖ Pour dressing over salad and toss until evenly coated.
- ❖ Serve cold or at room temperature. Store leftovers in an airtight container in the refrigerator for up to 1 week.

---

259) TOFU AND WATERMELON SALAD

Preparation Time: 10 minutes	Cooking Time: 0 minutes	Servings: 4

Ingredients:

- ✓ 2 tablespoons of freshly squeezed lemon juice
- ✓ 2 tablespoons of avocado oil
- ✓ 1 teaspoon of dried oregano
- ✓ ½ teaspoon of dried thyme
- ✓ ¼ teaspoon of garlic powder
- ✓ ¼ teaspoon of sea salt

Ingredients:

- ✓ 8 ounces (227 g) solid tofu, cubed
- ✓ ¼ cup balsamic vinegar
- ✓ 8 dates, pitted
- ✓ 4 cups crisp leafy greens
- ✓ 1 cup of diced watermelon
- ✓ ¼ cup chopped fresh basil

Directions:

- ❖ In a small bowl, combine the lemon juice, oil, oregano, thyme, garlic powder and salt. Add the tofu and let it absorb the flavors while you prepare the salad.
- ❖ In a high-speed blender, combine the vinegar and dates and blend until smooth.

- ❖ In each of 4 salad bowls, place 1 cup of leafy greens. Add ¼ cup watermelon to each.
- ❖ Using a slotted spoon, top each bowl with 2 tablespoons vegan feta (store remaining vegan feta in an airtight container in the refrigerator for up to 5 days).
- ❖ Garnish evenly with basil. Pour a spoonful of balsamic mixture over each salad and serve.

❖

260) SPINACH AND STRAWBERRY SALAD WITH LEMON VINAIGRETTE

Preparation Time: 5 minutes	Cooking Time: 0 minutes	Servings: 4

For the lemon vinaigrette:
- ✓ 3 tablespoons of avocado oil
- ✓ Juice of 1 small lemon
- ✓ 1 teaspoon of Dijon or yellow mustard
- ✓ ¼ teaspoon ground turmeric
- ✓ ⅛ teaspoon sea salt

- ✓ 1 teaspoon maple syrup (optional)

For the salad:
- ✓ 4 cups baby spinach
- ✓ 1 cup of strawberries cut in half
- ✓ ¼ cup sliced almonds

Directions:

- ❖ To make the lemon vinaigrette
- ❖ In a small bowl, whisk together the oil, lemon juice, mustard, turmeric and salt until well combined. Add the maple syrup (if using) and mix well.

- ❖ To make the salad
- ❖ In a large bowl, mix the spinach, strawberries and almonds.
- ❖ Pour dressing over salad and toss gently. Serve immediately. Or, if you plan to serve later, store the unseasoned salad and dressing in separate, airtight containers in the refrigerator and add the dressing to the salad when you are ready to serve.

261) RAINBOW SALAD WITH CITRUS MANGO DRESSING

Preparation Time: 5 minutes	Cooking Time: 0 minutes	Servings: 4

For the citrus mango salsa:
- ✓ 2 cups of chopped mango
- ✓ 1 cup chopped fennel
- ✓ ⅓ cup of chopped shallots
- ✓ ¼ cup chopped fresh basil
- ✓ 3 tablespoons of freshly squeezed lemon juice
- ✓ ¼ teaspoon of sea salt

For the Rainbow Salad:
- ✓ 1 (15-ounce / 425-g) may low-sodium chickpeas, drained (liquid reserved) and rinsed
- ✓ ½ cup chopped bell pepper
- ✓ 1 teaspoon chopped fresh cilantro, for garnish

Directions:

- ❖ To make the citrus mango salsa
- ❖ In a medium bowl, combine the mango, fennel, shallots, basil, lemon juice and salt and mix well. For best results, cover and refrigerate for several hours or up to overnight to let the flavors meld.

- ❖ To make the rainbow salad
- ❖ In a large bowl, combine the chickpeas, bell bell pepper, and ¼ cup sauce. (Store remaining sauce in an airtight container in the refrigerator for 5-7 days).
- ❖ Garnish the salad with the cilantro and serve.

262) ROASTED CABBAGE AND BEET SALAD

Preparation Time: 10 minutes	Cooking Time: 20 minutes	Servings: 1-2

- ✓ 4 small beets, peeled and diced
- ✓ 1 teaspoon of avocado oil
- ✓ ¼ teaspoon of dried rosemary
- ✓ ⅛ teaspoon of garlic powder
- ✓ Pinch of sea salt
- ✓ Pinch of freshly ground black pepper
- ✓ 2 cups of bite-sized pieces of kale

- ✓ ⅛ teaspoon sea salt
- ✓ 2 tablespoons of avocado oil
- ✓ 1 tablespoon freshly squeezed lemon juice
- ✓ 1 tablespoon brown rice syrup
- ✓ 1 garlic clove, crushed
- ✓ Pinch of sea salt
- ✓ Pinch of freshly ground black pepper

Directions:

- ❖ Preheat the oven to 400°F (205°C). Line a baking sheet with baking paper.
- ❖ In a small bowl, toss the beets with the avocado oil to coat. Sprinkle with the rosemary, garlic powder, salt and pepper and toss to coat. Transfer the beets to the prepared baking dish and roast for 15-20 minutes, or until slightly crispy.

- ❖ Meanwhile, in a medium bowl, sprinkle the cabbage with the salt, and gently massage the cabbage with your hands, mashing it until it becomes soft and slightly mushy, about 3 minutes. Transfer to a serving dish.
- ❖ In a small bowl, whisk together the avocado oil, lemon juice, brown rice syrup, garlic, salt and pepper until well combined.
- ❖ Add beets to bowl with cabbage and drizzle with dressing. Transfer to 1 large or 2 small plates and enjoy.

❖

263)   SPELT PASTA WITH AVOCADO

Preparation Time: 20 minutes	Cooking Time: 0 minutes	Servings: 4

Ingredients:

- ✓ 4 cups of cooked spelt pasta
- ✓ 1 medium avocado, diced
- ✓ 2 cups of cherry tomatoes cut in half
- ✓ 1 fresh basil chopped

Ingredients:

- ✓ 1 teaspoon of agave syrup
- ✓ 1 tablespoon of lime juice
- ✓ ¼ cup olive oil

Directions:

- ❖ Place the cooked pasta in a large bowl.
- ❖ Add the diced avocado, halved cherry tomatoes, and chopped basil to the bowl.
- ❖ Mix all ingredients together until well combined.

- ❖ Whisk the agave syrup, olive oil, pure sea salt and lime juice in a separate bowl.
- ❖ Pour it over the pasta and stir until well combined.
- ❖ Serve immediately.

❖

264)   HAMBURGER OF LETTUCE AND MUSHROOMS WITH BASIL

Preparation Time: 15 minutes	Cooking Time: 20 minutes	Servings: 2

- ✓ 2 cups portobello mushroom caps
- ✓ 1 avocado sliced
- ✓ 1 sliced plum tomato
- ✓ 1 cup of torn lettuce
- ✓ 1 cup of purslane

- ✓ ½ teaspoon of cayenne
- ✓ 1 teaspoon of oregano
- ✓ 2 teaspoons of basil
- ✓ 3 tablespoons of olive oil

- ❖ Preheat the oven to 425ºF (220ºC).
- ❖ Remove the mushroom stems and cut a ½-inch slice from the top slice, as if slicing a sandwich.
- ❖ Mix the onion powder, cayenne, oregano, olive oil and basil well in a medium bowl.
- ❖ Cover a baking sheet with aluminum foil and brush with grapeseed oil to prevent sticking.
- ❖ Place mushroom caps on baking sheet and brush with prepared marinade. Marinate for 10 minutes before baking.

- ❖ Bake for 10 minutes until golden brown and then flip. Continue baking for another 10 minutes.
- ❖ Spread the mushroom cap on a serving platter. This will serve as the bottom for the mushroom burger. On top of it, layer the sliced avocado, tomatoes, lettuce and purslane.
- ❖ Top the burger with another mushroom cap. Repeat steps 7 and 8 with the remaining mushrooms and vegetables.
- ❖ Serve and enjoy.

265)   ZOODLES WITH TOMATO SAUCE AND AVOCADO

Preparation Time: 10 minutes	Cooking Time: 15-20 minutes	Servings: 3

- ✓ 3 medium zucchini
- ✓ 1½ cups of cherry tomatoes
- ✓ 1 avocado
- ✓ 2 sliced green onions
- ✓ ⅓ cup of fresh parsley
- ✓ 1 garlic clove

- ✓ 3 tablespoons of olive oil
- ✓ Juice of 1 key lemon
- ✓ 1 tablespoon of spring water
- ✓ Pure sea salt, to taste
- ✓ Cayenne, to taste

- ❖ Preheat the oven to 400ºF (205ºC).
- ❖ Cover a baking sheet with a piece of baking paper.
- ❖ Place cherry tomatoes on covered baking sheet. Drizzle with 1 tablespoon olive oil and season with pure sea salt and cayenne.
- ❖ Cook the tomatoes for about 15-20 minutes until they start to split.
- ❖ Add the avocado quarters, torn parsley leaves, sliced green onions, garlic, spring water, key lemon juice and ½ teaspoon pure sea salt to a food processor.

- ❖ Blend until a creamy consistency is reached. If the sauce is too thick, add more spring water.
- ❖ Cut off the ends of the zucchini. Using a spiralizer, make zucchini noodles.
- ❖ Mix zucchini noodles with prepared avocado sauce.
- ❖ Divide among 3 small bowls and serve with cherry tomatoes.
- ❖ Enjoy your zoodles with sauce!

❖

266) MUSHROOM AND BELL PEPPER FAJITAS

Preparation Time: 10 minutes	Cooking Time: 10 minutes	Servings: 3

✓ 6 tortillas ✓ 3 large portobello mushrooms ✓ 1 onion ✓ 2 peppers ✓ 1 teaspoon of onion powder	✓ 1 teaspoon of habanero pepper ✓ ⅛ teaspoon of cayenne powder ✓ Juice of ½ key lime ✓ 1 tablespoon of grape seed oil

❖ Rinse portobello mushrooms and remove stems. Cut into ⅓-inch slices. ❖ Cut the onion and peppers into thin slices. ❖ Add the grapeseed oil to a large skillet and heat over medium heat. Add the sliced onions and peppers and cook for 2 minutes.	❖ Place the sliced mushrooms and seasonings in the skillet. Cook for 7-8 minutes, stirring occasionally. Remove from heat. ❖ Take a small skillet, place the tortillas on it and heat for 30-60 seconds on each side. ❖ Place the filling mixture in the center of the tortillas and drizzle the lime juice over the vegetables. ❖ Serve and enjoy.

267) CHICKPEA AND MUSHROOM SAUSAGES

Preparation Time: 15 minutes	Cooking Time: 5 minutes	Servings: 8-10

✓ 2 cups of cooked chickpeas ✓ 1 quart of Roma tomato ✓ 1 cup of quartered mushrooms ✓ ½ cup chopped onion ✓ ½ cup of chickpea flour ✓ 1 tablespoon of onion powder ✓ 1 teaspoon of ground sage ✓ 1 teaspoon of basil	✓ 1 teaspoon of oregano ✓ 1 teaspoon of dill ✓ ½ teaspoon of ground cloves ✓ 1 teaspoon of pure sea salt ✓ ½ teaspoon of cayenne powder ✓ 2 tablespoons of grape seed oil

❖ Place all ingredients, except chickpea flour and grapeseed oil, in a food processor. ❖ Blend for 15 seconds. ❖ Add the chickpea flour to the mixture and blend for another 30 seconds until well combined. ❖ Place the mixture in a piping bag and cut a small piece from the bottom corner.	❖ Add the grapeseed oil to a skillet and heat over high heat. ❖ Reduce to medium heat. Squeeze the prepared mixture into the pan to form sausages. ❖ Cook them for about 3 to 4 minutes on all sides. Turn carefully to prevent them from falling apart. ❖ Serve and enjoy.

268) MUSHROOM AND BLACK CABBAGE RAVIOLI

Preparation Time: 25 minutes	Cooking Time: 10 minutes	Servings: 5

Filling: ✓ 1 cup of chickpea flour ✓ 1 quart of Roma tomato ✓ 2 cups of quartered mushrooms ✓ 1 cup chopped cabbage ✓ ⅓ cup of diced onions ✓ 1 cup diced green and red peppers ✓ 1 tablespoon of onion powder ✓ 1 teaspoon of ginger ✓ 2 teaspoons of oregano ✓ 2 teaspoons of dill ✓ 2 teaspoons of basil ✓ 2 teaspoons of thyme ✓ 1 teaspoon of pure sea salt ✓ ½ teaspoon of cayenne	Dough: ✓ ½ cup of chickpea flour ✓ 1½ cups of spelt flour ✓ ½ teaspoon of oregano ✓ ½ teaspoon of basil ✓ 1 teaspoon of pure sea salt ✓ ¾ cup of spring water Cheese: ✓ ½ cup of soaked Brazil nuts (overnight or for at least 3 hours) ✓ 2 teaspoons of onion powder ✓ ½ teaspoon of oregano ✓ 1 teaspoon of pure sea salt ✓ ½ teaspoon of cayenne powder ✓ ½ cup of spring water

❖ Blend all filling ingredients, except chickpea flour, in a food processor for 30-40 seconds. ❖ Add the chickpea flour to the mixture and blend until well combined. ❖ Add the grapeseed oil to a skillet and heat over high heat. ❖ Reduce to medium heat. Spread the ravioli filling into the pan and cook for 3 to 4 minutes on all sides. ❖ Break up the filling and cook for another 3 minutes, then transfer to a medium bowl. ❖ Add all the ingredients for the cheese to the food processor and blend until the consistency is creamy. If it's too thick, add a little spring water. ❖ Mix the filling with the cheese mixture in the bowl.	❖ Place all the dry ingredients for the dough in the food processor and blend for 10-20 seconds. Slowly add the spring water while blending, until the dough can be shaped into a ball. ❖ Spread the flour on the work space. Take ¼ of the dough and roll it out into a thin sheet. ❖ Place rounded teaspoons of filling and cheese 1 inch apart on one side of dough. Fold dough over and press together around filling to seal. Cut into individual ravioli with a pastry cutter or knife. ❖ Repeat steps 9 and 10 with the remaining dough and filling. ❖ Bring a pot of spring water to a boil. add a little pure sea salt and grapeseed oil, then cook the ravioli for about 4-6 minutes. ❖ Strain and serve.

269) LETTUCE WRAP AND ZUCCHINI HUMMUS

Preparation Time: 10 minutes	**Cooking Time:** 8 minutes	**Servings: 2**

Ingredients:

- ✓ ½ cup iceberg lettuce
- ✓ 1 zucchini, sliced
- ✓ 2 cherry tomatoes, sliced
- ✓ 2 spelt flour tortillas

Directions:

- ❖ Take a grill pan, grease it with oil and preheat it over medium-high heat.
- ❖ Meanwhile, place zucchini slices in a large bowl, sprinkle with salt and cayenne pepper, drizzle with oil and then toss until coated.
- ❖ Place the zucchini slices on the grill pan and then cook for 2 to 3 minutes per side until grill marks develop.

Ingredients:

- ✓ 4 tablespoons of homemade hummus
- ✓ ¼ teaspoon salt
- ✓ ⅛ teaspoon of cayenne pepper
- ✓ 1 tablespoon of grape oil

- ❖ Assemble the tortillas and for that, heat the tortilla on the grill pan until warm and grill marks develop and spread 2 tablespoons of hummus on each tortilla.
- ❖ Spread grilled zucchini slices over tortillas, top with lettuce and tomato slices, then wrap tightly.
- ❖ Serve immediately.

270) BUTTERNUT APPLE AND PUMPKIN BURGER

Preparation Time: 10 minutes	**Cooking Time:** 1 hour	**Servings: 2**

Ingredients:

- ✓ ¾ cup diced pumpkin
- ✓ ½ cup diced apples
- ✓ 1 cup of cooked wild rice
- ✓ ¼ cup chopped shallots
- ✓ ½ tablespoon of thyme

Directions:

- ❖ Turn on the oven, then set it to 400°F (205°C) and let it preheat.
- ❖ Meanwhile, take a cookie sheet, line it with a sheet of parchment, spread the pumpkin pieces on it and then sprinkle with ⅛ teaspoon of salt.
- ❖ Cook the squash for 15 minutes, then add the shallot and apple, sprinkle with the remaining salt and cook for 20-30 minutes until cooked through.
- ❖ When done, let the vegetable mixture cool for 15 minutes, transfer it to a food processor, add the thyme, and then pulse until the mixture is chunky.

Ingredients:

- ✓ ¼ teaspoon of sea salt, divided
- ✓ 1 tablespoon unsalted pumpkin seeds
- ✓ 1 tablespoon of grape oil
- ✓ 2 spelt burgers, halved, toasted

- ❖ Add the pumpkin seeds and cooked wild rice, pulse until combined, and then tip the mixture into a bowl.
- ❖ Taste the mixture to adjust it and then shape it into two meatballs.
- ❖ Take a frying pan, put it over medium heat, add the oil and when it's hot, put in the meatballs and cook them 5 to 7 minutes per side until golden brown.
- ❖ Sandwich patties into hamburger buns and then serve.

271) CABBAGE AND AVOCADO

Preparation Time: 5 minutes	**Cooking Time:** 0 minutes	**Servings: 2**

Ingredients:

- ✓ 1 bundle of cabbage, cut into thin strips
- ✓ 1 small white onion, peeled, chopped
- ✓ 12 cherry tomatoes, chopped

Directions:

- ❖ Take a large bowl, place the cabbage strips in it, sprinkle with salt and then massage for 2 minutes.
- ❖

Ingredients:

- ✓ 1 tablespoon salt
- ✓ 1 avocado, peeled, pitted, sliced

- ❖ Cover the bowl with plastic wrap or its lid, let it sit for a minimum of 30 minutes, and then stir in the onion and tomatoes until well combined.
- ❖ Let the salad sit for 5 minutes, add the avocado slices and then serve.

272) ZUCCHINI BACON

Preparation Time: 10 minutes	Cooking Time: 20 minutes	Servings: 2

Ingredients:

- ✓ 2 zucchini, cut into strips
- ✓ 1 tablespoon of onion powder
- ✓ 1 tablespoon of sea salt
- ✓ ½ teaspoon of cayenne powder
- ✓ ¼ cup of date sugar

Ingredients:

- ✓ 2 tablespoons of agave syrup
- ✓ 1 teaspoon of liquid smoke
- ✓ ¼ cup of spring water
- ✓ 1 tablespoon of grape oil

Directions:

- ❖ Take a medium saucepan, place it over medium heat, add all the ingredients except the zucchini and oil and then cook until the sugar has dissolved.
- ❖ Then place the zucchini strips in a large bowl, pour the mixture from the casserole dish, stir until coated, and then let marinate for a minimum of 1 hour.

- ❖ When you're ready to cook, turn on the oven, set it to 400°F (205°C) and let it preheat.
- ❖ Take a baking sheet, line it with a sheet of parchment, grease it with oil, place the marinated zucchini strips on top and then bake for 10 minutes.
- ❖ Then flip the zucchini, continue cooking for 4 minutes and then let cool completely.
- ❖ Serve immediately.

273) MUSHROOM AND BELL PEPPER FRITTERS

Preparation Time: 10 minutes	Cooking Time: 10 minutes	Servings: 2

Ingredients:

- ✓ 1 cup of chickpea flour
- ✓ 7 ounces (198 g) mushrooms, chopped
- ✓ 1 medium green bell pepper, core, chopped
- ✓ 1 tablespoon of onion powder
- ✓ 2 medium white onions, peeled, chopped
- ✓ 1 teaspoon of sea salt

Ingredients:

- ✓ 1 tablespoon of oregano
- ✓ ⅛ teaspoon of cayenne pepper
- ✓ 1 tablespoon of grape oil
- ✓ 1 tablespoon basil leaves, chopped
- ✓ ½ cup of spring water

Directions:

- ❖ Take a large bowl, put in all the vegetables, add all the seasonings, basil and oregano, mix until combined and then let the mixture sit for 5 minutes.
- ❖ Add the chickpea flour, stir until combined and then stir in the water until well combined and smooth.

- ❖ Take a large skillet, place it over medium heat, add the oil, and when hot, pour the vegetable mixture into portions, press each portion down, and then cook for 3 to 4 minutes per side until cooked and golden brown.
- ❖ Serve immediately.

274) CURRY OF CHICKPEAS, PEPPERS AND MUSHROOMS

Preparation Time: 5 minutes	Cooking Time: 12 minutes	Servings: 2

Ingredients:

- ✓ 1 cup of cooked chickpeas
- ✓ 1 small white onion, peeled, diced
- ✓ ½ of a medium green bell pepper, core, chopped
- ✓ 1 cup diced mushrooms

Ingredients:

- ✓ 8 cherry tomatoes, chopped
- ✓ ½ teaspoon salt
- ✓ ¼ teaspoon cayenne pepper
- ✓ 1 teaspoon of grape oil

Directions:

- ❖ Take a medium skillet, put it over medium heat, add the oil and when hot, add the onion, tomatoes and bell bell pepper and cook for 2 minutes.

- ❖ Add the chickpeas and mushrooms, season with and cayenne pepper, stir until combined, and turn the heat to medium-low and then simmer for 10 minutes until cooked through, covering the pan with its lid.
- ❖ Serve immediately.

Chapter 4. SNACK AND DESSERTS

275) BEAN BURGERS

Preparation Time: 20 minutes	Cooking Time: 25 minutes	Servings: 8

✓ ½ cup of walnuts ✓ 1 carrot, peeled and chopped ✓ 1 celery stalk, chopped ✓ 4 shallots, chopped ✓ 5 cloves of garlic, minced	✓ 2¼ cups canned black beans, rinsed and drained ✓ 2½ cups sweet potato, peeled and grated ✓ ½ teaspoon of red pepper flakes, crushed ✓ ¼ teaspoon cayenne pepper ✓ Sea salt and freshly ground black pepper, to taste

Directions:	
❖ Preheat oven to 400 degrees F. Line a baking sheet with baking paper. ❖ In a food processor, add the walnuts and pulse until finely ground. ❖ Add the carrot, celery, shallot and garlic and pass through a meat grinder until finely chopped. ❖ Transfer the vegetable mixture to a large bowl. ❖ In the same food processor, add the beans and pulse until chopped.	❖ Add 1 1/2 cups sweet potato and pulse until it forms a chunky mixture. ❖ Transfer the bean mixture to the bowl with the vegetable mixture. ❖ Stir in remaining sweet potato and spices and mix until well combined. ❖ Make 8 equal-sized patties from the dough. ❖ Arrange the meatballs on the prepared baking sheet in a single layer. ❖ Bake for about 25 minutes. ❖ Serve hot.

276) GRILLED WATERMELON

Preparation Time: 10 minutes	Cooking Time: 4 minutes	Servings: 4

✓ 1 watermelon, peeled and cut into 1 inch thick wedges ✓ 1 garlic clove, finely chopped ✓ 2 tablespoons fresh lime juice	✓ Pinch of cayenne pepper ✓ Pinch of sea salt

Directions:	
❖ Preheat the grill to high heat. Grease the grill grate. ❖ Grill the watermelon pieces for about 2 minutes on both sides.	❖ Meanwhile, in a small bowl mix together the remaining ingredients. ❖ Drizzle the watermelon slices with the lemon mixture and serve.

277) MANGO SAUCE

Preparation time: 15 minutes		Servings: 6

Ingredients:	Ingredients:
✓ 1 avocado, peeled, pitted and cut into cubes ✓ 2 tablespoons fresh lime juice ✓ 1 mango, peeled, pitted and cut into cubes ✓ 1 cup cherry tomatoes, halved	✓ 1 jalapeño bell pepper, seeded and chopped ✓ 1 tablespoon fresh cilantro, chopped ✓ Sea salt, to taste

Directions:	
❖ In a large bowl, add the avocado and lime juice and mix well.	❖ Add remaining ingredients and stir to combine. ❖ Serve immediately.

278) AVOCADO GAZPACHO

Preparation Time: 15 minutes		Servings: 6

Ingredients:	Ingredients:
✓ 3 large avocados, peeled, pitted and chopped ✓ 1/3 cup fresh coriander leaves ✓ 3 cups of homemade vegetable broth ✓ 2 tablespoons fresh lemon juice	✓ 1 teaspoon of ground cumin ✓ ¼ teaspoon cayenne pepper ✓ Sea salt, to taste
❖ Add all ingredients to a high speed blender and pulse until smooth.	❖ Transfer the soup to a large bowl. ❖ Cover the bowl and refrigerate to chill for at least 2-3 hours before serving.

279) ROASTED CHICKPEAS

Preparation Time: 10 minutes	Cooking Time: 45 minutes	Servings: 12

✓ 4 cups of cooked chickpeas ✓ 2 garlic cloves, minced ✓ ½ teaspoon dried oregano, crushed ✓ ½ teaspoon of smoked paprika	✓ ¼ teaspoon ground cumin ✓ Sea salt, to taste ✓ 1 tablespoon of olive oil

Directions: ❖ Preheat oven to 400 degrees F. Grease a large baking sheet. ❖ Place the chickpeas on the prepared baking sheet in a single layer. ❖ Roast for about 30 minutes, stirring the chickpeas every 10 minutes. ❖ Meanwhile, in a small bowl, mix together garlic, thyme and spices.	❖ Remove the baking sheet from the oven. ❖ Pour the garlic mixture and oil over the chickpeas and toss to coat well. ❖ Roast for another 10-15 minutes or so. ❖ Now, turn off the oven but leave the pan in for about 10 minutes before serving.

280) BANANA CHIPS

Preparation time: 10 minutes	Cooking Time: 1 hour and 10 minutes	

Ingredients:	Ingredients:
✓ 2 large bananas, peeled and cut into ¼ inch thick slices	

Directions: ❖ Prepare oven for 250 degrees F. Line a large baking sheet with baking paper.	❖ Arrange the banana slices on the prepared baking sheet in a single layer. ❖ Bake for about 1 hour.

281) ROASTED CASHEWS

Preparation Time: 10 minutes	Cooking Time: 10 minutes	Servings: 12

Ingredients:	Ingredients:
✓ 2 cups of raw cashews ✓ ½ teaspoon of ground cumin ✓ ¼ teaspoon cayenne pepper	✓ Pinch of salt ✓ 1 tablespoon fresh lemon juice

Directions: ❖ Preheat oven to 400 degrees F. Line a large baking sheet with a piece of foil. ❖ In a large bowl, add the cashews and spices and stir to coat well.	❖ Transfer cashews to the prepared baking dish. ❖ Roast for about 8-10 minutes. ❖ Drizzle with lemon juice and serve.

282) DRIED ORANGE SLICES

Preparation Time: 10 minutes	Cooking Time: 1 hour	Servings: 15

Ingredients:	Ingredients:
✓ 4 navel oranges without seeds, cut into thin slices (DO NOT peel the oranges)	

❖ Set the dehydrator to 135 degrees F.	❖ Arrange the orange slices on the sheets of the dehydrator. ❖ Dehydrate for about 10 hours.

283) CHICKPEA HUMMUS

Preparation Time: 10 minutes		Servings: 12

Ingredients:

- ✓ 2 (15-ounce) cans of chickpeas, rinsed and drained
- ✓ ½ cup of tahini
- ✓ 1 garlic clove, minced
- ✓ 2 tablespoons fresh lemon juice

Ingredients:

- ✓ Sea salt, to taste
- ✓ Filtered water, if necessary
- ✓ 1 tablespoon olive oil plus more for sprinkling
- ✓ Pinch of cayenne pepper

❖ Transfer hummus to a large bowl and drizzle with oil.
❖ Sprinkle with cayenne pepper and serve immediately.

Directions:

❖ In a blender, add all ingredients and pulse until smooth.

284) AVOCADO FRIES IN THE OVEN

Preparation Time: 7 minutes	Cooking Time: 17 minutes	Servings: 4

- ✓ ½ cup of almond flour
- ✓ ½ teaspoon ground paprika, plus more for dusting
- ✓ 2 tablespoons of nutritional yeast
- ✓ ½ teaspoon of garlic powder

- ✓ 2 avocados, slightly unripe
- ✓ ½ cup of almond milk
- ✓ ½ teaspoon of sea salt

Directions:

❖ Preheat the oven to 420°F.
❖ In a small bowl, mix together the almond flour, nutritional yeast, garlic powder, paprika and salt until well combined.
❖ Halve and pit the avocados, and split each half from pole to pole. Remove the skin.
❖ Add the almond milk to another small bowl.
❖ Line a baking sheet with baking paper.

❖ Dip an avocado slice first in the milk and then in the coating mixture, turning it gently to make sure it is completely covered, and place it on the prepared baking sheet. Repeat with the other avocado slices.
❖ Bake for 15-17 minutes, being careful not to overcook or burn them.
❖ Remove from oven, sprinkle with more paprika and serve immediately.

285) DRIED APPLES WITH CINNAMON

Preparation Time: 3 minutes	Cooking Time: 3 hours	Servings: 1

- ✓ 2 apples, sliced
- ✓ 1 teaspoon ground cinnamon

- ✓ 1 teaspoon of olive oil

❖ Bake for 3 hours at 200 degrees F.
❖ Serve and enjoy!

Directions:

❖ Spread all the apple slices on a baking sheet.
❖ Cough up the slices with cinnamon and olive oil.

286) GUACAMOLE SAUCE

Preparation time: 5 minutes		Servings: 1

- ✓ ½ cup sauce,
- ✓ 2 crushed avocados,

- ✓ 2 tablespoons of chopped coriander
- ✓ Salt, to taste

❖ Mix all ingredients together in a bowl.

❖ Serve and enjoy!

287)   APPLE CHIPS

Preparation Time: 3 minutes	Cooking Time: 40 minutes	Servings: 2

Ingredients:

- ✓ 2 apples, cored and thinly sliced
- ✓ 2 tbsp white sugar

Directions:

- ❖ Preheat the oven to 225 degrees F.
- ❖ Place the apple slices on a baking sheet.

Ingredients:

- ✓ ½ teaspoon ground cinnamon

- ❖ Sprinkle cinnamon and sugar.
- ❖ Bake for 40 minutes and then serve.

288)   ALKA-GOULASH FAST

Preparation Time: 10 minutes	Cooking Time: 15 minutes	Servings: 4

Ingredients:

- ✓ 1 onion, finely chopped
- ✓ 1 garlic clove, crushed
- ✓ 2 carrots, diced
- ✓ 3 zucchini, diced
- ✓ 2 tablespoons of olive oil
- ✓ 1 tablespoon of paprika
- ✓ ¼ teaspoon ground nutmeg

Directions:

- ❖ Sauté onion, garlic, carrot and zucchini in olive oil over medium heat for 5 minutes until softened.
- ❖ Add the paprika, nutmeg, parsley and tomato puree.

Ingredients:

- ✓ 1 tablespoon fresh parsley, chopped
- ✓ 1 tablespoon of tomato puree
- ✓ 2 cups of tomatoes, peeled
- ✓ 2 cups of cooked, drained and rinsed red beans
- ✓ ½ cup of tomato juice
- ✓ Salt and black pepper to taste

- ❖ Add the tomatoes, red beans and tomato juice and stir.
- ❖ Simmer for 10 minutes until heated through.
- ❖ Serve immediately. Enjoy!

289)   EGGPLANT CAVIAR

		Servings: 2-4

Ingredients:

- ✓ 2 medium eggplants
- ✓ 2 tablespoons of olive oil
- ✓ 1 onion, finely chopped
- ✓ 1 green bell pepper, seeds removed and finely chopped
- ✓ 2 spoons of tomato puree

Directions:

- ❖ Pierce eggplant several times with a sharp knife. Boil or steam until soft. Allow them to cool.
- ❖ Remove stems and scoop out pulp from eggplant. Finely chop the soft pulp.
- ❖ Add the olive oil to a large skillet over medium heat. Sauté the onion and green bell pepper until the onion is translucent.
- ❖ Add the eggplant, tomato puree, water, salt and black pepper to the skillet.

Ingredients:

- ✓ 4 tablespoons of water
- ✓ 2 tablespoons of lemon juice
- ✓ Salt and black pepper to taste
- ✓ Gluten-free bread or wrap of your choice

- ❖ Reduce the heat and cook over low heat. Stir frequently for 20-30 minutes, at which point the mixture will begin to thicken.
- ❖ Place the mixture in a bowl and stir in the lemon juice.
- ❖ Allow the mixture to cool and place in the refrigerator.
- ❖ Serve cold with a slice of gluten-free bread, a wrap, or chopped vegetables (e.g., carrots or cucumbers).

290)	SPICED NUT MIXTURE	
		Servings: 4

Ingredients:

- ✓ 1/3 cup sesame seeds
- ✓ 1/2 cup hazelnuts, blanched
- ✓ 3 tablespoons of coriander seeds
- ✓ 2 tablespoons of cumin seeds

Directions:

- ❖ Dry-fry sesame seeds in a large skillet over medium heat until golden brown. Remove from heat and let cool in a bowl.
- ❖ Toast the hazelnuts in the same pan until they are shiny and starting to turn golden brown. Add to the sesame seeds and let cool.
- ❖ Dry-fry the coriander and cumin seeds until fragrant, but be sure not to let them burn. Add them to the bowl of hazelnuts and sesame seeds and let cool.

Ingredients:

- ✓ Hot gluten-free tortillas of your choice, cut into strips or chopped vegetables
- ✓ Olive Oil
- ✓ 1/2 teaspoon salt
- ✓ Black pepper to taste

- ❖ Now place the mixture in a food processor and add salt and black pepper to taste. Process the mixture until it reaches the consistency of a coarse, dry powder.
- ❖ Serve with gluten-free tortilla wraps or veggies alongside a bowl of olive oil. To consume, dip the bread or raw veggies, into the oil and then into the spicy nut mixture.

291)	GARLIC MUSHROOMS	
		Servings: 4

Ingredients:

- ✓ 2 tablespoons of olive oil
- ✓ 2 garlic cloves, crushed
- ✓ 1/4 teaspoon of dried thyme
- ✓ 1/4 teaspoon of dried parsley
- ✓ 1/4 teaspoon of dried sage
- ✓ 2 cups of mushrooms, cut in quarters

Directions:

- ❖ Sauté garlic in olive oil until softened and beginning to brown.
- ❖ Add the dried herbs and mushrooms and season with salt and black pepper to taste.

Ingredients:

- ✓ Chopped raw vegetables of your choice (e.g. cucumbers, carrots, peppers)
- ✓ 2 tablespoons chives, chopped
- ✓ Salt and black pepper to taste

- ❖ Sauté this mixture over low heat for about 10 minutes, until the mushrooms are soft.
- ❖ Serve the mushrooms alongside the raw vegetables. Garnish with the chopped chives.
- ❖ Enjoy!

292)	HUMMUS	

Ingredients:

- ✓ 1 cup cooked chickpeas, stock reserve
- ✓ 4 tablespoons of light tahini
- ✓ Juice of 2 lemons

Directions:

- ❖ Blend chickpeas with 1/8 cup reserved broth from cooking.
- ❖ Add the lemon juice, garlic, tahini and half of the olive oil.
- ❖ Blend this mixture until smooth.

Ingredients:

- ✓ 6 tablespoons of olive oil
- ✓ 4 garlic cloves, crushed
- ✓ Salt to taste

- ❖ Allow to rest for about an hour before serving.
- ❖ To serve, drizzle the remaining olive oil over each individual serving. Serve alongside some raw vegetables.

293) PALEO VEGAN ZUCCHINI HUMMUS

Ingredients:

- ✓ 1 cup of sliced zucchini
- ✓ 4 tablespoons of light tahini
- ✓ Juice of 2 lemons

Directions:

- ❖ Combine the zucchini, lemon juice, garlic, tahini and half of the olive oil in a blender.
- ❖ Blend this mixture until smooth.

Ingredients:

- ✓ 6 tablespoons of olive oil
- ✓ 4 garlic cloves, crushed
- ✓ Himalayan salt to taste
- ❖ Allow to rest for about an hour before serving.
- ❖ To serve, drizzle the remaining olive oil over each individual serving. Serve alongside some raw vegetables or sprouted bread.

294) GERMAN STYLE SWEET POTATO SALAD

Servings: 2-4

Ingredients:

- ✓ 2 cups sweet potatoes, chopped
- ✓ 1 cup baby spinach
- ✓ 1 cup of cherry tomatoes
- ✓ 1 red bell pepper
- ✓ 4 tablespoons of olive oil

Directions:

- ❖ Clean and peel the potatoes. Boil them in a saucepan until tender. The time required will vary depending on their size.
- ❖ Meanwhile, sauté the garlic and scallions in a skillet over medium heat for 2-3 minutes, until slightly soft.
- ❖ Add the dill and sauté for about 1 minute.

Ingredients:

- ✓ 4 shallots, cut and finely chopped
- ✓ 1 garlic clove, crushed or minced
- ✓ 2 tablespoons fresh dill, finely chopped
- ✓ 2 tablespoons fresh parsley, chopped
- ✓ Salt and black pepper to taste
- ❖ Remove from heat and season to taste with salt and black pepper.
- ❖ Drain the potatoes once they are cooked, and pour the herb dressing over them while they are hot.
- ❖ Let cool and then add the rest of the ingredients and garnish with parsley. Serve fresh!

295) QUINOA SALAD

Servings: 2

Ingredients:

- ✓ 1 cup quinoa, cooked
- ✓ 1 garlic clove, minced
- ✓ 1 cucumber, chopped
- ✓ 1 cup of fresh arugula leaves
- ✓ 1 red bell pepper, chopped
- ✓ 1 large avocado, peeled, pitted and diced

Directions:

- ❖ Just combine all the ingredients in a large salad bowl.

Ingredients:

- ✓ 2 tablespoons of chia seeds (optional)
- ✓ 2 tablespoons of olive oil
- ✓ 2 tablespoons of coconut milk (I think)
- ✓ Himalayan salt and black pepper to taste
- ✓ Juice of 1 lime or lemon
- ❖ Mix well and drizzle with olive oil, coconut milk and lemon juice.
- ❖ Enjoy!

296) TASTY QUINOA AND COCONUT SALAD

Ingredients:

- ✓ 2 cups quinoa, cooked
- ✓ 3 tablespoons of coconut oil
- ✓ 1 garlic clove, minced
- ✓ 1 teaspoon of curry powder
- ✓ 1 teaspoon of coriander powder
- ✓ ½ teaspoon of garlic powder

Ingredients:

- ✓ 1 cup radish
- ✓ 1/2 cup arugula leaves
- ✓ 2 horse radishes, thinly sliced or spiraled
- ✓ ¼ cup of raisins
- ✓ Himalayan salt to taste
- ✓ 1 lime tree

Directions:

- ❖ Heat some coconut oil in a skillet (over low to medium heat).
- ❖ Add the garlic and sauté for a couple of minutes.
- ❖ Then add the quinoa, curry powder and garlic powder.
- ❖ Continue to stir over low heat so that the quinoa takes on a nice exotic flavor.
- ❖ Add a pinch of Himalayan salt to taste. You can also add coconut milk.
- ❖ Turn off the heat and allow the quinoa to cool.
- ❖ Meanwhile, combine the remaining ingredients in a salad bowl.
- ❖ Add the quinoa, mix well and drizzle a little lime juice.
- ❖ Serve chilled.
- ❖ Enjoy!

297) MAYO ALKALINE SALAD

Servings: 4

Ingredients:

- ✓ 2 cups sweet potato, boiled, sliced, cooled
- ✓ 1 cup soy sprouts (I'm not talking about soybeans, I'm talking about soy sprouts...)
- ✓ 2 red peppers, chopped
- ✓ 1 onion, chopped
- ✓ 1 cup of arugula leaves

Ingredients:

- ✓ ¼ cup almond, crushed
- ✓ ½ cup vegan mayonnaise
- ✓ Juice of 1 lime
- ✓ 2 tablespoons of olive oil
- ✓ Himalayan salt and black pepper to taste

Directions:

- ❖ Combine all ingredients in a large salad bowl.
- ❖ Add the vegan mayonnaise, olive oil, lemon juice, black pepper and salt.
- ❖ Mix well. Chill in the refrigerator for a couple of hours.
- ❖ Serve chilled and enjoy!

298) BLACK-EYED PEA AND ORANGE SALAD

Servings: 4

Ingredients:

- ✓ 1 cup black-eyed peas, soaked
- ✓ 1 bay leaf
- ✓ A slice of onion
- ✓ Zest and juice of 1 orange
- ✓ 5 tablespoons of olive oil
- ✓ 6 large olives, pitted and chopped

Ingredients:

- ✓ 4 shallots, cut and chopped
- ✓ 2 tablespoons fresh parsley, chopped
- ✓ 2 tablespoons fresh basil, chopped
- ✓ 4 whole oranges
- ✓ 1 large handful of watercress

Directions:

- ❖ Place the black eyed peas, bay leaf and onion slice in a saucepan filled with enough water to cover them by 1 inch.
- ❖ Boil over high heat for 10 minutes, then reduce to a simmer and cook for 60 minutes, until black-eyed peas are soft.
- ❖ Whisk the olive oil, orange zest and juice in a bowl.
- ❖ Add the olives, shallots and herbs, then stir.
- ❖ Drain the black-eyed peas and add them to the mixture.
- ❖ Season to taste and make sure the black-eyed peas are well coated with the mixture.
- ❖ Serve the mixture on individual plates, and add a few orange segments and a pile of watercress on each.

299) ALKA-GOULASH FAST

Servings: 4

Ingredients:

- ✓ 1 onion, finely chopped
- ✓ 1 garlic clove, crushed
- ✓ 2 carrots, diced
- ✓ 3 zucchini, diced
- ✓ 2 tablespoons of olive oil
- ✓ 1 tablespoon of paprika
- ✓ 1/4 teaspoon ground nutmeg

Ingredients:

- ✓ 1 tablespoon fresh parsley, chopped
- ✓ 1 tablespoon of tomato puree
- ✓ 2 cups of tomatoes, peeled
- ✓ 2 cups of cooked, drained and rinsed red beans
- ✓ 1/2 cup of tomato juice
- ✓ Salt and black pepper to taste

Directions:

- ❖ Sauté onion, garlic, carrot and zucchini in olive oil over medium heat for 5 minutes, until softened.
- ❖ Add the paprika, nutmeg, parsley and tomato puree.

- ❖ Add the tomatoes, red beans and tomato juice and stir.
- ❖ Simmer for 10 minutes until heated through.
- ❖ Serve immediately. Enjoy!

300) PEA RISOTTO

Servings: 4

Ingredients:

- ✓ 1 cube of vegetable stock
- ✓ 2 tablespoons of olive oil
- ✓ 1 onion, finely chopped
- ✓ 3 garlic cloves, finely chopped
- ✓ 1 cup of basmati rice

Ingredients:

- ✓ 1 cup frozen peas
- ✓ 1 cup fresh spinach leaves
- ✓ 1 lemon, grated and squeezed
- ✓ Salt and black pepper to taste
- ✓ 3 cups of water

Directions:

- ❖ Crumble the vegetable stock cube into 3 cups of boiling water. Allow it to dissolve and then reduce the heat.
- ❖ Thaw peas in hot water, drain and set aside for later.
- ❖ Season onion with salt and black pepper to taste, and then sauté in olive oil over medium heat for about 5 minutes, until softened.
- ❖ Add the garlic to the pan and sauté for a few minutes, making sure it doesn't burn.
- ❖ Add the rice to the pan and stir well. Pour in a little vegetable stock so that the rice is just barely covered.

- ❖ Simmer over medium heat, stirring constantly, for several minutes, until the liquid has been almost completely absorbed.
- ❖ Add the rest of the broth one ladle at a time, stirring constantly until each batch of broth has been absorbed.
- ❖ When each ladleful has been absorbed and the rice is fully cooked, add the thawed peas, spinach leaves and lemon juice.
- ❖ Stir until the spinach leaves are wilted and serve hot.
- ❖ Enjoy!

301) ALKA-SATISFYING LUNCH SMOOTHIE

Servings: 1-2

Ingredients:

- ✓ 1 large avocado
- ✓ 1.5 cup of coconut milk or almond milk
- ✓ 2 tablespoons of fresh coriander leaves
- ✓ 2 tablespoons of coconut oil

Ingredients:

- ✓ 1 lemon, squeezed
- ✓ 4 tablespoons of chia seeds
- ✓ Himalayan salt to taste

Directions:

- ❖ Simply blend all the ingredients except the seeds and oil.

- ❖ Mix well, add chia seeds and enjoy with Himalayan salt.
- ❖ Enjoy!

302)   ALKALINE PIZZA BREAD

		Servings: 1

Ingredients:

- ✓ Flaxseed, 100g
- ✓ Sunflower seeds, 200g
- ✓ Pepper, a pinch
- ✓ Dried tomatoes, 50g

Ingredients:

- ✓ Organic salt or sea salt, a pinch
- ✓ Extra virgin olive oil (cold pressed), 4 teaspoons
- ✓ Optional: Fresh wild garlic

Directions:

- ❖ Note: You must soak the sunflower seeds for at least four hours.
- ❖ Blend the flaxseeds in a blender until reduced to a powder.
- ❖ Once the sunflower seeds have lasted up to four hours, place them in a blender and blend for a few seconds.

- ❖ Now add all the ingredients into a mixing bowl.
- ❖ Using your hands, form a dough until it reaches the right consistency.
- ❖ The idea is to form a couple of pizza/bread crusts.
- ❖ Place them in a dehydrator or oven and dehydrate for up to twelve hours. Serve.

303)   ALKALINE FILLED AVOCADO

Ingredients:

- ✓ Oregano, 1 teaspoon
- ✓ Ripe avocado, 1
- ✓ Lime juice (fresh), 1 teaspoon
- ✓ Fresh basil, 1 teaspoon

Ingredients:

- ✓ Chopped onions, 1 teaspoon
- ✓ Tomato, ½
- ✓ Extra virgin oil (cold pressed), 4 teaspoons
- ✓ Pepper and sea salt

- ❖ Mix the olive oil, chopped onion, lime juice and chopped tomato and place in the avocado holes.
- ❖ Sprinkle the oregano and basil on top and serve.

Directions:

- ❖ Cut the avocado into two equal halves and remove the seed.
- ❖ Use salt and pepper to season both halves.

304)   ALKALIZED POTATO SALAD

		Servings: 4

Ingredients:

- ✓ Cauliflower, 1 cup
- ✓ Dill, 2 tablespoons
- ✓ Vegenaise, 1 teaspoon
- ✓ Red onion, 1
- ✓ English cucumber (small), 1
- ✓ Broccoli, 2 cups

Ingredients:

- ✓ Green/red pepper (small), 1
- ✓ Red potatoes, 600g
- ✓ Juice of 1 lemon
- ✓ Sea Salt
- ✓ Olive oil (cold pressed), 3 tablespoons

- ❖ Mix well and set aside.
- ❖ Take a small bowl and mix the veganaise, olive oil and lemon juice until smooth.
- ❖ Mix it into the potato salad and toss gently.
- ❖ You can serve it immediately but it's best to set it aside for a few hours (because it tastes better that way).
- ❖ You are free to add other toppings according to your taste.

Directions:

- ❖ Steam the cauliflower and broccoli for a few minutes and make sure they are crispy.
- ❖ Also, steam the potatoes until slightly soft and let them cool.
- ❖ Once they have cooled, slice the potatoes but do not remove the skin and toss them in a large bowl.
- ❖ Next, add the chopped cucumber, cauliflower, bell bell pepper, broccoli, along with the dill, finely chopped onion and salt.

305) ALMONDS WITH SAUTÉED VEGETABLES

		Servings: 4

Ingredients:

- ✓ Young beans, 150g
- ✓ Broccoli flower, 4
- ✓ Oregano and cumin, ½ teaspoon
- ✓ Lemon juice (fresh), 3 tablespoons
- ✓ Garlic clove (finely chopped), 1

Directions:

- ❖ Add the broccoli, beans and other vegetables to a large skillet and fry until the beans and broccoli turn dark green.
- ❖ Make sure the vegetables are crispy as well.
- ❖ Now add the chopped garlic and onion, sauté and stir for a few minutes.

Ingredients:

- ✓ Cauliflower, 1 cup
- ✓ Olive oil (cold pressed), 4 tablespoons
- ✓ Pepper and salt to taste
- ✓ Some soaked almonds (sliced), for garnish
- ✓ Yellow onion, 1

- ❖ Then, put the dressing together.
- ❖ Take a small bowl, add the lemon juice, oregano, cumin and oil and mix well.
- ❖ Add some vegetables, stir slowly and taste for pepper and salt.
- ❖ Finally, use the sliced almonds for garnish.
- ❖ Serve.

306) ALKALINE SWEET POTATO MASH

		Servings: 3-4

Ingredients:

- ✓ Sea salt, 1 tablespoon
- ✓ Curry powder, ½ table spoon
- ✓ Sweet potatoes (large), 6

Directions:

- ❖ First, get a large mixing bowl.
- ❖ Wash and cut the sweet potatoes and add them to the cooking pot and cook for about twenty minutes.

Ingredients:

- ✓ Coconut milk (fresh), 1 ½ - 2 cups
- ✓ Extra virgin olive oil (cold pressed), 1 tablespoon
- ✓ Pepper, 1 pinch

- ❖ Then, remove the sweet potatoes and mash them to your desired consistency.
- ❖ Finally, all you have to do is add the remaining ingredients and serve.

307) MEDITERRANEAN PEPPERS

		Servings: 2

Ingredients:

- ✓ Oregano, 1 teaspoon
- ✓ Garlic cloves (crushed), 2
- ✓ Fresh parsley (chopped), 2 tablespoons
- ✓ Vegetable broth (no yeast), 1 cup
- ✓ Province herbs, 1 teaspoon

Directions:

- ❖ Heat the olive oil in a skillet over medium heat, add the bell bell pepper and onions and stir.
- ❖ Add the garlic and stir.

Ingredients:

- ✓ Red bell pepper (sliced) 2 + Yellow bell pepper (sliced) 2
- ✓ Red onions (thinly sliced), 2 medium-sized
- ✓ Extra virgin olive oil (cold pressed), 2 tablespoons
- ✓ Salt and pepper to taste

- ❖ Then, add the vegetable stock and season with parsley and herbs, as well as pepper and salt to taste.
- ❖ Cover the pan and let it cook for fourteen to fifteen minutes.
- ❖ Serve.

308)   TOMATO AND AVOCADO SAUCE WITH POTATOES

Servings: 3

Ingredients:

- ✓ Red onion 1
- ✓ 2 Tomatoes
- ✓ ½ - 1 lemon (squeezed)
- ✓ Chives (fresh and chopped), 1 teaspoon
- ✓ Parsley (fresh and chopped), 1 teaspoon

Ingredients:

- ✓ Cayenne pepper, ½ teaspoon
- ✓ Avocado (ripe), 2
- ✓ Waxy potatoes (medium size), 6
- ✓ Saltwater
- ✓ Pepper and salt

Directions:

- ❖ Take a pan and cook the potatoes in salted water, (cook the potatoes with the skin intact).
- ❖ Next, peel the avocado, toss it in a bowl and mash it with a fork.

- ❖ Now, dice the onion and tomatoes, add them to the bowl along with the parsley, chives and cayenne.
- ❖ Mix well and season with pepper, lemon juice and salt.
- ❖ Serve along with the potatoes.

---

309)   ALKALINE GREEN BEANS AND COCONUT

Servings: 4

Ingredients:

- ✓ Ground cumin, ½ teaspoon
- ✓ Red chili pepper (chopped), 1-2
- ✓ Coconut milk (fresh), 3 tablespoons
- ✓ Dry flaked coconut, 1 tablespoon
- ✓ Garlic (chopped), 2 cloves
- ✓ Cayenne pepper, 1 pinch

Ingredients:

- ✓ Sea salt, 1 pinch
- ✓ Extra virgin olive oil (cold pressed), 3 tablespoons
- ✓ Fresh herbs of your choice, 1 teaspoon
- ✓ One (1) pound of green beans, cut into 1-inch pieces
- ✓ Fresh ginger (chopped), ½ teaspoon

Directions:

- ❖ Heat the oil in a skillet and add the beans, cumin, garlic, ginger and frosting and sauté for about six minutes.

- ❖ Add the coconut flakes and oil and sauté until the milk is completely steamed (this may take three or four minutes).
- ❖ Season with pepper, salt and herbs to taste. Serve.

---

310)   ALKALIZED VEGETABLE LASAGNA

Servings: 1

Ingredients:

- ✓ Parsley root, 1
- ✓ Leek (small), 1
- ✓ Radish (small), 1
- ✓ Corn salad, 1
- ✓ Tomatoes (large), 3
- ✓ Garlic, 1 clove

Ingredients:

- ✓ Avocado (soft), 2
- ✓ Lemon (squeezed), 1-2
- ✓ Arugula, 1
- ✓ Parsley (few)
- ✓ Red bell pepper, 1

Directions:

- ❖ Take a blender and add the lemon juice, garlic clove and avocado.
- ❖ Cut the bell bell pepper into thin strips, cut the leek into thin rings and finely grate the parsley root and radish. When you are done, mix everything with the avocado cream.

- ❖ Let's start with the first layer of the lasagna.
- ❖ Deposit corn salad in a casserole dish, add avocado spread well.
- ❖ For the second layer, add the sliced tomatoes.
- ❖ Finally, add the arugula and parsley for the final layer.
- ❖ Serve.

311) ALOO GOBI

		Servings: 1 Bowl

✓ Cauliflower, 750g	✓ Cilantro/coriander leaves, 1/3 cup
✓ Fresh ginger, 20g	✓ Large potatoes, 4
✓ Large onions, 2	✓ Garam masala, 2 teaspoons
✓ Mint, 1/3 cup	✓ Green chilli, 4
✓ Turmeric, 2 teaspoons	✓ Water, 3 cups
✓ Diced tomatoes, 400g	✓ Extra virgin olive oil (cold pressed), 125 ml
✓ Fresh garlic, 2 cloves	✓ Salt to taste
✓ Cayenne pepper, 2 teaspoons	

Directions:

- ❖ Blend the chili, garlic and ginger.
- ❖ Fry oil in a wok for three minutes and add onion until golden brown.
- ❖ Add ground pasta and sauté for a few seconds, then add; garam masala, chili, turmeric, tomatoes and salt.

- ❖ Cook for about five minutes and add all other ingredients.
- ❖ Stir for three minutes and add the water.
- ❖ Cook until sauce is thick.
- ❖ Serve with Basmati rice or as a side dish.

312) CHOCOLATE CRUNCH BARS

Preparation Time: 3 hours	Cooking Time: 5 minutes	Servings: 4

✓ 1 1/2 cups sugar-free chocolate chips	✓ 1/4 cup of coconut oil
✓ 1 cup of nut butter	✓ 3 cups pecans, chopped
✓ Stevia for taste	

Directions:

- ❖ Prepare an 8-inch baking dish with baking paper.
- ❖ Mix chips chocolate with butter, coconut oil and sweetener in a bowl.
- ❖ Melt in the microwave for 2 to 3 minutes until melted.

- ❖ Stir in the nut and dice. Stir gently.
- ❖ Put this wand inside the oven and then it won't open anymore.
- ❖ Refrigerate for 2 to 3 hours.
- ❖ Slice and serve.

313) NUT BUTTER BARS

Preparation Time: 40 minutes.	Cooking Time: 10 minutes.	Servings: 6

✓ 3/4 cup of walnut flour	✓ 1/2 wooden walnut
✓ 2 ounces of nut butter	✓ 1/2 teaspoon vanilla
✓ 1/4 cup Swerve	

- ❖ Combine all the ingredients to get a better result.
- ❖ Transfer your contents to a small 6-inch baking dish. Press firmly.

- ❖ Refrigerate for 30 minutes.
- ❖ Cut into slices and serve.

314) HOMEMADE PROTEIN BAR

Preparation Time: 5 mnutes	Cooking Time: 10 minutes	Servings: 4

✓ 1 knob of butter	✓ To taste, ½ teaspoon of sea salt Optional Ingredients:
✓ 4 tablespoons of coconut oil	✓ 1 teaspoon cinnamon
✓ 2 scoops of vanilla protein	

- ❖ Mix coconut oil with butter, protein, stevia and salt in a dish.
- ❖ Mix cinnamon and chocolate chips.

- ❖ Presss the dough is firmly and freeze until firmed.
- ❖ Cut the crust into small bars.
- ❖ Serve and enjoy.

315) SHORTBREAD COOOKIES

Preparation Time: 10 minutes	Cooking Time: 1 hour and 10 minutes	Servings: 6

Ingredients:

- ✓ 2 1/2 cups coconut flour
- ✓ 6 tablespoons of nut butter

Directions:

- ❖ Preheat our oven to 350 degrees.
- ❖ Place on a cookie sheet with the parchment paper.
- ❖ Beat the butter with the erythritol until fluffy.
- ❖ Add the vanilla essence and coconut flour.

Ingredients:

- ✓ 1/2 cup erythritol
- ✓ 1 teaspoon of vanilla essence

- ❖ Mix everything together until crumbled.
- ❖ Spoon out a tablespoon of cookie dough onto the cookie sheet.
- ❖ Add more dough to make a pile.
- ❖ Bake for 15 minutes until golden brown.
- ❖ Serve.

288 Fat: 25.3g. Carbohydrates: 9.6g. Protein: 7.6g. Fiber: 3.8g.

316) COCONUT COOKIES CHIP

Preparation Time: 10 minutes	Cooking Time: 15 minutes	Servings: 4

Ingredients:

- ✓ 1 cup of walnut flour
- ✓ ½ cup cacao nibs
- ✓ ½ cup coconut flakes, unsweetened
- ✓ 1/3 cup erythritol
- ✓ ½ cup nut butter

Directions:

- ❖ Prepare your oven for 350 degrees F.
- ❖ Layer a cookie sheet with parchment paper.
- ❖ Add and combine all ingredients dry in a glass bowl.
- ❖ Coconut milk, coconut milk, vanilla, stevia and peanut butter.
- ❖ Beat well compared to stir in the battery. Mix well.

Ingredients:

- ✓ ¼ cup peanut thrower, more than once
- ✓ ¼ cup of coconut milk
- ✓ Stevia, to taste
- ✓ ¼ teaspoon of sea salt

- ❖ Spoon out a tablespoon of cookie dough on the coookie shet.
- ❖ Add more dough to make 16 coookies.
- ❖ Fluctuate each cookie using your fingers.
- ❖ Water for 25 minutes until dawn.
- ❖ Let them rest for 15 minutes.
- ❖ Serve.

192 Fat: 17.44g. Carbohydrates: 2.2g. Protein: 4.7g. Fiber: 2.1g.

317) COCONUT COOKIES

Preparation Time: 10 mnutes	Cooking Time: 20 minutes	Servings: 6

Ingredients:

- ✓ 6 tablespoons coconut flour
- ✓ ¾ teaspoons baking powder
- ✓ 1/8 teaspoon sea salt
- ✓ 3 tablespoons of nut butter

Directions:

- ❖ Preheat our oven to 375 degrees F. Layer a cookie sheet with parchment.
- ❖ Place all wet ingredients in a blender. Blend all the mixture in a blender.
- ❖ Add the wet mixture and mix well until it is used up.

Ingredients:

- ✓ 1/6 cup coconut oil
- ✓ 6 tablespoon data sugar
- ✓ 1/3 cup coco nut milk
- ✓ 1/2 teaspoon vanilla essence

- ❖ Place a spoonful of cookie dough on the cookie sheet.
- ❖ Add a little more butter to make many coookies. Bake until golden brown (about 10 minutes). We'll see.

151 Fat: 13.4g. Carbs: 6.4g. Protein: 4.2g. Fiber: 4.8g

318)   BERRY MOUSSE

Preparation Time: 5 minutes	Cooking Time: 5 minutes	Servings: 2

✓ 1 teaspoon Seville orange zest ✓ 3 oz. raspberries or blueberries.	✓ ¼ teaspoon vanilla essence ✓ 2 cups coconut cream

❖ Blend the rice in an electric blender until the fluff is dissolved. ❖ Add the vanilla and Seville zest. Stir well. ❖ Toss in the walnuts and berries.	❖ Cover the glove with a plastic wrench. ❖ Refrigerate for 3 hours. ❖ Garnish as desired. Serve.

265 Fat: 13g. Carbohydrates: 7.5g. Protein: 5.2g. Fiber: 0.5g.

319)   COCONUT PULP COOOKIES

Preparation Time: 5 minutes.	Cooking Time: 10 hours.	Servings: 4

✓ 3 cups coconut pulp ✓ 1 Granny Smith apple ✓ 1-2 teaspoon cinnamon	✓ 2-3 tablespoons of raw honey ✓ 1/4 cup coco walnut flakes

❖ Blend the coconut with the remaining ingredients in a processor food. ❖ Make lots of cookies with this mixture. ❖ Arrange them on a kitchen table, lined with parchment.	❖ Place the dough in a food grade oven for 6-10 hours at 115 degrees Fahrenheit. ❖ Serve.

240 Fat: 22.5g. Carbohydrates: 17.3g. Protein: 14.9g. Fiber: 0g.

320)   AVOCADO PUDDING

Preparation Time: 10 minutes	Cooking Time: 0 minutes	Servings: 2

✓ 2 avocados ✓ 3/4-1 cup coconut milk ✓ 1/3-1/2 cup of raw cacao powder	✓ 1 teaspoon 100% pure organic vanilla (optional) ✓ 2-4 tablespoons of date sugar

❖ Blend all ingredients in a blender.	❖ Refrigerate for 4 hours in a container. ❖ Serve.

609 Fats: 50.5g. Carbs: 9.9g. Protein: 29.3g. Fiber: 1.5g.

321)   COCONUT RAISINS COOOKIES

Preparation Time: 10 minutes.	Cooking Time: 10 minutes.	Servings: 4

✓ 1 1/4 cups of coconut flour 1 cup of nut flour ✓ 1 teaspoon baking soda ✓ 1/2 Celtic teaspoon sea salt ✓ 1 button for peanuts cup ✓ 1 cup coconut date sugar	✓ 2 teaspoons of vanilla ✓ ¼ cup coconut milk ✓ 3/4 cup organic raisins ✓ 3/4 cup coconut chips or flakes

❖ Turn on the oven to 357 degrees F. ❖ Mix the flour with salt and baking soda. ❖ Fluff with sugar until starting and then stirs in walnut milk and vinavilla.	❖ Mix well, then place in a container for the powder. Stir until fine. ❖ Add all remaining ingredients. ❖ Make small coookies out this dough. ❖ Arrange the cookies on a baking sheet. ❖ Bake for 10 minutes until set.

237 Fat: 19.8g. Carbs: 55.1g. Protein: 17.8g. Fiber: 0.9g.

322) CRACKER PUMPKIN SPICE

Preparation Time: 10 minutes.	Cooking Time: 1 hour.	Servings: 6

Ingredients:

- ✓ 1/3 cup coco walnut flour
- ✓ 2 tablespoons pumpkin pie spice
- ✓ ¾ cup sunflower seds
- ✓ ¾ cup flaxseed
- ✓ 1/3 cup sesame seeds

Ingredients:

- ✓ 1 tablespoon gron psyllium husk powder
- ✓ 1 teaspoon sea salt
- ✓ 3 tablespoons coco walnut oil, melted
- ✓ 1⅓ cups water

Directions:

- ❖ Heat our oven to 300 degrees F. Combine all ingredients in a bowl.
- ❖ Add the salt and oil to the mixture and mix well.
- ❖ Let the dough sit for 2 to 3 minutes.

- ❖ Roll out the dough on a cookie sheet lined with parchment paper.
- ❖ Bake for 30 minutes.
- ❖ Reduce the amount of food to 30 m weight and let it rest for another 30 m.
- ❖ Crush the bread into small pieces. Serve

248 Fat: 15.7g. Carbs: 0.4g. Protein: 24.9g. Fiber: 0g.

323) SPICY TOASTED NUTS

Preparation Time: 10 minutes.	Cooking Time: 15 minutes.	Servings: 4

Ingredients:

- ✓ 8 ounces of pecans or coconuts or walnuts
- ✓ 1 teaspoon of sea salt
- ✓ 1 tablespoon olive oil or coconut oil

Ingredients:

- ✓ 1 teaspoon of ground cumin
- ✓ 1 teaspoon of paprika powder or chili powder

Directions:

- ❖ Add all ingredients to an oven. Brown nuts until golden brown.

- ❖ Serve and enjoy.

287 Fat: 29.5g. Carbohydrates: 5.9g. Protein: 4.2g. Fiber: 4.3g.

324) WHEAT CRACKERS

Preparation Time: 10 minutes.	Cooking Time: 20 minutes.	Servings: 4

Ingredients:

- ✓ 1 3/4 cup of walnut flour
- ✓ 1 1/2 cups coconut flour
- ✓ 3/4 teaspoon sea salt

Ingredients:

- ✓ 1/3 vegetable oil
- ✓ 1 kitchen basket
- ✓ Sea salt for sprinkling

Directions:

- ❖ Set your oven to 350 degrees F.
- ❖ Mix the coconut flour, nut flour and salt in a bowl.
- ❖ Stir in vegetable oil and salt. Mix well until done.
- ❖ Pour the dough onto a flat surface in a thin dish.

- ❖ Cut small squares out of the sheet.
- ❖ Arrange dough squares on a sheet of baking paper lined with parchment paper.
- ❖ Wet for 20 minutes until light comes on.
- ❖ Serve.

64 Fat: 9.2g. Carbs: 9.2g. Protein: 1.5g. Fiber: 0.9g.

325) CHIPS POTATO

Preparation Time: 10 mnutes.	Cooking Time: 5 minutes.	Servings: 4

Ingredients:

✓ 1 tablespoon of vegetable oil

Ingredients:

✓ 1 potato, sliced paper thin Sea salt, to taste

❖ Bake in oven for 5 minutes until golden brown.
❖ Serve.

Directions:

❖ Toss potato with oil and sea salt.
❖ Distribute the slices in a sandwich dish in a single row.

80 Fat: 3.5g. Carbohydrates: 11.6g. Protein: 1.2g.

326) ZUCCHINI PEPPER CHIPS

Preparation Time: 10 minutes.	Cooking Time: 15 minutes.	Servings: 4

Ingredients:

✓ 1 2/3 cups vegetable oil
✓ 1 teaspoon onion powder
✓ 1/2 teaspoon of black pepper

Ingredients:

✓ 3 tablespoons crushed red pepper flakes
✓ 2 zucchini, thinly sliced

❖ Refrigerate for 10 minutes.
❖ Spread the zucchini slices on a greased baking sheet.
❖ Bake for 15 minutes
❖ Serve.

Directions:

❖ Mix the oil with all the spices in a bowl.
❖ Add the zucchini slices and mix well.
❖ Transfer the mixture into a container Zip lock and seal il.

172 Fat: 11.1g. Carbs: 19.9g. Protein: 13.5 g. Fiber: 0.2g.

327) FLAT BREAD

	Cooking Time: 20 Minutes	Servings: 6

Ingredients:

✓ 2 cups of Spelt Flour
✓ 2 teaspoons of Oregano
✓ 2 teaspoons of Onion powder
✓ 1/4 teaspoon of Cayenne

Ingredients:

✓ 2 teaspoons of basil
✓ 1 tablespoon of Pure Sea Salt
✓ 3/4 cup of spring water
✓ 2 tablespoons of Grape Seed Oil

❖ Roll out each loaf into a circles container about 4 inches in diameter.
❖ Prepare a wooden skillet. Place one flatbred in the skillet and cook over medium heat.
❖ Flip the dish for 2 to 3 minutes and work until dry. Small pieces of sugar paper should be placed on both sides.
❖ Continue to look at the upper body.
❖ Serve and enjoy your Flatbread!

Directions:

❖ Add spelt flour and all grains to a bowl and mix well.
❖ Add the Grape Seed Oil and 1/2 cup of Spring Water and continue to mix.
❖ Try to form a thick ball. If it is too thick, add more Spring Water.
❖ Make a place to roll the mud and sprinkle it with flour.
❖ Knead the slurry for about 5 minutes until it has become desired consistencyn.
❖ Divite the dough into 6 equal balls.

Useful Tips: You can add seasonings according to your taste.

328) HEALTHY CRACKERS

	Cooking Time: 30 minutes	**Servings: 50 Crackers**

Ingredients:

- ✓ 1/2 cup of rye flour
- ✓ 1 cup of flour Spelt
- ✓ 2 teaspoons of Sesame Seed
- ✓ 1 teaspoon of Agave Syrup

Ingredients:

- ✓ 1 teaspoon of Pure Sea Salt
- ✓ 2 tablespoons of Grape Seed Oil
- ✓ 3/4 cup of Spring Water

Directions:

- ❖ Preheat our oven to 350 degrees Fahrenheit.
- ❖ Add all ingredients to a glass container and mix everything together.
- ❖ Make a ball of dough. If the dough is too thick, add more flour.
- ❖ Prepare a place to spread the dough and cover it with a piece of parchment paper.
- ❖ Degrease the container well with Grape Seed Oil and place the dart on it.
- ❖ Roll out the dough with a rolling pin, adding more flour to keep it from falling apart.

- ❖ When your dough is ready, take a pastry cutter and insert it into the container. If you don't have a cutter, you can use a cookie cutter.
- ❖ Place the squares on a kitchen basket and place them in the corner of a ech square using a fork or a skewer.
- ❖ Brush the dish with a little grain oil and sprinkle with a little pure sea salt, if needed.
- ❖ Bake for 12 to 15 minutes or until crackers are golden brown.
- ❖ Everything that was done was done with the help of another person.
- ❖ Serve and enjoy your Healthy Crackers!

Useful Tips: You can add any seasonings from Doctor Sebi's food list according to your desire. You can make crackers with our tomato sauce, avocado sauce or cheese. Sauce.

329) TORTILLAS

	Cooking Time: 20 Minutes	**Servings: 8**

Ingredients:

- ✓ 2 cups of flour Spelt
- ✓ 1 teaspoon of Pure Sea Salt

Ingredients:

- ✓ 1/2 cup of spring Water

Directions:

- ❖ In a food processor* mix the spelt flour with the pure salt. Blend for about 15 minutes.
- ❖ Blend, slowly add Grape seed oil until well distributed.
- ❖ Slowly add the soy water while stirring until a color forms.
- ❖ Prepare a piece of wallpaper and pour some parchment paper on it. Dust with some flour.

- ❖ Process the nut for about 1 to 2 minutes until it reaches the right consistency.
- ❖ Pour the dough into 8-inch pieces.
- ❖ Roll out each ball into a very thin circle.
- ❖ Prepare a lunchbox, cook one tortilla at a time in a microwave for about 30-60 minutes.
- ❖ Serve and enjoy your Tortillas!

Useful Tips: If you don't have a refrigerator, you can use a mixer or blender. However, you will have a better result with a food that has nothing to do with food. You can serve Tortillas with our Sweet Butter Sauce, Avocado Sauce or Cheese. Salsa.

330) TORTILLA CHIPS

	Cooking Time: 30 minutes	Servings: 8

Ingredients:

- ✓ 2 cups of Spelt Flour
- ✓ 1 teaspoon of Pure Sea Salt

Directions:

- ❖ Set your oven to 350 degrees Fahrenheit.
- ❖ Place spelt flour and pure salt in a food processor*. Blend for about 15 seconds.
- ❖ While stirring, slowly add the soybean oil until well combined.
- ❖ Continue to blend and slowly add Spring Water to a dough is formed.
- ❖ Prepare a work surface and cover it with a piece of parchment paper. Sprinkle the flour on it.
- ❖ Knead the dough for about 1 to 2 minutes, until it's just right.
- ❖ Cover a baking pan with a little Grape Seed Oil.

Ingredients:

- ✓ 1/2 cup of rinse water
- ✓ 1/3 cup of ground olive oil

- ❖ Place the prepared dart in the baking dish.
- ❖ Brush the mixture with a little grape oil and, if desired, a little pure sea salt.
- ❖ Cut the dough into 8 pieces with a pizza knife.
- ❖ Bake for about 10-12 minutes or until the chips are starting to become golden brown.
- ❖ Allow to cool before serving.
- ❖ Serve and enjoy your Tortilla Chips!

Useful Tips: If you don't have a refrigerator, you can use a hand mixer or blender. However, you will get better results with an immersion blender. You can serve Tortillas with our Sweet Barbecue Sauce, Guacamole, or "Cheese". Sauce .

331) ONION RINGS

	Cooking Time: 30 Minutes.	Servings: 8

Ingredients:

- ✓ White onion or yellow onion
- ✓ 1 cup of Spelt Flour
- ✓ 1/2 cup of homemade Hempseed Milk
- ✓ 1/2 cup of Aquafaba *
- ✓ 2 teaspoons of Onion Powder.

Directions:

- ❖ Preheat our oven to 450 degrees Fahrenheit.
- ❖ Pour Homemade Hempseed Milk and Aquafaba into a medium bowl and blend well.
- ❖ Add 1 teaspoon of Oregano, 1 teaspoon of Onion Powder, 1/2 teaspoon of Cayenne, and 1 teaspoon of Pure Sea Salt to the wet ingredients and mix.
- ❖ Peel the Onions, slice the ends.
- ❖ Cut peeled onion into slices about 1/4 inch thick. Cut the onion into rings.
- ❖ Add the Spelt flour, 1 teaspoon of Oregano, 1 teaspoon of Onion Powder, 1/2 teaspoon of Cayenne, and 1
- ❖ taspoon of Pure Sea Salt in a container with one quart. Shake out all the liquid.

Ingredients:

- ✓ 2 teaspoons of Oregano
- ✓ 1 teaspoon of Cayenne powder
- ✓ 2 teaspoons of Pure Sea Salt
- ✓ 3 tablespoons of grape oil

- ❖ Brush a baking sheet with Grape Seed Oil 8. Place a couple onion rings over the water mixture.
- ❖ Put the water onion rings in the dry mixture and turn until coated on both sides.
- ❖ Place the covered onion rings on the baking sheet.
- ❖ Repeat steps 8 through 10 until all onion rings are covere.
- ❖ Lightly spray the rings with Grape seed oil.
- ❖ Water for about 10-15 minutes until it shines.
- ❖ All that is possible for coool them before serving.
- ❖ Serve and enjoy our onion rings!

Useful Tips: If you haven't made Aquafaba, add 1/2 extra millet of Homemade hemp seed milk. You can use Onion Rings with our Sweet Bärbecue Sauce , or "Cheese" Sauce .

332)	GRAPE AND CHARD SMOOTHIE	
Preparation Time: 10 minutes		**Servings: 2**
✓ 2 cups of green grapes without seeds ✓ 2 cups fresh beets, cut and chopped ✓ 2 tablespoons of maple syrup	✓ 1 teaspoon fresh lemon juice ✓ 1½ cups of water ✓ 4 ice cubes	
❖ Place all ingredients in a high speed blender and pulse until creamy.	❖ Pour the smoothie into two glasses and serve immediately.	

333)	MATCHA SMOOTHIE	
Preparation Time: 10 minutes		**Servings: 2**
✓ 2 tablespoons of chia seeds ✓ 2 teaspoons of matcha green tea powder ✓ ½ teaspoon fresh lemon juice ✓ ½ teaspoon xanthan gum	✓ 8-10 drops of liquid stevia ✓ 4 tablespoons of coconut cream ✓ 1½ cups unsweetened almond milk ✓ ¼ cup ice cubes	
❖ Place all ingredients in a high speed blender and pulse until creamy.	❖ Pour the smoothie into two glasses and serve immediately.	

334)	BANANA SMOOTHIE	
Preparation Time: 10 minutes		**Servings: 2**
✓ 2 cups of cooled unsweetened almond milk ✓ 1 large frozen banana, peeled and sliced	✓ 1 tablespoon almonds, chopped ✓ 1 teaspoon of organic vanilla extract	
❖ Place all ingredients in a high speed blender and pulse until creamy.	❖ Pour the smoothie into two glasses and serve immediately.	

335)	STRAWBERRY SMOOTHIE	
Preparation Time: 10 minutes		**Servings: 2**
✓ 2 cups of cooled unsweetened almond milk ✓ 1½ cups of frozen strawberries	✓ 1 banana, peeled and sliced ✓ ¼ teaspoon of organic vanilla extract	
❖ Add all ingredients to a high speed blender and pulse until smooth.	❖ Pour the smoothie into two glasses and serve immediately.	

336)	RASPBERRY AND TOFU SMOOTHIE	
Preparation Time: 15 minutes		**Servings: 2**
✓ 1½ cups of fresh raspberries ✓ 6 ounces of hard-boiled silken tofu, drained ✓ 1/8 teaspoon of coconut extract	✓ 1 teaspoon of stevia powder ✓ 1½ cups unsweetened almond milk ✓ ¼ cup ice cubes, crushed	
❖ Add all ingredients to a high speed blender and pulse until smooth.	❖ Pour the smoothie into two glasses and serve immediately.	

337)   MANGO SMOOTHIE

Preparation Time: 10 minutes		**Servings: 2**

Ingredients:

- ✓ 2 cups frozen mango, peeled, pitted and chopped
- ✓ ¼ cup almond butter
- ✓ Pinch of ground turmeric

Ingredients:

- ✓ 2 tablespoons fresh lemon juice
- ✓ 1¼ cup unsweetened almond milk
- ✓ ¼ cup ice cubes

❖ Pour the smoothie into two glasses and serve immediately.

Directions:

❖ Add all ingredients to a high speed blender and pulse until smooth.

338)   PINEAPPLE SMOOTHIE

Preparation Time: 10 minutes		**Servings: 2**

Ingredients:

- ✓ 2 cups pineapple, chopped
- ✓ ½ teaspoon fresh ginger, peeled and chopped
- ✓ ½ teaspoon ground turmeric
- ✓ 1 teaspoon of natural immune support supplement*.

Ingredients:

- ✓ 1 teaspoon of chia seeds
- ✓ 1½ cups of cold green tea
- ✓ ½ cup ice, crushed

❖ Pour the smoothie into two glasses and serve immediately.

Directions:

❖ Add all ingredients to a high speed blender and pulse until smooth.

339)   CABBAGE AND PINEAPPLE SMOOTHIE

Preparation Time: 15 minutes		**Servings: 2**

Ingredients:

- ✓ 1½ cups fresh cabbage, chopped and shredded
- ✓ 1 frozen banana, peeled and chopped
- ✓ ½ cup of fresh pineapple chunks

Ingredients:

- ✓ 1 cup unsweetened coconut milk
- ✓ ½ cup of fresh orange juice
- ✓ ½ cup of ice

❖ Pour the smoothie into two glasses and serve immediately.

Directions:

❖ Add all ingredients to a high speed blender and pulse until smooth.

340)   GREEN VEGETABLE SMOOTHIE

Preparation Time: 15 minutes		Servings: 2

Ingredients:

- ✓ 1 medium avocado, peeled, pitted and chopped
- ✓ 1 large cucumber, peeled and chopped
- ✓ 2 fresh tomatoes, chopped
- ✓ 1 small green bell pepper, seeded and chopped

Ingredients:

- ✓ 1 cup fresh spinach, torn
- ✓ 2 tablespoons fresh lime juice
- ✓ 2 tablespoons of homemade vegetable broth
- ✓ 1 cup of alkaline water

❖ Pour smoothie into glasses and serve immediately.

Directions:

❖ Add all ingredients to a high speed blender and pulse until smooth.

❖

341)   AVOCADO AND SPINACH SMOOTHIE

Preparation Time: 10 minutes		Servings: 2

- ✓ 2 cups of fresh spinach
- ✓ ½ avocado, peeled, pitted and chopped
- ✓ 4-6 drops of liquid stevia

- ✓ ½ teaspoon ground cinnamon
- ✓ 1 tablespoon of hemp seeds
- ✓ 2 cups of cooled alkaline water

❖ Pour the smoothie into two glasses and serve immediately.

Directions:

❖ Add all ingredients to a high speed blender and pulse until smooth.

342)   CUCUMBER SMOOTHIE

Preparation Time: 15 minutes		Servings: 2

- ✓ 1 small cucumber, peeled and chopped
- ✓ 2 cups fresh mixed greens (spinach, kale, chard), chopped and shredded
- ✓ ½ cup of lettuce, torn
- ✓ ¼ cup fresh parsley leaves
- ✓ ¼ cup fresh mint leaves

- ✓ 2-3 drops of liquid stevia
- ✓ 1 teaspoon fresh lemon juice
- ✓ 1½ cups of filtered water
- ✓ ¼ cup ice cubes

❖ Pour the smoothie into two glasses and serve immediately.

Directions:

❖ Add all ingredients to a high speed blender and pulse until smooth.

343) APPLE AND GINGER SMOOTHIE

Preparation Time: 10 minutes	Cooking Time: 0 minutes	Servings: 1

✓ 1 apple, peeled and diced ✓ ¾ cup (6 ounces) of coconut yogurt	✓ ½ teaspoon of ginger, freshly grated

Directions: ❖ Add all ingredients to a blender. ❖ Blend well until smooth.	❖ Refrigerate for 2 to 3 hours. ❖ Serve.

344) GREEN TEA BLUEBERRY SMOOTHIE

Preparation Time: 10 minutes	Cooking Time: 5 minutes	Servings: 1

Ingredients:	Ingredients:
✓ 3 tablespoons of alkaline water ✓ 1 green tea bag ✓ 1½ cups of fresh blueberries	✓ 1 pear, peeled, stoned and diced ✓ ¾ cup of almond milk

Directions: ❖ Boil 3 tablespoons of water in a small saucepan and transfer to a cup. ❖ Dip the tea bag into the cup and let it sit for 4 to 5 minutes. ❖ Discard the tea bag and ❖ Transfer the green tea to a blender	❖ Add all other ingredients to blender. ❖ Blend well until smooth. ❖ Serve with fresh blueberries.

❖

345) APPLE AND ALMOND SMOOTHIE

Preparation Time: 10 minutes	Cooking Time: 0 minutes	Servings: 1

✓ 1 cup of apple cider ✓ 1/2 cup of coconut yogurt ✓ 4 tablespoons almonds, crushed	✓ 1/4 teaspoon of cinnamon ✓ 1/4 teaspoon nutmeg ✓ 1 cup of ice cubes

❖ Add all ingredients to a blender.	❖ Blend well until smooth. ❖ Serve.

346) CRANBERRY SMOOTHIE

Preparation Time: 10 minutes	Cooking Time: 0 minutes	Servings: 1

✓ 1 cup of cranberries ✓ ¾ cup of almond milk ✓ ¼ cup raspberries	✓ 2 teaspoons fresh ginger, finely grated ✓ 2 teaspoons of fresh lemon juice

❖ Add all ingredients to a blender.	❖ Blend well until smooth. ❖ Serve with fresh berries on top.

Bibliography

FROM THE SAME AUTHOR

THE ALKALINE DIET *Cookbook* - 120+ Easy-to-Follow Recipes for Beginners to start a Healthier Lifestyle!

THE ALKALINE DIET FOR BEGINNERS *Cookbook* - 120+ Super Easy Recipes to Start a Healthier Lifestyle! The Best Recipes You Need to Jump into the Alkaline and Anti-inflammatory Diet!

THE ALKALINE DIET FOR MEN *Cookbook* - The Best 120+ Recipes to Stay HEALTHY and FIT with Alkaline Diet!

THE ALKALINE DIET FOR WOMEN *Cookbook* - The Best 120+ recipes to stay TONE and HEALTHY! Reboot your Metabolism before Summer with the Lightest Alkaline Meals!

THE ALKALINE DIET FOR KIDS *Cookbook* - The Best 120+ recipes for children, tested BY Kids FOR Kids! Stay really HEALTHY with one of the most complete diet, HAVING FUN!

THE ALKALINE DIET FOR TWO *Cookbook* - 220+ Easy-to-Follow Recipes for Dad and Kids to start a Healthier Lifestyle! Stay HEALTHY and FIT making your meals together, HAVING FUN!

THE ALKALINE DIET FOR COUPLE *Cookbook* - 220+ Simple Recipes to make together! Stay HEALTHY and Eat Delicious Meals with the most complete guide about the kitchen for two!

THE ALKALINE DIET FOR MUM *Cookbook* - The Best 220+ Recipes For Mum and Kids to start a Healthier Lifestyle! HAVE FUN preparing these delicious and alkaline meals with your family!

Conclusion

Thanks for reading "The Alkaline Diet for Healthy Women *Cookbook*"!

Follow the right habits it is essential to have a healthy Lifestyle, and the Alkaline diet is

the best solution!

I hope you liked this Cookbook!

I wish you to achieve all your goals!

Sarah Johnson

CPSIA information can be obtained
at www.ICGtesting.com
Printed in the USA
BVHW060126180521
607551BV00011B/1158